The
Economist

Pocket
World
in
Figures

The Economist

Pocket
World
in
Figures

The
Economist
Books

Hutchinson

First published in Great Britain by
Hutchinson Business Books Limited
An imprint of Random Century Limited, Random Century House,
20 Vauxhall Bridge Road, London SW1V 2SA

Editor Penny Butler
Art Editor Keith Savage
Material researched and compiled by Jill Leyland Associates
Editorial Assistants Jennifer Mussett, Alan Duff, Sarah Harper

Editorial Director Stephen Brough
Art Director Douglas Wilson
Managing Editor Fay Franklin
Production Manager Robert Gray

The greatest care has been taken in compiling this book. However,
no responsibility can be accepted by the publishers or contributors
for the accuracy of the information presented.
Where opinion is expressed it is that of the author and does not
necessarily coincide with the editorial views of The Economist
newspaper.

Any correspondence regarding this publication should be addressed
to: The Editorial Director, The Economist Books, Axe and Bottle
Court, 70 Newcomen Street, London SE1 1YT

A CIP catalogue record for this book is available from the British Library

ISBN 0-09-174913-1

Map by Oxford Illustrators Ltd, Oxford, England
Printed in Hong Kong produced by Mandarin Offset

Contents

Part II Country Profiles

Notes

All the relevant major international statistical sources have been used in the preparation of this book. In addition, extensive use has been made of the substantial publications and information sources of The Economist Group including Business International, and notably of The Economist Intelligence Unit, EIU. Further details of EIU publications can be obtained from:

The Marketing Department,
The Economist Intelligence Unit,
40 Duke Street, London W1A 1DW
Telephone: 071 493 6711
Fax: 071 499 9767

Coverage

The country profiles cover 60 major countries; the world rankings consider 146: all those with a population of at least 1m or a GDP of at least $1bn. The extent and quality of the statistics available varies from country to country. Every care has been taken to specify the broad definitions on which the data are based and to indicate cases where data quality or technical difficulties are such that interpretation of the figures is likely to be seriously affected. Nevertheless, figures from individual countries will often differ from standard international statistical definitions. Data for Cyprus normally refer to Greek Cyprus only.

Statistical basis

The all-important factor in a book of this kind is to be able to make reliable comparisons between countries. Although this is never quite possible for the reasons stated above, the best route, which this book takes, is to compare data for the same year or period and to use actual, not estimated, figures. The research for this first edition of The Economist Pocket World in Figures was carried out in 1990 using the latest published sources that present data on an internationally comparable basis. The data, therefore, unless otherwise indicated, refer to the year ending 31 December 1988. (This is why East and West Germany are shown as separate countries, as are North and South Yemen). General exceptions are: population under 15 and over 65 and number of men per 100 women refer to estimates for 1990; crude birth, death and fertility rates are based on 1985-90 averages; energy data refer to 1987; household data and marriage and divorce data refer to the latest year with available figures, 1980-88. In a number of cases, data are shown for the latest year within a range, for example; 1985-88, means that data can refer to 1985, 1986, 1987 or 1988.

Other definitions

Data shown on country profiles may not always be consistent with those shown on the world rankings because the definitions or years covered can differ. Data may also differ between two different rankings.

Statistics for principal exports and principal imports are normally based on customs statistics. These are generally compiled on different definitions to the visible exports and imports figures shown in the balance of payments section.

The overall balance in the balance of payments section in the country profiles is equal to current plus capital account plus errors and ommissions. The change in reserves is shown here without the practice of reversing the sign often followed in balance of payments presentations.

Definitions of the statistics shown are given in the glossary at the end of the book. Figures may not add exactly to totals, or percentages to 100, because of rounding. Sums of money have generally been converted to US dollars at the official exchange rate ruling at the time to which the figures refer; in the case of GDP estimates, special exchange rates have been used for a small number of

Abbreviations

countries whose official exchange rate was considered to be unrealistic. This is explained in more detail on page 22.

Energy consumption data are not always reliable, particularly for the major oil producing countries. Consumption per head data may therefore be higher than in reality. Energy exports can exceed production and imports can exceed consumption if transit operations distort trade data or oil is imported for refining and re-exported.

bn	billion (one thousand million)	m	million
kg	kilogram	NMP	Net Material Product
km	kilometre	PPP	Purchasing Power Parity
GDP	Gross Domestic Product	-	zero
GNP	Gross National Product	...	not available
GRT	Gross Tonnage		

=== Part I ===
WORLD RANKINGS

Countries: *natural facts*

Countries: *the largest*
'000 sq km

1	USSR	22,403	36	Chile	757
2	China	9,561	37	Zambia	753
3	USA	9,373	38	Morocco	711
4	Canada	9,221	39	Burma	677
5	Brazil	8,512	40	Afghanistan	647
6	Australia	7,682	41	Somalia	638
7	Indonesia	5,086	42	CAR	623
8	India	3,288	43	Madagascar	592
9	Argentina	2,777	44	Kenya	583
10	Sudan	2,506	45	Botswana	558
11	Algeria	2,382	46	France	547
12	Zaire	2,344	47	Thailand	514
13	Saudi Arabia	2,150	48	Spain	505
14	Mexico	1,973	49	Cameroon	475
15	Libya	1,760	50	Papua New Guinea	465
16	Iran	1,648	51	Sweden	450
17	Mongolia	1,565	52	Iraq	442
18	Peru	1,285	53	Paraguay	407
19	Chad	1,284	54	Zimbabwe	391
20	Niger	1,267	55	Norway	387
21	Angola	1,247	56	Japan	378
22	Mali	1,240	57	Congo	342
23	South Africa	1,223	58	Finland	338
	Ethiopia	1,223	59	South Yemen	337
25	Colombia	1,142	60	Malaysia	330
26	Bolivia	1,099		Vietnam	330
27	Mauritania	1,031	62	Côte d'Ivoire	322
28	Egypt	998	63	Poland	313
29	Tanzania	945	64	Oman	300
30	Nigeria	924		Philippines	300
31	Venezuela	912	66	Italy	294
32	Namibia	824	67	Burkina Faso	274
33	Mozambique	799	68	Ecuador	271
34	Pakistan	796	69	New Zealand	268
35	Turkey	771		Gabon	268

Mountains: *the highest*

	Name	Location	Height (m)
1	Everest	Nepal-China	8,848
2	K2 (Godwin Austen)	Pakistan	8,611
3	Kanchenjunga	Nepal-India	8,598
4	Makalu	China-Nepal	8,481
5	Dhaulagiri	Nepal	8,172
6	Nanga Parbat	Pakistan	8,126
7	Annapurna	Nepal	8,079
8	Gasherbrum	Pakistan	8,068
9	Gosainthan	China	8,013
10	Nanda Devi	India	7,817

Rivers: *the longest*

	Name	Location	Length (km)
1	Nile-Kagera	Africa	6,671
2	Amazon-Ucayali	South America	6,449
3	Yangtze	Asia	6,301
4	Mississippi-Missouri	North America	6,019
5	Huang (Yellow)	Asia	5,464
6	Ob'-Irtysh	Asia	5,411
7	Plata-Parana	South America	4,699
8	Mekong	Asia	4,500
	Parana	South America	4,500
10	Amur	Asia	4,416
11	Lena	South America	4,400
12	Mackenzie	North America	4,241
13	Congo	Africa	4,200
14	Niger	Africa	4,160
15	Yenisey	Asia	4,093
16	Mississippi	North America	3,779
17	Missouri	North America	3,724
18	Volga	Europe	3,531
19	Madeira-Mamore	South America	3,199
	Purus	South America	3,199
21	Yukon	North America	3,185
22	Indus	Asia	3,180
23	Rio Grande	North America	3,034
24	Syr-Dar'ya	Asia	2,992
25	Sao Francisco	South America	2,900
	Brahmaputra	Asia	2,900
27	Danube	Europe	2,860
28	Salween	Asia	2,849
29	Euphrates	Asia	2,760
30	Orinoco	South America	2,736

Waterfalls: *the highest*

	Name	Location	Height (m)
1	Angel	Venezuela	978
2	Tugela	South Africa	947
3	Utigard	Norway	800
4	Mongefossen	Norway	774
5	Yosemite	California, USA	739
6	Mardalsfoss	Norway	656
7	Tyssestrengane	Norway	646
8	Kukenaam	Venezuela	609
9	Takkakaw	Canada	503
10	Ribbon	California, USA	491

Notes: Estimates of the lengths of different rivers vary widely according to the rules adopted concerning the selection of tributaries to be followed, the path to take through a delta, where hydrological systems begin and end and so forth. The Nile is normally taken as the world's longest river but some estimates put the Amazon as longer if a southerly path through its delta leading to the River Para is followed. Likewise, difficulties in waterfall measurements exist depending on which breaks in the fall are counted. The more famous waterfalls, Niagara and Victoria, are surprisingly small, 53m and 355m respectively; their notoriety evolving from their width and accessibility.

Population: *explosions revealed*

Largest populations 1988
Millions

1	China	1,104.00	31	Canada	25.95
2	India	796.60	32	Morocco	23.91
3	USSR	283.68	33	Kenya	23.88
4	USA	246.33	34	Algeria	23.84
5	Indonesia	174.95	35	Sudan	23.80
6	Brazil	144.43	36	Yugoslavia	23.56
7	Japan	122.61	37	Tanzania	23.20
8	Pakistan	105.41	38	Romania	23.05
9	Nigeria	104.96	39	North Korea	21.90
10	Bangladesh	104.53	40	Peru	21.26
11	Mexico	82.73	41	Taiwan	19.90
12	Vietnam	64.23	42	Afghanistan	19.60
13	West Germany	61.20	43	Venezuela	18.75
14	Philippines	58.72	44	Nepal	18.23
15	Italy	57.44	45	Iraq	17.25
16	UK	57.08	46	Uganda	17.19
17	France	55.87	47	Malaysia	16.92
18	Thailand	54.54	48	East Germany	16.67
19	Iran	52.52	49	Sri Lanka	16.59
20	Turkey	52.42	50	Australia	16.53
21	Egypt	51.90	51	Czechoslovakia	15.62
22	Ethiopia	47.88	52	Mozambique	14.93
23	South Korea	41.97	53	Netherlands	14.76
24	Burma	40.08	54	Ghana	14 13
25	Spain	39.05	55	Saudi Arabia	14.02
26	Poland	37.86	56	Chile	12.75
27	Zaire	33.46	57	Côte d'Ivoire	11.61
28	Argentina	31.96	58	Syria	11.34
29	Colombia	30.24	59	Madagascar	11.24
30	South Africa	29.60	60	Cameroon	11.10

Largest populations 2010
Millions

1	China	1,382.46	16	Egypt	78.45
2	India	1,225.30	17	Turkey	76.64
3	USSR	326.41	18	Thailand	71.59
4	USA	281.22	19	Zaire	67.44
5	Indonesia	231.95	20	Burma	60.56
6	Nigeria	216.23	21	France	59.43
7	Brazil	207.45	22	West Germany	57.90
8	Pakistan	191.41	23	UK	57.56
9	Bangladesh	188.19	24	Italy	57.29
10	Japan	131.67	25	Tanzania	56.27
11	Mexico	125.16	26	Kenya	53.46
12	Vietnam	98.04	27	South Africa	51.82
13	Iran	94.69	28	South Korea	51.58
14	Philippines	92.03	29	Sudan	44.00
15	Ethiopia	82.01	30	Colombia	43.84

Notes: Projections are UN data based on "medium growth" assumptions.

Fastest growing populations 1983-88
Av. ann. growth %

1	Macao	5.9	11	Libya	4.0
2	Burkina Faso	5.8	12	Jordan	3.9
3	Saudi Arabia	5.6		Oman	3.9
4	Kenya	4.9	14	Zambia	3.8
5	Bahrain	4.8	15	Botswana	3.7
6	Kuwait	4.5	16	Madagascar	3.6
	Côte d'Ivoire	4.5	17	Somalia	3.5
8	UAE	4.4		Iran	3.5
9	Liberia	4.2		Uganda	3.5
10	Qatar	4.1		Ghana	3.5

Slowest growing populations 1983-88
Av. ann.growth %

1	Hungary	-0.2		Ireland	0.2
2	West Germany	-0.1	12	UK	0.3
3	East Germany	0.0		Sweden	0.3
	Barbados	0.0		Czechoslovakia	0.3
	Luxembourg	0.0		Greece	0.3
6	Denmark	0.1		Norway	0.3
	Bulgaria	0.1	17	Finland	0.4
	Belgium	0.1		Switzerland	0.4
	Austria	0.1		France	0.4
10	Italy	0.2		Romania	0.4

Fastest growing populations 1990-2010
Av. ann. growth %

1	Kenya	3.8	11	Afghanistan	3.3
	Côte d'Ivoire	3.8		Nigeria	3.3
	Jordan	3.8		Liberia	3.3
	Saudi Arabia	3.8		Botswana	3.3
5	Tanzania	3.7		Benin	3.3
6	Zambia	3.6		Malawi	3.3
7	Uganda	3.5		Syria	3.3
	Libya	3.5		Madagascar	3.3
9	Oman	3.4	19	Rwanda	3.2
	North Yemen	3.4		Zaire	3.2

Slowest growing populations 1990-2010
Av. ann. growth %

1	West Germany	-0.2		Bulgaria	0.0
	UK	-0.2		Belgium	0.0
3	Austria	-0.1	13	Greece	0.1
	Switzerland	-0.1		Finland	0.1
5	Luxembourg	0.0	15	Netherlands	0.2
	Hungary	0.0		Norway	0.2
	Sweden	0.0		Portugal	0.2
	East Germany	0.0	18	France	0.3
	Denmark	0.0		Spain	0.3
	Italy	0.0		Japan	0.3

Population: *city living*

Biggest cities
Pop. m 1980s

1	Seoul	Korea	9.64
2	Mexico City	Mexico	8.83
3	Moscow	USSR	8.82
4	São Paulo	Brazil	8.49
5	Tokyo	Japan	8.38
6	Bombay	India	8.24
7	New York	USA	7.32
8	London	UK	6.77
9	Jakarta	Indonesia	6.50
10	Shanghai	China	6.29
11	Lima	Peru	6.05
	Cairo	Egypt	6.05
13	Tehran	Iran	6.02
14	Beijing (Peking)	China	5.53
15	Istanbul	Turkey	5.48
16	Rio de Janeiro	Brazil	5.18
17	Tianjin	China	5.15
18	Karachi	Pakistan	5.10
19	Leningrad	USSR	4.95
20	Delhi	India	4.88
21	Bangkok	Thailand	4.70
22	Detroit	USA	4.60
23	Santiago	Chile	4.10
24	Bogotá	Colombia	4.07
25	Pusan	South Korea	3.40
26	Calcutta	India	3.29
27	Madras	India	3.27
28	Madrid	Spain	3.19
29	Yokohama	Japan	3.15
30	Shenyang	China	3.03

Highest urban pop.
% pop. living in urban areas 1985

1	Macao	100.0
	Singapore	100.0
3	Belgium	96.3
4	Kuwait	93.7
5	Hong Kong	92.4
6	UK	91.7
7	Israel	90.3
8	Iceland	89.4
9	Netherlands	88.4
10	Qatar	88.0

Lowest urban pop.
% pop. living in urban areas 1985

1	Bhutan	4.5
2	Burundi	5.6
3	Rwanda	6.2
4	Nepal	7.7
5	Burkina Faso	7.9
6	Oman	8.8
7	Uganda	9.4
8	Cambodia	10.8
9	Ethiopia	11.6
10	Bangladesh	11.9

Highest population density
Pop. per sq km

1	Macao	25,882	21	India	242
2	Hong Kong	5,308		Trinidad & Tobago	242
3	Singapore	4,288	23	UK	234
4	Bermuda	1,132	24	Jamaica	223
5	Malta	1,076	25	Israel	219
6	Bangladesh	726	26	Haiti	199
7	Bahrain	695	27	Philippines	196
8	Mauritius	591	28	Italy	195
9	Barbados	580		Vietnam	195
10	Taiwan	553	30	Neth Antilles	191
11	South Korea	423	31	Burundi	185
12	Netherlands	396	32	North Korea	178
13	Puerto Rico	370	33	Switzerland	160
14	Japan	325	34	East Germany	154
15	Belgium	300	35	Luxembourg	143
16	Lebanon	272	36	Dominican Republic	141
17	Rwanda	256	37	Pakistan	132
18	Sri Lanka	253	38	Nepal	130
19	West Germany	246	39	Czechoslovakia	122
20	El Salvador	243	40	Poland	121

Lowest population density
Pop. per sq km

1	Mongolia	1.3	21	Papua New Guinea	7.7
2	Mauritania	1.9	22	Sudan	9.5
3	Namibia	2.1	23	Paraguay	9.9
	Australia	2.1	24	Zambia	10.0
5	Botswana	2.2		Algeria	10.0
6	Libya	2.4	26	Norway	10.8
	Iceland	2.4	27	Somalia	11.2
8	Canada	2.8	28	Argentina	11.5
9	Chad	4.2	29	New Zealand	12.3
10	CAR	4.5	30	USSR	12.7
	Gabon	4.5	31	Zaire	14.3
12	Oman	4.6	32	Finland	14.6
13	Guyana	4.7	33	Laos	16.3
14	Niger	5.3	34	Peru	16.5
15	Congo	5.5	35	Chile	16.8
16	Bolivia	6.4	36	Brazil	17.0
17	Saudi Arabia	6.5	37	Bahamas	17.2
18	South Yemen	7.0	38	Uruguay	17.6
19	Mali	7.2	39	UAE	17.9
20	Angola	7.5	40	Mozambique	18.7

a Capital city.
Notes: Estimates of cities' populations vary according to where geographical boundaries are defined. As far as possible the data refer to complete conurbations but some figures may refer to administrative areas and exclude the outer suburbs.

Estimates of population density refer to the total land area of a country. In countries such as Japan and Canada, where much of the land area is virtually uninhabitable, the effective population densities of the habitable areas are much greater than the figures suggest.

Population: *age and sex*

Youngest populations
% aged under 15

1	Kenya	52.1		Namibia	45.8
2	Côte d'Ivoire	49.4		Nicaragua	45.8
3	Zambia	49.1	23	Pakistan	45.7
	Tanzania	49.1		Liberia	45.7
5	Rwanda	48.9	25	Burundi	45.6
6	Kuwait	48.7	26	Guatemala	45.5
7	Uganda	48.5	27	Saudi Arabia	45.4
	Botswana	48.5		Ghana	45.4
9	Nigeria	48.4	29	Togo	45.3
10	North Yemen	48.1		Sudan	45.3
	Syria	48.1	31	Madagascar	45.1
12	Jordan	47.9	32	Ethiopia	44.9
13	Somalia	47.6		Angola	44.9
14	Benin	47.5	34	Zimbabwe	44.8
15	Niger	47.3	35	South Yemen	44.7
16	Mali	46.6	36	Mauritania	44.6
17	Zaire	46.2		Honduras	44.6
18	Malawi	46.1	38	El Salvador	44.5
19	Libya	45.8		Sierra Leone	44.5
	Oman	45.8		Senegal	44.5

Oldest populations
% aged over 65

1	Sweden	18.3	21	Japan	11.7
2	Norway	16.4	22	Czechoslovakia	11.6
3	UK	15.5	23	Canada	11.4
	Denmark	15.5	24	Uruguay	11.2
5	West Germany	15.4	25	Australia	11.0
6	Switzerland	15.3		New Zealand	11.0
7	Austria	15.0	27	Iceland	10.4
8	Belgium	14.7	28	Romania	10.3
9	Italy	14.2		Cyprus	10.3
10	France	13.8		Ireland	10.3
11	Greece	13.7	31	Barbados	10.2
12	Luxembourg	13.4		Malta	10.2
	Hungary	13.4	33	Poland	10.0
14	Finland	13.2	34	USSR	9.6
15	East Germany	13.1	35	Argentina	9.1
16	Spain	13.0		Yugoslavia	9.1
	Bulgaria	13.0	37	Israel	8.9
18	Portugal	12.9	38	Hong Kong	8.8
	Netherlands	12.9	39	Puerto Rico	8.6
20	USA	12.6	40	Cuba	8.4

Notes: Data refer to 1985-90.

Most male populations
No. men per 100 women[a]

1	UAE	206.8	Iran	103.5
2	Qatar	167.3	23 Singapore	103.4
3	Bahrain	145.3	Cuba	103.4
4	Kuwait	132.9	25 Dominican Republic	103.3
5	Saudi Arabia	119.1	26 Egypt	103.1
6	Oman	110.4	27 Côte d'Ivoire	102.8
7	Libya	110.1	28 Paraguay	102.6
8	Pakistan	108.6	29 Tunisia	102.4
9	Papua New Guinea	107.8	Syria	102.4
10	Bhutan	107.2	31 Liberia	102.2
11	India	107.0	Costa Rica	102.2
12	Hong Kong	106.5	33 Guatemala	102.1
13	Bangladesh	106.3	34 Venezuela	101.8
14	Albania	106.0	Honduras	101.8
	China	106.0	36 Malaysia	101.6
16	Afghanistan	105.9	37 Peru	101.5
17	Turkey	105.4	38 Ecuador	101.2
	Nepal	105.4	39 Iceland	101.1
	Jordan	105.4	40 Laos	101.0
20	Iraq	103.9	Philippines	101.0
21	Panama	103.5		

Most female populations
No. men per 100 women

1	USSR	89.9	21 Switzerland	95.3
2	Somalia	91.2	UK	95.3
3	Barbados	91.4	23 France	95.4
	North Yemen	91.4	Poland	95.4
5	East Germany	91.6	25 Romania	95.5
6	Botswana	91.7	26 Belgium	95.6
	Austria	91.7	27 Vietnam	96.0
8	Lesotho	92.6	28 Burundi	96.1
	West Germany	92.6	29 El Salvador	96.2
10	Hungary	93.2	30 Haiti	96.4
11	Portugal	93.3	31 Sierra Leone	96.6
12	Finland	94.2	32 Uruguay	96.7
13	Lebanon	94.4	Japan	96.7
14	Italy	94.6	34 Denmark	96.9
15	Mali	94.7	35 Spain	97.0
16	CAR	94.8	Malawi	97.0
17	Puerto Rico	94.9	Benin	97.0
18	Luxembourg	95.1	38 Angola	97.1
	Czechoslovakia	95.1	Greece	97.1
20	USA	95.2	Gabon	97.1

a Large numbers of immigrant workers, mostly men, result in the high male ratios of
several Middle East countries.

Notes: Data refer to 1988.

Population: *matters of breeding*

Highest crude birth rates
No. live births per 1,000 pop. 1985-90

1	Kenya	53.9		Madagascar	45.7
2	Malawi	53.0		Senegal	45.7
3	Zambia	51.2	28	Zaire	45.6
4	Rwanda	51.0	29	Mozambique	45.0
5	Niger	50.9		Liberia	45.0
	Côte d'Ivoire	50.9	31	Togo	44.9
7	Somalia	50.8	32	Sudan	44.6
8	Tanzania	50.5	33	Congo	44.4
	Benin	50.5	34	Ghana	44.3
10	Mali	50.1		CAR	44.3
	Uganda	50.1	36	Chad	44.2
12	Nigeria	49.8	37	Syria	44.1
13	Afghanistan	49.3	38	Namibia	44.0
14	Sierra Leone	48.2	39	Libya	43.9
15	North Yemen	47.9	40	Ethiopia	43.7
16	Botswana	47.3	41	Bolivia	42.8
	South Yemen	47.3	42	Iraq	42.6
18	Burkina Faso	47.2	43	Iran	42.4
	Angola	47.2	44	Bangladesh	42.2
20	Pakistan	47.0	45	Saudi Arabia	42.0
21	Guinea	46.6	46	Nicaragua	41.8
22	Mauritania	46.2	47	Zimbabwe	41.7
23	Oman	46.0	48	Cameroon	41.6
24	Jordan	45.9	49	Cambodia	41.4
25	Burundi	45.7	50	Laos	41.3

Highest fertility rates
Av. no. children per woman 1985-90

1	Rwanda	8.29		Madagascar	6.60
2	Kenya	8.12	22	Liberia	6.50
3	Côte d'Ivoire	7.41		Pakistan	6.50
4	Zambia	7.20		Mauritania	6.50
5	Oman	7.17		Sierra Leone	6.50
	Saudi Arabia	7.17		Burkina Faso	6.50
	Jordan	7.17	27	Sudan	6.44
8	Niger	7.10	28	Ghana	6.39
	Tanzania	7.10		Mozambique	6.39
10	Benin	7.00		Angola	6.39
	Malawi	7.00		Senegal	6.39
	Nigeria	7.00	32	Iraq	6.35
13	North Yemen	6.97	33	Burundi	6.31
14	Afghanistan	6.90	34	Botswana	6.25
	Uganda	6.90	35	Guinea	6.19
16	Libya	6.87	36	Ethiopia	6.15
17	Syria	6.76	37	Zaire	6.09
18	Mali	6.70		Namibia	6.09
19	South Yemen	6.66		Togo	6.09
20	Somalia	6.60	40	Bolivia	6.06

Lowest crude birth rates
No. live births per 1,000 pop. 1985-90

1	West Germany	10.4		Czechoslovakia	14.0
2	Denmark	10.7	22	Canada	14.1
3	Italy	10.8	23	Malta	14.7
4	Sweden	11.2	24	Australia	15.0
5	Japan	11.4		Yugoslavia	15.0
6	Luxembourg	11.5	26	USA	15.1
7	Austria	11.6	27	Romania	15.5
	Hungary	11.6	28	New Zealand	15.6
9	Switzerland	11.7	29	Hong Kong	15.9
	Belgium	11.7	30	Cuba	16.0
11	Netherlands	11.8	31	Poland	16.4
12	Greece	11.9	32	Singapore	16.5
13	Norway	12.4	33	Iceland	16.8
14	Finland	12.5	34	Ireland	18.1
15	Bulgaria	12.7	35	USSR	18.4
16	Spain	12.8	36	Mauritius	18.5
17	East Germany	12.9		Barbados	18.5
18	UK	13.4	38	Cyprus	18.6
19	Portugal	13.5	39	South Korea	18.8
20	France	14.0	40	Uruguay	18.9

Lowest fertility rates
Av. no. children per woman 1985-90

1	West Germany	1.38		Portugal	1.75
2	Denmark	1.45	22	UK	1.80
	Netherlands	1.45	23	US	1.83
	Italy	1.45	24	France	1.85
	Luxembourg	1.45		Australia	1.85
6	Austria	1.50	26	Malta	1.90
7	Switzerland	1.55		New Zealand	1.90
	Belgium	1.55		Bulgaria	1.90
9	Finland	1.65	29	Mauritius	1.94
	Singapore	1.65	30	Yugoslavia	1.95
	Sweden	1.65	31	Czechoslovakia	2.00
	Canada	1.65		Barbados	2.00
13	Norway	1.69		South Korea	2.00
14	Spain	1.70	34	Iceland	2.05
	Greece	1.70	35	Romania	2.15
	Japan	1.70	36	Poland	2.20
	East Germany	1.70	37	Cyprus	2.31
	Hong Kong	1.70	38	China	2.36
19	Cuba	1.71	39	USSR	2.38
20	Hungary	1.75	40	Puerto Rico	2.44

Notes: The crude birth rate is the number of live births in one year per 1,000 population. In addition to the fertility rate (see below) it depends on the population's age structure and will tend to be higher if there is a large proportion of women of childbearing age.

The fertility rate is the average number of children born to a woman who completes her childbearing years.

Economic strength

Biggest economies
GDP $bn 1988

1	USA	4,881	36	Algeria	54
2	Japan	2,859	37	Yugoslavia	53
3	West Germany	1,208		Iraq	53
4	France	949	39	Greece	52
5	Italy	828	40	Czechoslovakia[a]	42
6	UK	826	41	Portugal	41
7	USSR[a]	583		Israel	41
8	Canada	488	43	Pakistan	40
9	Brazil	354	44	Colombia	39
10	Spain	338	45	Philippines	38
11	China	332	46	New Zealand	37
12	India	267	47	Malaysia	34
13	Australia	232	48	Ireland	32
14	Netherlands	227	49	Romania[b]	31
15	Switzerland	183	50	Peru	30
16	Sweden	178		Nigeria	30
17	Mexico	173	52	Egypt	29
18	South Korea	171	53	Hungary	27
19	Belgium	152	54	Cuba	26
20	Austria	126	55	Libya	24
21	Taiwan	118	56	Singapore	23
22	Denmark	107		UAE	23
23	Finland	104	58	Chile	22
24	Norway	91	59	Kuwait	19
25	Argentina	88		Bulgaria[a]	19
26	East Germany[a]	87	61	North Korea[b]	18
	South Africa	87		Bangladesh	18
28	Indonesia	82		Morocco	18
29	Saudi Arabia	74		Puerto Rico	18
30	Turkey	72	65	Syria	14
31	Poland[a]	65	66	Cameroon	12
32	Iran	64	67	Sudan	11
33	Venezuela	63	68	Tunisia	10
34	Thailand	58		Burma[a]	10
35	Hong Kong	54	70	Côte d'Ivoire	9

a Estimate.
b Estimate based on very limited information.

Notes: Several East European and other planned (or formerly planned) economies use national accounting methods which provide estimates of Net (or Gross) Material Product (NMP or GMP see glossary for fuller details).

In most instances, official exchange rates for 1988 have been used to convert GDP figures from national currencies into US dollars. For a few countries, where the official rate is (or was) extremely unrealistic, a compromise rate has been used. These are:

East Europe		**Asia**	
Bulgaria	$1 = Lv1.66	Laos	$1 = K400
Czechoslovakia	$1 = Kcs51.6		
East Germany	$1 = EM3.5	**Middle East**	
Romania	$1 = Lei28.56	Iran	$1 = IR313.3
USSR	$1 = Rb1.22	Iraq	$1 = ID0.53

Human development index

1	Japan	99.6	41	Romania	86.3
2	Sweden	98.7	42	Venezuela	86.1
3	Switzerland	98.6	43	Kuwait	83.9
4	Netherlands	98.4	44	Jamaica	82.4
5	Canada	98.3	45	Colombia	80.1
	Norway	98.3	46	Malaysia	80.0
7	Australia	97.8	47	Albania	79.0
8	France	97.4	48	Sri Lanka	78.9
9	Denmark	97.1		North Korea	78.9
10	UK	97.0	50	Mauritius	78.8
11	Finland	96.7	51	Brazil	78.4
	West Germany	96.7		Paraguay	78.4
13	Belgium	96.6	53	Thailand	78.3
	New Zealand	96.6	54	UAE	78.2
	Italy	96.6	55	Iraq	75.9
16	Spain	96.5	56	Ecuador	75.8
17	USA	96.1	57	Peru	75.3
	Ireland	96.1	58	Jordan	75.2
	Austria	96.1	59	Turkey	75.1
20	Israel	95.7	60	Nicaragua	74.3
21	East Germany	95.3	61	Mongolia	73.7
22	Greece	94.9	62	Lebanon	73.5
23	Hong Kong	93.6	63	South Africa	73.1
24	Czechoslovakia	93.1	64	Libya	71.9
	Chile	93.1	65	China	71.6
26	USSR	92.0	66	Philippines	71.4
27	Bulgaria	91.8	67	Saudi Arabia	70.2
28	Costa Rica	91.6	68	Dominican Republic	69.9
	Uruguay	91.6	69	Syria	69.1
30	Hungary	91.5	70	Iran	66.0
31	Yugoslavia	91.3	71	Tunisia	65.7
32	Poland	91.0	72	El Salvador	65.1
	Argentina	91.0	73	Botswana	64.6
34	South Korea	90.3	74	Algeria	60.9
35	Singapore	89.9	75	Vietnam	60.8
36	Portugal	89.9	76	Guatemala	59.2
37	Trinidad & Tobago	88.5	77	Indonesia	59.1
38	Panama	88.3	78	Lesotho	58.0
39	Cuba	87.7	79	Zimbabwe	57.6
40	Mexico	87.6	80	Honduras	56.3

GDP or GDP per head is often taken as a measure of how developed a country is but its usefulness is limited as it only refers to economic welfare.

In 1990 the UN Development Programme published its first estimate of a Human Development Index, which combines statistics on two other indicators – adult literacy and life expectancy – with income levels to give a better, though still far from perfect, indicator of human development. The index is shown here scaled from 0 to 100; countries scoring over 80 are considered to have high human development, those scoring from 50 to 79 have medium human development and those under 50 have low human development. Technical details are shown in the glossary.

World economies: *rich and poor*

Highest GDP per head
$ 1988

1	Switzerland	27,748
2	Bermuda	23,793
3	Iceland	23,640
4	Japan	23,325
5	Norway	21,724
6	Finland	21,156
7	Sweden	21,155
8	Denmark	20,988
9	USA	19,815
10	West Germany	19,743
11	Canada	18,834
12	Luxembourg	18,000
13	France	17,004
14	Austria	16,675
15	Qatar	15,909
16	UAE	15,560
17	Netherlands	15,421
18	Brunei[a]	15,417
19	Belgium	15,394
20	UK	14,477
21	Italy	14,432
22	Australia	14,083
23	New Zealand	11,544
24	Bahamas	10,833
25	Kuwait	10,189
26	Hong Kong	9,613
27	Israel	9,368
28	Ireland	9,181
29	Singapore	9,019
30	Spain	8,668
31	Neth Antilles	7,895
32	Cyprus	7,709
33	Bahrain	7,583
34	Taiwan	5,975
35	Macao	5,909
36	Libya	5,853
37	Barbados	5,840
38	Oman	5,500
39	Puerto Rico	5,384
40	Saudi Arabia	5,311
41	East Germany[a]	5,256
42	Greece	5,244
43	Malta	5,057
44	South Korea	4,081
45	Portugal	4,017
46	Venezuela	3,400
47	Trinidad & Tobago	3,379
48	Iraq	3,090
49	South Africa	2,958
50	Argentina	2,759
51	Czechoslovakia[a]	2,737
52	Gabon	2,733
53	Hungary	2,625
54	Uruguay	2,595
55	Cuba	2,509
56	Brazil	2,451
57	Yugoslavia	2,279
58	Algeria	2,269
59	Bulgaria[a]	2,217
60	Mexico	2,102
61	USSR[a]	2,055
62	Malaysia	2,045
63	Panama	1,918
64	Lebanon[b]	1,887
65	Mauritius	1,855
66	Chile	1,732
67	Poland[a]	1,719
68	Costa Rica	1,638
69	Paraguay	1,545
70	Botswana	1,488

Lowest GDP per head
$ 1988

1	Mozambique[a]	78
2	Cambodia[b]	83
3	Ethiopia[a]	114
4	Tanzania	123
5	Laos	129
6	Madagascar	139
7	Afghanistan[b]	143
8	Vietnam	154
9	Chad	159
10	Nepal	160
11	Bangladesh	179
12	Malawi	186
13	Zaire	193
14	Bhutan[a]	197
15	Burkina Faso	204
	Uganda	204
17	Burundi	214
18	Mali	217
19	Sierra Leone	233
20	Somalia	241

a Estimate.

b Estimate based on limited information.

Highest purchasing power[a]
GDP per head in PPP (USA = 100)

1	USA	100.0	36	Argentina	26.4
2	Canada	92.5	37	Mexico	26.3
3	Switzerland	87.0	38	Mauritius	24.8
4	Norway	84.4	39	Poland	24.5
5	Iceland	79.0		Brazil	24.5
	Luxembourg	79.0	41	Venezuela	24.4
7	Kuwait	78.6	42	South Korea	24.3
8	Sweden	76.9	43	Panama	22.8
9	Denmark	74.2	44	Malaysia	21.9
10	West Germany	73.8	45	Turkey	21.8
11	Singapore	72.6	46	Costa Rica	21.3
12	Japan	71.5	47	Trinidad & Tobago	20.8
13	Australia	71.1	48	Colombia	20.0
14	Finland	69.5	49	Tunisia	19.8
15	France	69.3	50	Jordan	17.9
16	UAE	69.2	51	Peru	17.8
17	Netherlands	68.2	52	Thailand	17.0
18	Austria	66.1	53	Congo	16.4
	UK	66.1	54	Botswana	16.1
20	Italy	65.6	55	Egypt	15.8
21	Belgium	64.7	56	Ecuador	15.3
22	New Zealand	60.9	57	Algeria	14.9
23	Hong Kong	60.4	58	Paraguay	14.8
24	Israel	52.1	59	Jamaica	14.2
25	Saudi Arabia	47.2	60	Cameroon	14.0
26	Spain	46.0	61	Morocco	13.1
27	Ireland	40.9	62	Nicaragua	12.5
28	Greece	36.0	63	China	12.1
29	Portugal	33.8	64	Gabon	11.7
30	Hungary	31.2		Sri Lanka	11.7
31	Yugoslavia	29.2	66	Guatemala	11.1
32	Uruguay	28.7	67	Philippines	10.7
33	Iran	28.3	68	Papua New Guinea	10.5
	South Africa	28.3	69	Côte d'Ivoire	10.2
35	Chile	27.6	70	Zimbabwe	9.9

Lowest purchasing power[a]
GDP per head in PPP (USA=100)

1	Zaire	1.4	11	Malawi	3.6
2	Ethiopia	1.6	12	Rwanda	3.8
3	Mali	2.4		Togo	3.8
4	Burundi	2.6	14	Madagascar	3.9
	Tanzania	2.6	15	Liberia	4.0
	Niger	2.6	16	Nepal	4.1
7	Ghana	2.7	17	Sudan	4.3
8	Uganda	2.9	18	Haiti	4.4
9	Sierra Leone	3.0	19	Kenya	4.5
10	CAR	3.4	20	India	4.7

a See glossary for explanation of purchasing power parity.

Economic growth

Fastest economic growth 1980-88
Av. ann. % increase in real GDP

1	China	11.4	21	Egypt	5.4
2	Botswana	10.6		Chad	5.4
3	Oman	9.8	23	Congo	5.3
4	Laos[a]	9.1		Turkey	5.3
5	South Korea	9.0	25	Malaysia	5.1
6	Bhutan[b]	8.1	26	Cuba	4.7
7	North Yemen	8.0	27	Bulgaria[d]	4.5
8	Macao[c]	7.7	28	Kenya	4.3
9	Hong Kong	7.6	29	Sri Lanka	4.2
10	Taiwan	7.5		Cameroon	4.2
11	Nepal	7.0	31	Japan	4.1
12	Singapore	6.6	32	East Germany[d]	4.0
13	Mongolia[de]	6.4		Indonesia	4.0
14	Pakistan	6.3	34	Vietnam[f]	3.7
15	Burkina Faso	6.1		Puerto Rico	3.7
16	Cambodia[f]	5.8		Mali	3.7
	Mauritius	5.8	37	North Korea[f]	3.6
18	India	5.7		Morocco	3.6
19	Cyprus	5.6	39	Burundi	3.5
20	Thailand	5.5		Senegal	3.5

Slowest economic growth 1980-88
Av. ann. % increase in real GDP

1	Libya[g]	-7.3	21	Panama	-0.3
2	Saudi Arabia	-5.1	22	Togo	0.0
3	Iraq	-4.3	23	Sudan	0.1
4	UAE	-3.7		Guatemala	0.1
5	Trinidad & Tobago	-3.3		Fiji	0.1
6	Guyana	-3.1	26	Zambia	0.2
7	South Yemen	-2.2	27	Niger	0.4
8	Liberia	-1.9	28	Yugoslavia	0.5
9	Brunei	-1.7	29	Côte d'Ivoire	0.6
10	Nigeria	-1.3		Namibia[b]	0.6
11	Nicaragua	-1.2	31	Peru	0.7
12	Kuwait	-1.1	32	Venezuela	0.9
	Mozambique	-1.1	33	Poland	1.0
	Bolivia	-1.1		Barbados	1.0
15	Argentina	-0.9		Mexico	1.0
	Madagascar	-0.9	36	Sierra Leone	1.1
17	Haiti	-0.8	37	Jamaica	1.2
	El Salvador	-0.8	38	Philippines	1.3
19	Uruguay	-0.5		Ethiopia	1.3
20	Gabon	-0.4	40	Greece	1.4

a 1980-85.
b 1981-86.
c 1982-88.
d Net Material Product.
e 1980-86.
f Estimate based on total agricultural output.
g 1980-87.

Fastest economic growth 1965-80

Av. ann. % increase in real GDP

1	Oman	15.2	11	Brazil	9.0
2	Botswana	14.2	12	North Yemen[a]	8.9
3	Saudi Arabia	11.3	13	Ecuador	8.7
4	Iraq[a]	10.5		Syria	8.7
5	Malta	10.1	15	Hong Kong	8.6
	Singapore	10.1	16	Indonesia	8.0
7	Jordan[a]	10.0	17	Bulgaria[b]	7.6
8	Taiwan	9.8	18	Algeria	7.5
9	Gabon	9.5	19	Malaysia	7.4
	South Korea	9.5	20	Thailand	7.2

Slowest economic growth 1965-80

Av. ann. % increase in real GDP

1	Cambodia[ac]	-8.1	11	Chile	1.9
2	Lebanon	-1.2		Zambia	1.9
3	Chad	0.1		Nepal	1.9
4	Niger	0.3	14	Switzerland	2.0
5	Uganda	0.8		Mauritania	2.0
6	Zaire	1.3	16	Senegal	2.1
	Jamaica	1.3		Benin	2.1
	Kuwait	1.3		UK	2.1
9	Ghana	1.4	19	Uruguay	2.4
10	Madagascar	1.6		Bangladesh	2.4

Highest industrial growth 1980-88

Av. ann. % increase in real terms

1	Botswana	16.9	6	South Korea	10.8
2	China	13.4	7	Congo	10.5
3	North Yemen	12.5	8	Mali	9.1
4	Chad	11.2		Laos[d]	9.1
5	Oman	11.1	10	Mauritius	8.3

Highest services growth 1980-88

Av. ann. % increase in real terms

1	Laos[d]	15.6		Oman	8.6
2	North Yemen	11.6	7	Hong Kong	8.3
3	Iceland	9.6	8	Burkina Faso	8.2
4	Botswana	8.8	9	Taiwan	8.0
5	South Korea	8.6	10	Cyprus	7.0

Highest agricultural growth 1980-88

Av. ann. % increase in real terms

1	Kuwait	20.9	6	Mauritius	6.3
2	UAE	9.3	7	Burkina Faso	6.0
3	Nepal	7.5	8	South Korea	5.8
4	Burma	7.1	9	Pakistan	5.7
5	China	6.6	10	Oman	5.5

a 1970-80.
b Net Material Product.
c Estimate based on total agricultural output.
d 1980-85.

Trading places

Biggest traders
% total world exports (visible & invisible) 1988

1	USA	13.99	26	Finland	0.73
2	West Germany	10.80	27	Malaysia	0.65
3	Japan	9.93	28	Ireland	0.59
4	UK	7.74	29	Thailand	0.58
5	France	6.72	30	Indonesia	0.56
6	Italy	4.50	31	Poland	0.52
7	Belgium[a]	3.90	32	India	0.50
8	Netherlands	3.72	33	Kuwait	0.46
9	Canada	3.64		Yugoslavia	0.46
10	Switzerland	2.26	35	Turkey	0.42
11	South Korea	1.91	36	Portugal	0.39
12	Spain	1.79		Israel	0.39
13	Hong Kong	1.66	38	Romania[b]	0.38
14	Sweden	1.65	39	Greece	0.34
15	Austria	1.43		Venezuela	0.34
16	China	1.41	41	UAE	0.33
17	Singapore	1.36	42	New Zealand	0.31
18	Australia	1.15		Hungary	0.31
19	USSR	1.09	44	Argentina	0.30
	Saudi Arabia	1.09	45	Philippines	0.28
21	Mexico	1.07	46	Iran[c]	0.25
	Denmark	1.07		Iraq	0.25
23	Brazil	0.96	48	Egypt	0.24
24	Norway	0.94		Nigeria	0.24
25	South Africa	0.77	50	Algeria	0.23

Most trade dependent
Trade as % GDP[d] 1988

1	Singapore	215.8
2	Neth Antilles	149.5
3	Liberia	135.0
4	Hong Kong	115.7
5	Bahrain	110.7
6	Belgium	97.0
7	Lesotho	89.8
8	Kuwait	87.3
9	Malta	83.8
10	Guyana	77.2
11	Bahamas	75.3
12	Malaysia	71.2
13	Mauritius	68.9
14	Ireland	68.5
15	Papua New Guinea	62.7

Least trade dependent
Trade as % GDP[d] 1988

1	Mongolia	3.6
2	North Korea	5.0
3	Cuba	5.2
	Vietnam	5.2
5	Albania	6.6
6	Rwanda	6.9
7	USSR	7.1
8	India	7.2
9	East Germany	7.4
10	Sudan	8.2
11	Bangladesh	8.7
12	Benin[c]	8.8
13	Uganda	9.8
14	Brazil	10.3
15	USA	10.9

Notes: The figures are drawn from balance of payment statistics and, therefore, have differing technical definitions from trade statistics taken from customs or similar sources.

The invisible trade figures do not show some countries, notably Eastern European, due to unavailable data.

Biggest visible traders

% world visible exports 1988

1	West Germany	11.94	21	Mexico	1.08
2	USA	11.83	22	Saudi Arabia	1.05
3	Japan	9.79	23	Denmark	1.02
4	France	6.20	24	South Africa	0.95
5	UK	5.36	25	Norway	0.83
6	Italy	4.74	26	Finland	0.80
7	Canada	4.29	27	Malaysia	0.78
8	Netherlands	3.81	28	Indonesia	0.72
9	Belgium[a]	3.40	29	Ireland	0.69
10	Hong Kong	2.33	30	Poland	0.63
11	South Korea	2.26	31	Thailand	0.59
12	Switzerland	1.87	32	India	0.57
13	Sweden	1.84	33	Romania[b]	0.52
14	China	1.76	34	Yugoslavia	0.47
15	USSR	1.53		UAE	0.47
16	Spain	1.49	36	Portugal	0.39
17	Singapore	1.45	37	Venezuela	0.38
18	Brazil	1.25		Hungary	0.37
19	Australia	1.21	39	Turkey	0.37
20	Austria	1.14	40	Israel	0.36

Biggest invisible traders

% world invisible exports 1988

1	USA	19.35	21	Kuwait	0.80
2	UK	13.67	22	Finland	0.56
3	Japan	10.27	23	China	0.55
4	France	8.03		Turkey	0.55
5	West Germany	7.95		Thailand	0.55
6	Belgium[a]	5.14	26	Greece	0.50
7	Italy	3.91	27	Israel	0.47
8	Netherlands	3.50	28	Egypt	0.46
9	Switzerland	3.25	29	Yugoslavia	0.45
10	Spain	2.52	30	Portugal	0.37
11	Austria	2.15	31	India	0.35
12	Canada	2.01	32	Ireland	0.33
13	Saudi Arabia	1.21		Philippines	0.33
14	Norway	1.19	34	Malaysia	0.32
15	Sweden	1.18	35	South Africa	0.30
	Denmark	1.18	36	New Zealand	0.27
17	Singapore	1.13	37	Poland	0.25
18	South Korea	1.03	38	Venezuela	0.24
	Mexico	1.03	39	Brazil	0.23
20	Australia	1.01	40	Argentina	0.20

---

a Data for Belgium include Luxembourg.
b 1986.
c 1984.
d Average of imports and exports as % GDP.

Current account

Largest surpluses
$bn 1988

1	Japan	79.6	14	Singapore	1.7
2	West Germany	48.6	15	Turkey	1.5
3	South Korea	14.2	16	Romania	1.4
4	Taiwan	10.2	17	South Africa	1.3
5	Zimbabwe	9.0	18	Oman	0.9
6	Switzerland	8.3	19	Puerto Rico	0.8
7	Netherlands	5.3	20	Ireland	0.7
8	Brazil	4.9		Panama	0.7
9	Kuwait	4.7	22	Botswana	0.5
10	Belgium^a	3.4		Morocco	0.5
11	UAE	2.8	24	Czechoslovakia^c	0.3
12	Yugoslavia	2.5	25	Algeria	0.1
13	Malaysia	1.8			

Largest deficits
$bn 1988

1	USA	-126.2	29	Cameroon	-0.9
2	UK	-26.0	30	New Zealand	-0.8
3	Australia	-10.1	31	Austria	-0.7
4	Saudi Arabia	-9.6		Zaire	-0.7
5	Canada	-8.3		Nicaragua^b	-0.7
6	Italy	-5.4	34	Hungary	-0.6
7	India	-5.2		Israel	-0.6
8	Venezuela	-4.7		Ecuador	-0.6
9	China	-3.9		Gabon	-0.6
10	Spain	-3.8		Portugal	-0.6
11	Norway	-3.7	39	Colombia	-0.5
12	France	-3.5		North Yemen	-0.5
13	Finland	-3.0		Kenya	-0.5
14	Mexico	-2.9		East Germany	-0.5
15	Sweden	-2.5	43	Philippines	-0.4
16	Denmark	-1.8		South Yemen	-0.4
17	Thailand	-1.7		Iran	-0.4
18	Argentina	-1.6		Jordan	-0.4
	Cuba	-1.6		Sri Lanka	-0.4
20	USSR	-1.5	48	Tanzania	-0.3
21	Pakistan	-1.4		Sudan	-0.3
22	Côte d'Ivoire	-1.3		Senegal^c	-0.3
23	Egypt	-1.2		Poland	-0.3
	Indonesia	-1.2		Bangladesh	-0.3
25	Iraq	-1.1		Ethiopia	-0.3
	Peru	-1.1		Congo	-0.3
27	Greece	-1.0		Nepal	-0.3
	Nigeria	-1.0		Burma	-0.3
				Costa Rica	-0.3

a Data for Belgium include Luxembourg.
b 1986.
c Estimate.

Largest surpluses as % GDP
1988

1	South Yemen	28.2	15	West Germany	4.0
2	Botswana	27.2	16	Fiji	2.9
3	Kuwait	23.6	17	Japan	2.8
4	Panama	16.6	18	Jamaica	2.6
5	UAE	12.0	19	Morocco	2.5
6	Oman	11.2	20	Netherlands	2.3
7	Liberia	10.9	21	Belgium[a]	2.2
8	Taiwan	8.6	22	Tunisia	2.1
9	South Korea	8.3	23	Ireland	2.0
10	Singapore	6.9	24	South Africa	1.5
11	Malaysia	5.2	25	Brazil	1.4
12	Yugoslavia	4.6	26	Czechoslovakia[b]	0.7
13	Switzerland	4.5	27	Algeria	0.3
14	Puerto Rico	4.1	28	Zimbabwe	0.2

Largest deficits as % GDP
1988

1	Nicaragua[a]	-34.8	28	Costa Rica	-5.7
2	Guyana[c]	-26.7		Burundi	-5.6
3	Gabon	-18.8	30	Uganda	-5.5
4	Lesotho	-17.7		Senegal[d]	-5.5
5	Congo	-14.8	32	Mali	-5.4
6	Mauritania	-14.7	33	Rwanda	-5.2
7	Côte d'Ivoire	-12.9	34	Bahamas	-5.1
	Saudi Arabia	-12.9	35	Togo	-4.8
9	Zaire	-10.7	36	Australia	-4.3
10	Nepal	-9.6	37	Bahrain	-4.2
11	Tanzania	-9.0	38	Egypt	-4.0
12	Madagascar[a]	-8.7		Norway	-4.0
13	Ecuador	-8.5		Burkina Faso[b]	-4.0
14	North Yemen	-8.2	41	Niger	-3.9
15	Jordan	-7.7	42	Peru	-3.7
16	Venezuela	-7.4	43	Barbados	-3.6
17	Honduras	-7.3		Pakistan	-3.6
18	Cameroon	-7.1	45	Benin[c]	-3.4
19	CAR	-6.7	46	Nigeria	-3.3
20	Zambia	-6.5		Neth Antilles	-3.3
21	Papua New Guinea	-6.2		Bolivia	-3.3
	Kenya	-6.2	49	UK	-3.1
23	Cuba	-6.1	50	Thailand	-2.9
24	Ethiopia[a]	-6.0		Sudan	-2.9
25	Guatemala	-5.9		Chad	-2.9
	Trinidad & Tobago	-5.9		Finland	-2.9
27	Sri Lanka	-5.8		Burma	-2.9

a 1986.
b Estimate.
c 1985.
d 1984.

Inflation

Highest inflation 1988-89
% consumer price inflation

1	Nicaragua	4,266.3	31	Mexico	20.0
2	Peru	3,398.6	32	Israel	19.8
3	Argentina	3,079.2	33	El Salvador[a]	19.7
4	Yugoslavia	1,250.0	34	Chile	17.0
5	Brazil	286.9	35	Burma[a]	16.1
6	Poland	244.0	36	Bolivia	16.0
7	Uganda[a]	183.7	37	Hungary	15.6
8	Zaire	104.1	38	Madagascar	15.0
9	Venezuela	84.5	39	South Africa	14.7
10	Somalia[a]	82.0	40	Jamaica	14.4
11	Turkey[a]	75.4	41	Sri Lanka[a]	14.0
12	Uruguay[a]	62.2	42	Greece	13.8
13	Syria	59.4	43	Chad[a]	12.8
14	Ecuador[a]	58.3		Zimbabwe	12.8
15	Zambia[a]	55.7	45	Mauritius	12.6
16	Iraq	45.0		Portugal	12.6
17	Dominican Republic[a]	44.4	47	Fiji[a]	11.7
18	Nigeria	40.9	48	Botswana	11.5
19	Guyana[a]	40.0	49	Lesotho[a]	11.4
20	Iran	37.5	50	Guatemala[a]	10.9
21	Sierra Leone[a]	34.3	51	Philippines	10.6
22	Malawi[a]	33.9	52	Kenya	10.4
23	Tanzania[a]	31.2		Pakistan	10.4
24	Ghana[a]	31.0	54	Bangladesh	10.0
25	Colombia[a]	28.1	55	Honduras	9.8
26	Paraguay[a]	22.7	56	Hong Kong	9.7
27	Afghanistan[a]	22.0	57	Liberia[a]	9.6
28	Egypt	21.3	58	Algeria	9.2
29	Costa Rica[a]	20.8	59	Nepal[a]	9.0
30	China	20.7	60	Cameroon	8.6

Highest inflation 1984-89
% av. ann. consumer price inflation

1	Peru	2,414.4	16	Turkey[b]	47.8
2	Nicaragua	1,539.9	17	Zambia[b]	41.0
3	Argentina	444.0	18	Iraq	38.0
4	Brazil	390.2	19	Sudan[b]	36.9
5	Peru	371.7	20	Ecuador[b]	33.5
6	Yugoslavia	345.2	21	Tanzania[b]	32.6
7	Bolivia	246.6	22	Venezuela	30.6
8	Uganda[b]	143.6	23	Ghana[b]	28.6
9	Sierra Leone[b]	81.9	24	Afghanistan[b]	26.5
10	Mexico	77.3	25	Dominican Republic[b]	26.3
11	Poland	75.6	26	Paraguay[b]	24.3
12	Zaire	69.6	27	Syria[c]	24.1
13	Uruguay[b]	65.8	28	Iceland	23.5
14	Israel	58.2	29	Guyana[b]	22.9
15	Somalia[b]	52.8	30	Colombia[a]	22.0

Lowest inflation 1988-89

% consumer price inflation

1	CAR[a]	-4.0		France	3.5
2	Senegal[a]	-1.9	27	Congo[a]	3.6
3	Niger[a]	-1.4	28	Haiti[a]	4.0
4	Gabon[a]	-0.9		Canada	4.0
5	Togo[a]	-0.2		Morocco	4.0
6	Panama[a]	0.3	31	Ireland	4.1
	Bahrain[a]	0.3	32	Burkina Faso[a]	4.2
8	Malta[a]	0.9	33	Taiwan	4.4
9	Netherlands	1.1	34	Burundi[a]	4.5
10	Saudi Arabia	1.2	35	Norway	4.6
11	Czechoslovakia	1.4	36	USA	4.8
	Mauritania[a]	1.4		Denmark	4.8
13	Kuwait[a]	1.5		Finland	4.8
14	Japan	2.3	39	Barbados[a]	4.9
15	Singapore	2.4	40	Papua New Guinea[a]	5.4
16	Neth Antilles[a]	2.6		Bahamas	5.4
	Austria	2.6	42	Thailand	5.5
18	Malaysia	2.8	43	South Korea	5.6
	West Germany	2.8	44	New Zealand	5.7
20	Rwanda[a]	2.9	45	Côte d'Ivoire	6.0
21	Belgium	3.1	46	Indonesia	6.1
22	Switzerland	3.2	47	Sweden	6.5
	Jordan[a]	3.2	48	Italy	6.6
24	Luxembourg	3.3	49	Spain	6.8
25	Cyprus[a]	3.5	50	Ethiopia[a]	7.0

Lowest inflation 1984-89

% av. ann. consumer price inflation

1	Saudi Arabia	-1.2	16	Jordan[b]	1.9
	Bahrain[b]	-1.2	17	Neth Antilles[b]	2.0
3	Niger[b]	-0.9		Burkina Faso[b]	2.0
4	Togo[b]	-0.3	19	Switzerland	2.1
5	Malta[b]	0.5	20	Austria	2.2
6	Singapore	0.7	21	Haiti[b]	2.3
	Netherlands	0.7	22	Belgium	2.4
	CAR[b]	0.7	23	Rwanda[b]	2.6
9	Panama[b]	0.8	24	Thailand	3.2
10	Kuwait[b]	1.1	25	France	3.5
	Japan	1.1	26	Barbados[b]	3.6
12	Taiwan	1.3		USA	3.6
	West Germany	1.3	28	Ireland	3.7
14	Malaysia	1.4		Liberia[b]	3.7
15	Luxembourg	1.8		Cyprus[b]	3.7

a 1987-88.
b 1983-88.

Notes: Inflation is measured as the % increase in the consumer price index between two dates. The figures shown are based on the average level of the index during the relevant years.

Debt

Highest foreign debt[b]
$m 1988

#	Country	Amount	#	Country	Amount
1	Brazil	114,591	21	Iraq	20,696
2	Mexico	101,566	22	Malaysia	20,541
3	Argentina	58,936	23	East Germany[a]	20,300
4	India	57,513	24	Morocco	19,923
5	Indonesia	52,600	25	Chile	19,645
6	Egypt	49,971	26	Peru	18,639
7	South Korea	43,183	27	Saudi Arabia	18,538
8	China	42,085	28	Hungary[a]	17,349
9	USSR	40,856	29	Portugal	17,313
10	Turkey	39,592	30	Pakistan	17,010
11	Poland[a]	39,200	31	Colombia	17,000
12	Venezuela	34,657	32	Côte d'Ivoire	14,125
13	Nigeria	30,719	33	Taiwan	13,869
14	Philippines	29,448	34	Sudan	11,859
15	Israel	25,100	35	Ecuador	10,865
16	Algeria	24,850	36	Bangladesh	10,220
17	Greece	23,514	37	Hong Kong	9,300
18	Thailand	21,756	38	Zaire	8,474
19	Yugoslavia	21,684	39	Nicaragua	8,052
20	South Africa	21,185	40	UAE	7,820

Highest debt service[c]
$m 1988

#	Country	Amount	#	Country	Amount
1	Brazil	16,599	21	Yugoslavia	3,334
2	Mexico	14,662	22	Colombia	3,096
3	Indonesia	9,133	23	Thailand	2,736
4	South Korea	9,023	24	South Africa	2,459
5	Turkey	6,650	25	Nigeria	2,064
6	Algeria	6,444	26	Saudi Arabia	1,918
7	Argentina	5,777	27	Chile	1,858
8	Malaysia	5,568	28	Egypt	1,826
9	Venezuela	5,445	29	Hong Kong	1,584
10	Poland[a]	5,250	30	Morocco	1,532
11	Israel	4,836	31	Pakistan	1,525
12	Portugal	4,687	32	Kuwait	1,440
13	China	4,578	33	Taiwan	1,340
14	Romania[a]	4,235	34	Tunisia	1,134
15	Greece	4,015	35	Bulgaria	1,129
16	East Germany	3,702	36	Côte d'Ivoire	1,085
	Hungary[a]	3,702	37	UAE	982
18	Iraq	3,465	38	Czechoslovakia	950
19	Philippines	3,409	39	Singapore	927
20	India	3,390		Jordan	927

Highest foreign debt burden
Foreign debt as % GDP 1988

1	Guyana	521.8	21	Guinea	105.0
2	Mozambique	436.0	22	Nigeria	100.5
3	Nicaragua	407.0	23	Malawi	97.1
4	Zaire	349.9	24	Costa Rica	95.6
5	Zambia	238.8	25	Chile	95.0
6	Mauritania	223.5	26	Togo	93.1
7	Congo	217.3	27	Laos	92.6
8	Somalia	214.8	28	Bolivia	91.6
9	South Yemen	211.9	29	Morocco	90.6
10	Madagascar	209.2	30	Dominican Republic	85.2
11	Egypt	182.6	31	Gabon	80.7
12	Tanzania	164.6	32	Senegal	75.8
13	Liberia	146.0	33	Honduras	75.4
14	Côte d'Ivoire	142.0	34	Philippines	75.1
15	Jamaica	135.2	35	Niger	74.6
16	Panama	124.4	36	Burundi	74.0
17	Jordan	120.8	37	Sri Lanka	73.7
18	Mali	108.1	38	Argentina	69.5
19	Sudan	106.7	39	Kenya	68.4
20	Ecuador	105.3	40	Tunisia	66.5

Highest debt service ratios[c]
% 1988

1	Algeria	79.0	21	Côte d'Ivoire	36.2
2	Niger	74.6	22	East Germany[a]	35.8
3	Nicaragua	64.7	23	Uruguay	33.7
4	Romania[a]	54.9	24	Iraq	32.6
5	Poland[a]	53.9	25	Congo	32.1
6	Madagascar	53.7	26	Israel	31.9
7	Argentina	51.2		Philippines	31.9
8	Burundi	47.8	28	Portugal	31.8
9	Uganda	47.2	29	Mozambique	31.6
10	Mexico	46.1		Papua New Guinea	31.6
11	Colombia	46.0	31	Cameroon	31.2
12	Brazil	44.4	32	Guatemala	29.9
13	Indonesia	43.0	33	Sierra Leone	28.8
14	Venezuela	42.5	34	Pakistan	28.7
15	Hungary[a]	40.6	35	Honduras	28.3
16	Ethiopia	39.2		Morocco	28.3
17	Turkey	37.4	37	Zimbabwe	27.8
18	Jordan	36.9	38	Sudan	27.2
19	Bolivia	36.6	39	Kenya	27.1
	Bulgaria[a]	36.6	40	USSR	27.0

a Convertible currency debt only. The debt service is calculated as a % of convertible currency exports.
b Foreign debt is debt owed to non-residents and repayable in foreign currency; the figures shown include liabilities of government, public and private sectors. Developed countries have been excluded.
c Debt service is the sum of interest and principal repayments (amortization) due on outstanding foreign debt. The debt service ratio is debt service expressed as a percentage of the country's exports of goods and services.

Aid

Largest donors
$m 1988

1	USA*	10,141	16	Finland*	608
2	Japan*	9,134	17	Belgium*	597
3	France**	6,865	18	Austria*	302
4	West Germany*	4,731	19	Spain	240
5	USSR	4,212	20	China	185
6	Italy*	3,183	21	East Germany	180
7	UK*	2,645	22	Libya	129
8	Canada*	2,342	23	India	126
9	Netherlands*	2,231	24	Kuwait	108
10	Saudi Arabia	2,098	25	New Zealand*	105
11	Sweden*	1,529	26	Portugal	83
12	Australia*	1,101	27	Ireland*	57
13	Norway*	985	28	Venezuela	49
14	Denmark*	922	29	Greece	38
15	Switzerland*	617	30	South Korea	20

Largest recipients
$m 1988

1	India	2,099	31	Papua New Guinea	377
2	China	1,973	32	Niger	371
3	Indonesia	1,626	33	Uganda	353
4	Bangladesh	1,590	34	Malawi	335
5	Egypt	1,537	35	French Polynesia	331
6	Pakistan	1,439	36	Tunisia	326
7	Israel	1,241	37	Honduras	323
8	Tanzania	975	38	Madagascar	304
9	Sudan	923	39	Burkina Faso	297
10	Ethiopia	912	40	Cameroon	286
11	Mozambique	882		Turkey	286
12	Philippines	854	42	Peru	272
13	Kenya	808	43	Zimbabwe	270
14	Réunion	608	44	Guadeloupe	266
15	Sri Lanka	592	45	Chad	264
16	Zaire	580	46	Guinea	262
17	Senegal	566	47	New Caledonia	261
18	Thailand	557	48	Rwanda	247
19	Morocco	481	49	Guatemala	232
20	Zambia	477	50	North Yemen	226
21	Ghana	474	51	Brazil	210
22	Martinique	461	52	Nicaragua	209
23	Burma	451	53	Syria	205
24	Somalia	447	54	Togo	199
25	Côte d'Ivoire	439	55	CAR	197
26	Jordan	431	56	Jamaica	193
27	Mali	427	57	Costa Rica	188
28	El Salvador	419	58	Mauritania	184
29	Nepal	399	59	Burundi	183
30	Bolivia	392	60	Mexico	173

Largest donors as % GNP
1988

1	Saudi Arabia	2.70	Switzerland*	0.32
2	Norway*	1.10	UK*	0.32
3	Netherlands*	0.98	18 Luxembourg	0.29
4	Denmark*	0.89	19 New Zealand*	0.27
5	Sweden*	0.87	20 Austria*	0.24
6	France*ᵃ	0.72	21 USA*	0.21
7	Finland*	0.59	22 Ireland*	0.20
8	Libya	0.51	23 Portugal	0.20
9	Canada*	0.49	Qatar	0.16
10	Australia*	0.47	25 Venezuela	0.08
11	Kuwait	0.41	26 Greece	0.07
12	Belgium*	0.40	27 Spain	0.07
13	Italy*	0.39	Nigeria	0.05
	West Germany*	0.39	29 UAEᵇ	0.03
15	Japan*	0.32	30 Algeria	0.02

Largest aid recipients per head
$ 1988

1	French Polynesia	2,068.8	26 Lebanon	49.8
2	French Guinea	1,686.0	27 Chad	48.9
3	Martinique	1,397.0	28 Mali	47.9
4	Réunion	1,147.2	29 Malawi	43.2
5	Pacific Islands Trust		30 Tanzania	42.0
	Territory	1,110.2	31 Tunisia	41.7
6	New Caledonia	1,003.8	32 Sudan	38.0
7	Guadeloupe	794.0	33 Côte d'Ivoire	37.8
8	Israel	280.1	34 Rwanda	36.6
9	Botswana	124.0	35 Benin	36.2
10	Jordan	109.4	36 Sri Lanka	35.7
11	Papua New Guinea	105.9	37 Burundi	35.5
12	Mauritania	95.8	38 Burkina Faso	34.9
13	El Salvador	82.0	39 Kenya	33.9
	Senegal	82.0	40 Ghana	33.5
15	Jamaica	78.8	41 Zimbabwe	30.4
16	CAR	68.3	42 Madagascar	27.0
17	Honduras	67.3	43 Guatemala	26.7
18	Zambia	63.3	44 Haiti	26.0
19	Somalia	62.9	45 Cameroon	25.8
20	Togo	61.2	46 North Yemen	23.0
21	Mozambique	59.0	47 Nepal	21.9
22	Nicaragua	57.7	48 Uganda	20.5
23	Bolivia	56.1	49 Morocco	20.1
24	Niger	55.5	50 Ethiopia	19.0
25	Guinea	51.7		

* Members of OECD Development Assistance Committee (DAC).
a Including overseas departments and territories. When these are excluded French aid amounted to $4,777m in 1988, equivalent to 0.50% of GNP.

Industry

Largest industrial output
$bn 1988

1	USA	1,250		21	Austria	51
2	Japan	1,155		22	Belgium	47
3	West Germany	480		23	Poland	40
4	USSR	327		24	Finland	36
5	France	305		25	South Africa	35
6	UK	295		26	Saudi Arabia	33
7	Italy	286		27	Denmark	31
8	China	174		28	Iraq	30
9	Canada	171			Czechoslovakia	30
10	Spain	127		30	Yugoslavia	29
11	Brazil	116			Indonesia	29
12	Netherlands	76			Norway	29
13	Sweden	75		33	Argentina	26
14	South Korea	74			Turkey	26
15	India	73		35	Israel	24
	Australia	73		36	Algeria	23
17	East Germany	65			Venezuela	23
18	Switzerland	63		38	Romania	22
19	Mexico	62		39	Iran	20
20	Taiwan	55		40	Thailand	19

Highest growth in output
Av. ann. real % growth 1965-88

1	Botswana	21.5		11	Indonesia	8.5
2	South Korea	14.5		12	Syria	8.2
3	North Yemen	14.3		13	Thailand	8.1
4	Jordan	11.9		14	Kenya	7.6
5	Taiwan	11.7			Cameroon	7.6
6	China	11.2			Bulgaria	7.6
7	Congo	10.4		17	Nigeria	7.3
8	Ecuador	10.0		18	Japan	7.2
9	Mongolia[a]	9.6		19	Turkey	7.0
10	Singapore	8.8		20	Niger	6.9

Lowest growth in output
Av. ann. real % growth 1965-88

1	Bahrain	0.1		11	Zimbabwe	0.8
	Somalia	0.1			Libya	0.8
3	South Africa	0.2			Ireland	0.8
	Lesotho	0.2		14	Ghana	0.9
	Barbados	0.2		15	Zaire	1.1
6	Malawi	0.5		16	Uruguay	1.2
7	Hungary	0.6			Rwanda	1.2
	New Zealand	0.6		18	Venezuela	1.3
9	Bolivia	0.7		19	Papua New Guinea	1.4
	Dominican Republic	0.7			Zambia	1.4

a 1970-86.

Largest chemicals output
$bn 1988

1	USA	124.95	11	Brazil	10.45
2	Japan	115.54	12	Netherlands	8.41
3	West Germany	47.97	13	Mexico	7.39
4	UK	32.45	14	South Korea	6.66
5	Italy	28.60	15	Belgium	6.09
6	France	27.45	16	Sweden	6.01
7	China	17.41	17	Australia	5.81
8	Canada	15.40	18	South Africa	3.90
9	Spain	11.39	19	Argentina	3.15
10	India	10.90	20	Denmark	3.08

Largest machinery and transport output
$bn 1988

1	Japan	439.06	11	Sweden	26.31
2	USA	437.34	12	Netherlands	21.41
3	West Germany	182.28	13	India	18.90
4	France	100.63	14	South Korea	17.76
5	UK	94.40	15	Australia	15.25
6	Italy	91.52	16	Austria	12.66
7	China	45.25	17	Poland	11.86
8	Canada	42.77	18	Belgium	10.78
9	Brazil	27.87	19	Mexico	8.62
10	Spain	27.85	20	Finland	8.52

Largest textiles and clothing output
$bn 1988

1	Japan	69.32	11	India	11.63
2	USA	62.48	12	Spain	11.39
3	Italy	37.18	13	Mexico	7.39
4	West Germany	23.98	14	Poland	6.32
5	China	22.63	15	Hong Kong	5.83
6	France	21.35	16	Australia	5.08
7	UK	17.70	17	Yugoslavia	4.98
8	Brazil	13.94	18	Algeria	4.58
9	South Korea	12.58	19	Iran	4.38
10	Canada	11.97	20	Austria	4.05

Largest processed food output
$bn 1988

1	USA	149.94	11	Mexico	14.78
2	Japan	115.54	12	Netherlands	14.53
3	West Germany	57.56	13	Australia	13.07
4	France	54.89	14	South Korea	11.10
5	UK	41.30	15	Belgium	8.91
6	Canada	25.66	16	Austria	8.61
7	China	22.63	17	India	8.00
8	Spain	21.52	18	Sweden	7.52
9	Italy	20.02	19	Denmark	6.77
10	Brazil	17.42	20	Indonesia	6.68

Agriculture

Most economically dependent on agriculture
% GDP from agriculture 1988

1	Cambodia[a]	90.0	21	CAR[d]	41.0
2	Laos[ab]	75.0	22	Burkina Faso[d]	38.0
3	Afghanistan[c]	69.5	23	Rwanda[d]	37.0
4	Somalia[d]	65.0	24	Malawi	36.5
5	Burundi[d]	56.5	25	Nigeria	35.9
6	Nepal	56.1	26	Mauritania[e]	35.3
7	Mozambique[d]	54.2	27	Togo	34.4
8	Tanzania[d]	53.1	28	Albania[af]	34.1
9	Bhutan[d]	51.0	29	Niger[d]	34.0
	Vietnam[c]	51.0		Sudan[d]	34.0
11	Ghana	49.3	31	Papua New Guinea[e]	33.9
12	Burma	48.6	32	China[dg]	33.8
13	Mali[c]	47.6	33	India[d]	33.3
14	Bangladesh	46.8	34	Haiti[e]	32.7
15	Chad[e]	46.1	35	Côte d'Ivoire	31.1
16	Benin[d]	46.0	36	Kenya	30.7
17	Sierra Leone[e]	44.7	37	Honduras[d]	29.1
18	Guinea	43.9	38	Philippines[d]	28.9
19	Madagascar	43.0	39	North Yemen	27.9
20	Ethiopia[e]	42.1	40	Zaire[c]	27.5

Least economically dependent on agriculture
% GDP from agriculture 1988

1	Neth Antilles[f]	0.4	21	Italy	3.8
2	Hong Kong[d]	0.5	22	Australia	4.0
3	Singapore	0.6	23	Oman	4.3
4	Brunei[f]	0.8		Netherlands	4.3
5	Qatar	1.3	25	Bahamas[e]	4.4
6	Bahrain	1.4	26	Sweden	4.5
	UK	1.4		Trinidad & Tobago	4.5
8	West Germany	1.5		Denmark	4.5
9	Puerto Rico[e]	1.6	29	Austria	4.7
10	Kuwait	1.7	30	Libya	5.0
11	UAE	1.9	31	Spain	5.1
12	Belgium	2.0	32	Venezuela	5.9
13	USA[d]	2.1		South Africa	5.9
14	Luxembourg	2.5	34	Taiwan	6.1
15	Japan	2.8	35	Saudi Arabia	6.6
16	Botswana	2.9		Finland	6.6
17	Canada	3.0	37	Barbados[d]	6.9
18	Switzerland[c]	3.5	38	Czechoslovakia[d]	7.6
	Norway	3.5	39	Jamaica	7.9
20	France	3.6	40	New Zealand[d]	8.1

a As % of NMP.
b 1984.
c 1985.
d 1987.
e 1986.
f 1982.
g As % of national income.

Fastest growth

% av. ann. growth per head 1977-88

1	Saudi Arabia	4.5	9	Jordan	2.2
2	Laos	3.7		Vietnam	2.2
	China	3.7	11	East Germany	2.1
4	Morocco	2.8	12	Belgium[a]	2.0
5	Indonesia	2.7	13	Gabon	1.9
6	Burma	2.6		Spain	1.9
7	Malaysia	2.4	15	Netherlands	1.8
8	Burkina Faso	2.3			

Slowest growth

% av. ann. growth per head 1977-88

1	Trinidad & Tobago	-7.5		Lesotho	-2.9
2	Hong Kong	-6.3	10	Guyana	-2.8
	Nicaragua	-6.3	11	Barbados	-2.4
4	Botswana	-4.8	12	South Yemen	-2.3
5	Singapore	-3.7	13	Mozambique	-2.2
6	Uganda	-3.6	14	Malawi	-2.1
7	Zambia	-3.1	15	Kenya	-1.9
8	Angola	-2.9			

Biggest producers

'000 tonnes 1988

Cereals

1	China	352,306	6	Indonesia	48,441
2	USA	206,467	7	Brazil	42,540
3	USSR	187,060	8	Canada	35,348
4	India	175,638	9	Romania	31,090
5	France	56,178	10	Turkey	30,985

Meat

1	USA	27,935	6	Brazil	4,735
2	China	24,996	7	Italy	3,822
3	USSR	19,213	8	Japan	3,654
4	France	5,477	9	Argentina	3,494
5	West Germany	5,428	10	UK	3,396

Fruit

1	Brazil	27,523	6	USSR	14,503
2	USA	25,735	7	France	11,145
3	India	24,649	8	Spain	11,024
4	Italy	18,846	9	Turkey	8,890
5	China	18,430	10	Mexico	7,937

Vegetables

1	China	112,954	6	Japan	15,250
2	India	48,528	7	Italy	13,662
3	USSR	33,781	8	Egypt	10,818
4	USA	27,894	9	Spain	9,754
5	Turkey	16,889	10	South Korea	8,712

a Data for Belgium include Luxembourg.

Commodities

Wheat

Top 10 producers
'000 tonnes 1988

1	China	87,505
2	USSR	84,500
3	USA	49,295
4	India	45,096
5	France	29,677
6	Turkey	20,500
7	Canada	15,655
8	Australia	14,102
9	Pakistan	12,675
10	West Germany	12,044

Top 10 consumers
'000 tonnes 1988

1	China	105,700
2	USSR	100,500
3	EC	60,000
4	India	51,000
5	Eastern Europe	41,000
6	USA	29,300
7	Canada	7,800
8	South Africa	6,000
9	Argentina	4,500
10	Australia	2,700

Rice[a]

Top 10 producers
'000 tonnes 1988

1	China	172,365
2	India	101,950
3	Indonesia	41,769
4	Bangladesh	21,900
5	Thailand	20,813
6	Vietnam	15,200
7	Burma	14,000
8	Japan	12,419
9	Brazil	11,804
10	Philippines	8,971

Top 10 consumers
'000 tonnes 1988

1	China	172,067
2	India	102,450
3	Indonesia	41,802
4	Bangladesh	22,250
5	Thailand	16,022
6	Vietnam	15,475
7	Burma	13,650
8	Japan	12,436
9	Brazil	11,879
10	Philippines	9,152

Sugar[b]

Top 10 producers
'000 tonnes 1988

1	EC	15,016
2	India	10,207
3	USSR	8,950
4	Cuba	8,119
5	Brazil	7,874
6	USA	6,415
7	China	4,875
8	Mexico	3,909
9	Australia	3,759
10	Thailand	2,638

Top 10 consumers
'000 tonnes 1988

1	USSR	13,950
2	EC	12,240
3	India	10,175
4	China	8,000
5	USA	7,428
6	Brazil	6,241
7	Mexico	4,070
8	Japan	2,905
9	Indonesia	2,545
10	Pakistan	1,978

Coarse grains[c]

Top 5 producers
'000 tonnes 1988

1	USA	149,935
2	USSR	99,660
3	China	92,436
4	India	28,593
5	France	26,435

Top 5 consumers
'000 tonnes 1988

1	USSR	122,179
2	USA	88,622
3	China	87,842
4	EC	80,300
5	Eastern Europe	66,000

Tea

Top 10 producers '000 tonnes 1988		*Top 10 consumers* '000 tonnes 1988	
1 India	700	1 India	430
2 China	540	2 USSR	236
3 Sri Lanka	227	3 UK	160
4 Kenya	164	4 Turkey	139
5 Turkey	140	5 Japan	120
6 Indonesia	130	6 Pakistan	88
7 USSR	120	7 USA	82
8 Japan	95	8 Egypt	73
9 Argentina	45	9 Iran	50
10 Bangladesh	43	10 Iraq	41

Coffee

Top 10 producers '000 tonnes 1988		*Top 10 consumers* '000 tonnes 1987-88	
1 Brazil	1,500	1 USA	1,149
2 Colombia	762	2 Brazil	660
3 Indonesia	360	3 West Germany	518
4 Mexico	306	4 France	296
5 Côte d'Ivoire	264	5 Japan	271
6 India	210	6 Italy	256
7 Ethiopia	180	7 Netherlands	159
Uganda	180	8 Spain	152
9 Guatemala	168	9 Colombia	126
10 Costa Rica	162	10 UK	116

Cocoa

Top 10 producers '000 tonnes 1987-88		*Top 10 consumers* '000 tonnes 1987-88	
1 Côte d'Ivoire	674	1 USA	524
2 Brazil	400	2 West Germany	186
3 Malaysia	227	3 USSR	160
4 Ghana	187	4 UK	141
5 Nigeria	145	5 France	126
6 Cameroon	133	6 Japan	104
7 Ecuador	76	7 Italy	62
8 Colombia	54	8 Brazil	56
9 Dominican Republic	50	9 Canada	53
10 Mexico	48	10 Spain	51

a Paddy (unmilled rice, in the husk).
b Raw value.
c Includes: maize (corn), barley, sorgum, rye, oats and millet.

Commodities

Copper[a]

Top 10 producers '000 tonnes 1988		Top 10 consumers '000 tonnes 1988	
1 USA	1,857	1 USA	2,211
2 USSR	1,380	2 Japan	1,331
3 Chile	1,013	3 USSR	1,250
4 Japan	955	4 West Germany	798
5 Canada	529	5 China	465
6 China	460	6 Italy	445
7 Zambia	448	7 France	409
8 Belgium	434	8 UK	328
9 West Germany	426	9 Belgium	318
10 Poland	401	10 South Korea	266

Lead[a]

Top 10 producers '000 tonnes 1988		Top 10 consumers '000 tonnes 1988	
1 USA	1,047	1 USA	1,201
2 USSR	795	2 USSR	790
3 UK	374	3 Japan	407
4 West Germany	345	4 West Germany	374
5 Japan	340	5 UK	303
6 Canada	268	6 China	250
7 France	256	7 Italy	246
8 China	241	8 France	216
9 Australia	180	9 South Korea	146
10 Mexico	179	10 Yugoslavia	129

Zinc[b]

Top 10 producers '000 tonnes 1988		Top 10 consumers '000 tonnes 1988	
1 USSR	1,035	1 USA	1,089
2 Canada	703	2 USSR	1,080
3 Japan	678	3 Japan	774
4 China	425	4 West Germany	446
5 West Germany	353	5 China	385
6 USA	330	6 France	290
7 Australia	303	7 Italy	250
8 Belgium	298	8 UK	193
9 France	274	9 Belgium	175
10 Spain	245	10 South Korea	173

Tin[a]

Top 5 producers '000 tonnes 1988		Top 5 consumers '000 tonnes 1988	
1 Malaysia	49.9	1 USA	37.6
2 Brazil	42.7	2 Japan	32.2
3 Indonesia	28.2	3 USSR	30.0
4 China	24.0	4 West Germany	19.4
5 USSR	17.0	5 China	14.0

Nickel[a]

Top 10 producers '000 tonnes 1988		*Top 10 consumers* '000 tonnes 1988	
1 USSR	215.0	1 Japan	161.7
2 Canada	136.6	2 USA	140.6
3 Japan	100.6	3 USSR	130.0
4 Norway	52.5	4 West Germany	86.2
5 Australia	37.4	5 France	39.6
6 China	30.0	6 UK	33.0
7 Dominican Republic	29.3	7 Italy	28.6
8 UK	28.0	8 China	27.5
9 South Africa	27.2	9 Spain	16.8
10 Cuba	25.0	10 Finland	16.3

Aluminium[a]

Top 10 producers '000 tonnes 1988		*Top 10 consumers* '000 tonnes 1988	
1 USA	3,945	1 USA	4,598
2 USSR	2,440	2 Japan	2,123
3 Canada	1,540	3 USSR	1,800
4 Australia	1,141	4 West Germany	1,233
5 Brazil	874	5 France	660
6 Norway	827	6 China	600
7 West Germany	744	7 Italy	581
8 China	610	8 Canada	437
9 Venezuela	443	9 UK	427
10 India	335	10 Turkey	399

Precious metals

Gold Top 10 producers tonnes 1988		*Silver* Top 10 producers tonnes 1988	
1 South Africa	617.9	1 Mexico	2,412.0
2 USSR[d]	273.0	2 USA	1,661.1
3 USA	200.9	3 USSR	1,580.0
4 Australia	157.0	4 Peru	1,551.6
5 Canada	127.8	5 Canada	1,371.5
6 China	96.0	6 Australia	1,113.6
7 Brazil	56.0	7 Poland	1,063.0
8 Philippines	35.3	8 Chile	486.2
9 Colombia	29.0	9 North Korea	310.0
10 Papua New Guinea	28.7	10 Japan	251.5

a Refined production.
b Smelter production.
c Mine production.
d 1987.

Commodities

Rubber (natural and synthetic)

Top 10 producers '000 tonnes 1988		Top 10 consumers '000 tonnes 1988	
1 USSR	2,435	1 East Europe	3,340
2 USA	2,335	2 USA	2,875
3 Malaysia	1,660	3 Japan	1,665
4 Japan	1,299	4 China	890
5 Indonesia	1,235	5 West Germany	675
6 Thailand	975	6 France	496
7 France	568	7 Italy	452
8 West Germany	493	8 Brazil	408
9 UK	313	9 India	394
10 Brazil	284	10 UK	367

Raw wool

Top 10 producers '000 tonnes 1988 [a]		Top 10 consumers '000 tonnes 1988 [b]	
1 Australia	914	1 USSR	318
2 USSR	477	2 China	299
3 New Zealand	346	3 Italy	140
4 China	209	4 Japan	126
5 Argentina	157	5 UK	87
6 South Africa	92	6 West Germany	58
7 Uruguay	89	USA	58
8 Turkey	85	8 South Korea	54
9 UK	62	9 Turkey	48
10 Pakistan	53	10 India	36

Cotton

Top 10 producers '000 tonnes 1988		Top 10 consumers '000 tonnes 1988	
1 China	4,143	1 China	4,297
2 USA	3,344	2 USSR	2,018
3 USSR	2,933	3 India	1,763
4 India	1,762	4 USA	1,638
5 Pakistan	1,390	5 Brazil	841
6 Brazil	740	6 Pakistan	839
7 Turkey	535	7 Japan	766
8 Egypt	309	8 Turkey	558
9 Mexico	307	9 South Korea	459
10 Australia	290	10 Italy	310

Major oil seeds [c]

Top 5 producers '000 tonnes 1988		Top 5 consumers '000 tonnes 1988	
1 USA	52,549	1 USA	44,801
2 China	35,563	2 China	32,624
3 Brazil	20,544	3 India	13,956
4 India	15,170	4 Brazil	12,356
5 Argentina	12,295	5 Argentina	7,168

Energy

Crude oil

Top 10 producers '000 b/d 1988		Top 10 consumers '000 b/d 1988	
1 USSR	11,679	1 USA	17,283
2 USA	8,140	2 USSR	8,855
3 Saudi Arabia[d]	5,288	3 Japan	4,732
4 China	2,728	4 West Germany	2,422
5 Iraq[d]	2,646	5 China	2,125
6 Mexico	2,512	6 Italy	1,807
7 Iran[d]	2,259	7 France	1,798
8 UK	2,232	8 UK	1,681
9 Venezuela[d]	1,903	9 Canada	1,601
10 Canada	1,610	10 Mexico	1,528
11 UAE[d]	1,606	11 Brazil	1,347
12 Kuwait[d]	1,492	12 India	1,065
13 Nigeria[d]	1,450	13 Spain	957
14 Indonesia[d]	1,328	14 Saudi Arabia[d]	915
15 Norway	1,158	15 Iran[d]	775

Dry natural gas

Top 10 producers bn cubic ft 1988		Top 10 consumers bn cubic ft 1988	
1 USSR	25,320	1 USSR	23,357
2 USA	16,630	2 USA	17,933
3 Canada	3,570	3 Canada	2,353
4 Netherlands	2,470	4 West Germany	2,075
5 UK	1,640	5 UK	1,990
6 Algeria	1,600	6 Japan	1,586
7 Indonesia	1,370	7 Netherlands	1,515
8 Romania	1,350	8 Romania	1,427
9 Saudi Arabia	1,150	9 Italy	1,283
10 Norway	1,090	10 France	1,007

Coal

Top 10 producers '000 tonnes 1988		Top 10 consumers '000 tonnes 1988	
1 China	956,443	1 China	956,561
2 USA	862,069	2 USA	801,107
3 USSR	784,936	3 USSR	745,862
4 East Germany	316,697	4 East Germany	316,960
5 Poland	284,029	5 Poland	251,443
6 India	196,007	6 India	196,416
7 West Germany	187,840	7 West Germany	191,770
8 South Africa	176,044	8 South Africa	133,485
Australia	176,044	9 Czechoslovakia	127,024
10 Czechoslovakia	127,042	10 Japan	113,593

a Greasy basis.
b Clean basis.
c Soybeans, sunflower seed, cottonseed, groundnuts and rapeseed.
d Opec members.

Energy

Largest producers
'000 tonnnes coal equivalent

#	Country	Value	#	Country	Value
1	USSR	2,335,805	21	Netherlands	96,235
2	USA	1,987,250	22	East Germany	95,931
3	China	884,742	23	Nigeria	94,053
4	Canada	332,315	24	Romania	91,315
5	UK	332,066	25	Libya	74,361
6	Saudi Arabia	330,869	26	Brazil	73,427
7	Mexico	249,646	27	Egypt	72,749
8	India	208,630	28	Czechoslovakia	67,914
9	Australia	193,494	29	France	67,111
10	Iran	186,445	30	Argentina	59,224
11	Poland	180,410	31	Malaysia	52,036
12	Venezuela	175,296	32	Oman	51,582
13	West Germany	151,416	33	North Korea	50,574
14	Iraq	150,948	34	Colombia	50,473
15	South Africa	134,983	35	Japan	49,121
16	Indonesia	131,819	36	Yugoslavia	35,692
17	UAE	131,792	37	Italy	30,254
18	Norway	124,789	38	Turkey	28,091
19	Algeria	123,759	39	Qatar	27,589
20	Kuwait	99,582	40	Spain	26,225

Largest consumers
'000 tonnes coal equivalent

#	Country	Value	#	Country	Value
1	USA	2,327,580	21	South Africa	81,382
2	USSR	1,878,085	22	South Korea	73,163
3	China	815,339	23	Iran	65,638
4	Japan	456,101	24	Argentina	60,228
5	West Germany	344,020	25	North Korea	57,924
6	UK	290,742	26	Yugoslavia	56,747
7	Canada	254,022	27	Belgium	55,155
8	India	214,877	28	Venezuela	55,139
9	France	206,944	29	Bulgaria	53,031
10	Italy	204,704	30	Turkey	51,247
11	Poland	181,145	31	Indonesia	46,629
12	Mexico	137,729	32	Sweden	42,034
13	East Germany	131,306	33	Hungary	40,520
14	Australia	111,231	34	Egypt	34,549
15	Brazil	108,492	35	Algeria	33,287
16	Netherlands	106,476	36	Austria	30,456
17	Romania	106,075	37	Norway	28,417
18	Czechoslovakia	98,262	38	Finland	28,062
19	Saudi Arabia	86,042	39	Denmark	27,425
20	Spain	81,776	40	UAE	27,306

Notes: Consumption data for small countries, especially oil producers, can be unreliable, often leading to unrealistically high consumption per head rates. Data refer to 1988.

Largest exporters

'000 tonnes coal equivalent

1	USSR	408,854	14	Australia	88,518
2	Saudi Arabia	217,644	15	Algeria	82,780
3	UK	141,177	16	Nigeria	81,313
4	Iraq	130,903	17	Kuwait	77,860
5	Canada	125,730	18	Libya	61,616
6	Iran	122,462	19	China	54,930
7	Netherlands	108,168	20	South Africa	42,787
8	Venezuela	106,425	21	Malaysia	40,278
9	Mexico	106,067	22	Oman	40,023
10	Norway	103,404	23	Singapore	39,280
11	UAE	102,873	24	Egypt	36,049
12	USA	99,441	25	Poland	27,701
13	Indonesia	94,937			

Largest importers

'000 tonnes coal equivalent

1	USA	487,204	14	East Germany	47,831
2	Japan	456,101	15	Czechoslovakia	43,590
3	West Germany	218,367	16	Sweden	36,036
4	Italy	192,087	17	USSR	35,589
5	France	170,988	18	Bulgaria	35,191
6	Netherlands	120,332	19	Poland	34,782
7	UK	95,595	20	Turkey	33,951
8	Spain	82,747	21	Romania	32,865
9	Belgium	74,837	22	India	32,842
10	South Korea	70,125	23	Finland	28,623
11	Singapore	68,018	24	Greece	28,457
12	Brazil	58,321	25	Denmark	26,349
13	Canada	48,940			

Largest consumption per head

Kg coal equivalent

1	Qatar	21,881	16	Czechoslovakia	6,311
2	UAE	18,832	17	Bulgaria	5,912
3	Bahrain	14,680	18	Trinidad & Tobago	5,770
4	Luxembourg	11,139	19	Finland	5,692
5	Brunei	9,988	20	West Germany	5,624
6	Canada	9,915	21	Belgium	5,560
7	USA	9,542	22	Denmark	5,346
8	Kuwait	9,191	23	Iceland	5,331
9	Oman	8,353	24	UK	5,107
10	East Germany	7,891	25	Sweden	5,004
11	Netherlands	7,263	26	Poland	4,810
12	Australia	6,845	27	Singapore	4,776
13	Norway	6,782	28	Bermuda	4,638
14	USSR	6,634	29	Romania	4,624
15	Saudi Arabia	6,322	30	Austria	4,018

Workers of the world

Highest % population in labour force
1984-87

1	Barbados	66.5		16	Switzerland	49.4
2	Bermuda[a]	58.2		17	New Zealand	49.3
3	Burundi	55.5		18	UK	48.3
4	Denmark	55.0		19	Singapore	47.9
	Netherlands	55.0			West Germany	47.9
6	Thailand	53.0		21	Australia	47.4
7	Norway	52.5		22	Cyprus	46.7
8	Finland	52.4		23	Portugal	46.0
	Sweden	52.4		24	Hungary	45.7
	Bulgaria	52.4		25	Nepal[b]	45.6
11	Canada	51.1		26	Ghana	45.4
12	Burkina Faso	51.0		27	Austria	45.3
13	USA	50.0			Jamaica	45.3
	Hong Kong	50.0		29	France	44.3
15	Japan	49.8		30	Colombia	44.0

Lowest % population in labour force
1984-87

1	Bahrain	26.6		16	Paraguay[c]	34.3
2	Morocco[c]	29.3		17	Venezuela	34.4
3	Pakistan	29.6		18	Benin	34.5
4	Bangladesh	30.2		19	Chile	35.1
5	Tunisia	30.6		20	Guyana	35.7
	Togo[b]	30.6		21	Turkey	36.2
7	Algeria	30.9		22	Spain	36.8
8	Bolivia	31.2			India[b]	36.8
9	Egypt	31.6		24	Botswana	37.0
10	Mexico[a]	33.0		25	South Africa	37.2
11	Zimbabwe[c]	33.1			Ireland	37.2
12	Guatemala	33.6		27	Argentina	37.4
13	Fiji	33.7		28	Costa Rica	37.5
14	Ecuador	33.8		29	Greece	39.2
15	Israel	34.2		30	Trinidad & Tobago	39.3

Most male workforce
% male workers

1	Bangladesh	90.8		12	Guatemala	75.5
2	Pakistan	90.6		13	India[b]	74.0
3	Algeria	88.4		14	Argentina	73.0
4	Bahrain	80.7		15	Costa Rica	72.4
5	Morocco[c]	80.3		16	Venezuela	72.3
	Kuwait	80.3		17	Mexico[a]	72.2
	Paraguay[c]	80.3		18	Guyana	70.1
8	Egypt	79.0		19	Chile	70.0
9	Fiji	78.8		20	Ecuador	69.9
10	Tunisia	78.7			Turkey	69.9
11	Bolivia	76.4				

Notes: Figures on the percentage of the workforce who are employees or self-employed may be underestimated or a proportion of the labour force may be unclassified in national statistics. Both categories exclude unpaid workers in a family business.

Highest no. employees
% labour force who are employees

1	Bulgaria	98.2	17	UK	79.3
2	USA	90.8	18	Netherlands	79.2
3	Canada	89.9	19	Australia	77.2
4	Sweden	89.1	20	New Zealand	75.7
5	Denmark	88.8	21	France	74.8
6	Bermuda	88.6	22	Belgium	74.6
7	West Germany	88.3	23	Trinidad & Tobago	73.4
8	Norway	86.7	24	Japan	72.8
9	Austria	85.7	25	Ireland	70.8
10	Hong Kong	85.2	26	Cyprus	70.6
11	Luxembourg	84.9		Uruguay	70.6
12	Finland	84.6	28	Costa Rica	70.5
13	Puerto Rico	84.5	29	Yugoslavia	65.7
14	Bahamas	81.4	30	Panama	65.5
15	Hungary	81.1		Spain	65.5
16	Singapore	80.2			

Highest no. self-employed
% labour force self-employed

1	Togo	70.3	16	Brazil	25.7
2	Ghana	67.7	17	Portugal	24.7
3	Haiti	51.6	18	Sri Lanka	24.4
4	Indonesia	45.2	19	Cyprus	24.2
5	Pakistan	44.7	20	Chile	23.7
6	Peru	41.2	21	Costa Rica	22.9
7	Philippines	35.7	22	Uruguay	22.7
8	Greece	32.7	23	Tunisia	22.5
9	Guatemala	30.9	24	Italy	21.3
10	South Korea	29.6	25	Trinidad & Tobago	18.7
11	Colombia	27.6	26	Spain	18.4
12	Mexico	27.0	27	Ireland	18.2
13	Egypt	26.5	28	Yugoslavia	17.2
14	Panama	26.0	29	New Zealand	16.0
	Venezuela	26.0	30	Japan	15.0

Most female workforce
% female workers

1	Botswana	53.1		Denmark	45.8
2	Burundi	52.8	12	Jamaica	45.6
3	Ghana	51.2	13	Bermuda[a]	45.2
4	Burkina Faso	49.1	14	Bahamas[a]	44.5
5	Sweden	48.0	15	USA	44.3
6	Bulgaria	47.7		Norway	44.3
7	Barbados	47.2	17	Madagascar	44.2
8	Finland	47.1	18	Togo[b]	43.8
9	Thailand	47.0	19	Canada	43.4
10	Hungary	45.8	20	France	43.3

a 1980.
b 1981.
c 1982.

Banking and business

Largest banks
By capital $m

1	Sumitomo Bank	Japan	13,357
2	Dai-Ichi Kangyo Bank	Japan	12,322
3	Fuji Bank	Japan	11,855
4	Crédit Agricole	France	11,802
5	Sanwa Bank	Japan	11,186
6	Mitsubishi Bank	Japan	10,900
7	Barclays Bank	UK	10,715
8	National Westminster Bank	UK	9,761
9	Deutsche Bank	West Germany	8,462
10	Industrial Bank of Japan	Japan	8,184
11	Union Bank of Switzerland	Switzerland	8,150
12	Citicorp	USA	7,319
13	Compagnie Financière de Paribas	France	6,968
14	Tokai Bank	Japan	6,821
15	Hong Kong Bank	Hong Kong	6,746
16	Bank of China	China	6,611
17	Long-Term Credit Bank of Japan	Japan	6,463
18	Banque Nationale de Paris	France	6,177
19	Swiss Bank Corp	Switzerland	6,153
20	Bank of Tokyo	Japan	5,928
21	Mitsui Bank	Japan	5,675
22	Crédit Lyonnais	France	5,617
23	Japan Development Bank	Japan	5,532
24	Société Générale	France	5,528
25	Banco do Brasil	Brazil	5,503
26	Dresdner Bank	West Germany	5,405
27	Rabobank Nederland	Netherlands	5,336
28	Sumitomo Trust & Banking	Japan	4,970
29	Westpac Banking Corporation	Australia	4,931
30	Crédit Suisse	Switzerland	4,898
31	Mitsubishi Trust & Banking Corporation	Japan	4,770
32	Bank America Corp	USA	4,764
33	Banco Bilbao Vizcaya	Spain	4,691
34	Taiyo Kobe Bank	Japan	4,556
35	Cariplo	Italy	4,513
36	National Australia Bank	Australia	4,404
37	Midland Bank	UK	4,372
38	Royal Bank of Canada	Canada	4,291
39	Banca Nazionale del Lavoro	Italy	4,153
40	Canadian Imperial Bank of Commerce	Canada	4,080

Notes: Capital is essentially equity and reserves.
Figures for Japanese banks refer to the year ended March 31, 1990, for Australian
banks to the year ended September 30, 1989, for Canadian banks to the year ended
October 31, 1989. Figures for all other countries refer to the year ended December 31,
1989.

Largest businesses

By sales $bn

1	General Motors	USA	127.0
2	Ford Motor	USA	96.9
3	Exxon	USA	86.7
4	Royal Dutch/Shell Group	UK/Netherlands	85.5
5	IBM	USA	63.4
6	Toyota Motor[a]	Japan	60.4
7	General Electric	USA	55.3
8	Mobil	USA	51.0
	Hitachi[b]	Japan	51.0
10	British Petroleum	UK	49.5
11	Iri	Italy	49.1
12	Matsushita Electric Industrial[b]	Japan	43.1
13	Daimler-Benz	West Germany	40.6
14	Philip Morris	USA	39.1
15	Fiat	Italy	36.7
16	Chrysler	USA	36.2
17	Nissan Motor[b]	Japan	36.1
18	Unilever	UK/Netherlands	35.3
19	El du Pont de Nemours	USA	35.2
	Samsung	South Korea	35.2
21	Volkswagen	West Germany	34.7
22	Siemens[c]	West Germany	32.7
23	Texaco	USA	32.4
24	Toshiba[b]	Japan	29.5
25	Chevron	USA	29.4
	Nestlé[d]	Switzerland	29.4
27	Renault[e]	France	27.5
28	ENI	Italy	27.1
29	Philips' Gloeilampenfabrieken	Netherlands	27.0
30	Honda Motor[b]	Japan	26.5
31	BASF[d]	West Germany	25.3
32	NEC[b]	Japan	24.6
33	Hoechst	West Germany	24.4
34	Amoco	USA	24.2
35	Peugeot	France	24.1
36	B.A.T Industries	UK	23.5
	Elf Aquitaine[e]	France	23.5
38	Bayer[d]	West Germany	23.0
39	CGE (Cie Générale d'Electricité)	France	22.6
40	Imperial Chemical Industries (ICI)	UK	21.9

a Year ended June 30, 1989.
b Year ended March 31, 1989.
c Year ended September 30, 1989.

d Includes some significant subsidiaries owned 50% or less, either fully or pro rata.
e Government owned.

Notes: All companies shown have derived at least half of their sales from manufacturing and/or mining. Figures refer to the year ended December 31, 1989, except where specified. They include sales of consolidated subsidiaries but exclude excise taxes collected by manufacturers, thus differing, in some instances, from figures published by the companies themselves.

Stockmarkets

Largest market capitalization
$bn 1989

1	Japan	4,392,597	26	Norway	25,285
2	USA	3,505,686	27	Mexico	22,550
3	UK	826,598	28	Austria	22,261
4	West Germany	365,176	29	New Zealand	13,487
5	France	364,841	30	Philippines	11,965
6	Canada	291,328	31	Portugal	10,618
7	Taiwan	237,012	32	Kuwait	9,932
8	Italy	169,417	33	Chile	9,587
9	Netherlands	157,789	34	Israel	8,227
10	South Korea	140,946	35	Turkey	6,783
11	Australia	136,626	36	Greece	6,376
12	South Africa	131,059	37	Argentina	4,225
13	Spain	122,652	38	Indonesia	2,514
14	Sweden	119,285	39	Pakistan	2,457
15	Switzerland	104,239	40	Jordan	2,162
16	Luxembourg	79,979	41	Venezuela	1,816
17	Hong Kong	77,496	42	Egypt	1,760
18	Belgium	74,596	43	Colombia	1,136
19	Brazil	44,368	44	Zimbabwe	1,067
20	Denmark	40,152	45	Nigeria	1,005
21	Malaysia	39,842	46	Jamaica	957
22	Singapore	35,925	47	Morocco	621
23	Finland	30,652	48	Bangladesh	476
24	India	27,316	49	Kenya	474
25	Thailand	25,648	50	Sri Lanka	471

Highest growth in market capitalization
% increase 1984-89

1	Portugal	14,445	21	Netherlands	407
2	Indonesia	2,857	22	West Germany	366
3	Taiwan	2,297	23	Sweden	364
4	Thailand	1,391	24	Chile	355
5	Austria	1,384	25	Norway	337
6	Philippines	1,335	26	Argentina	261
7	Luxembourg	1,103	27	UK	241
8	Mexico	926		India	241
9	Spain	829	29	Hong Kong	228
10	France	788	30	South Korea	217
11	Greece	732	31	Singapore	193
12	Finland	636	32	Australia	179
13	Turkey	609	33	Switzerland	169
14	Japan	582	34	Uruguay	167
15	Jamaica	574	35	Morocco	163
16	Italy	559	36	South Africa	145
17	Belgium	511	37	New Zealand	119
18	Zimbabwe	506	38	Canada	116
19	Bangladesh	447	39	Malaysia	105
20	Denmark	428	40	Pakistan	100

Highest growth in value traded
% increase 1984-89

1	Portugal	63,633	26	Hong Kong	454
2	Indonesia	26,950	27	Greece	448
3	Taiwan	11,687	28	Israel	432
4	Turkey	11,300	29	Belgium	389
5	Austria	10,168	30	Jordan	373
6	Denmark	8,260	31	New Zealand	364
7	South Korea	3,034	32	Costa Rica	350
8	Thailand	2,999	33	Singapore	346
9	West Germany	2,012	34	India	343
10	Colombia	1,900	35	Australia	320
11	Philippines	1,828	36	Egypt	259
12	Finland	1,666	37	Venezuela	244
13	Chile	1,598	38	Peru	221
14	Spain	1,457	39	Malaysia	209
15	France	1,295	40	Mexico	188
16	Jamaica	1,186	41	South Africa	181
17	Bangladesh	1,150	42	Canada	172
18	Japan	879	43	USA	156
19	Italy	858	44	Uruguay	150
20	Norway	825	45	Morocco	106
21	Luxembourg	745	46	Sweden	105
22	Netherlands	632	47	Brazil	68
23	Argentina	592	48	Côte d'Ivoire	57
24	UK	556	49	Pakistan	7
25	Zimbabwe	500			

Highest growth in no. listed companies[a]
% increase 1984-89

1	Portugal	691.3	19	Australia	32.3
2	Luxembourg	267.9	20	Austria	28.6
3	Egypt	213.6	21	Mexico	26.9
4	Indonesia	154.2	22	Pakistan	26.8
5	Bangladesh	107.1	23	Jamaica	25.0
6	Colombia	90.2	24	Canada	21.5
7	South Korea	86.3	25	Nigeria	19.4
8	Thailand	82.3	26	Netherlands	19.0
9	Peru	68.8	27	Malaysia	15.7
10	South Africa	59.1	28	Brazil	13.4
11	India	54.6	29	Spain	12.8
12	Italy	51.7	30	Singapore	12.4
13	Finland	50.0	31	Denmark	11.3
14	Taiwan	47.2	32	Chile	11.1
15	Switzerland	46.3	33	Kenya	5.5
16	West Germany	39.9	34	Greece	4.4
17	Japan	39.8	35	Jordan	2.9
18	France	32.5	36	New Zealand	2.1

a Only 36 stockmarkets experienced an increase in number of listed companies 1984-89.
Notes: Many of the newer stockmarkets shown were extremely small in 1984. Consequently their growth between 1984 and 1989 was massive by measures shown.

Transport: *roads and cars*

Longest road networks
Km 1985-88

1	USA	6,233,308	16	Mexico	225,684
2	Brazil	1,673,733	17	Indonesia	219,009
3	USSR	1,586,416	18	Argentina	211,369
4	India[a]	1,554,200	19	South Africa	182,968
5	Japan	1,104,282	20	Philippines	157,448
6	China[b]	982,200	21	Zaire	145,000
7	Australia	852,986	22	Iran[c]	136,400
8	Canada	844,386	23	Sweden	131,048
9	France	805,070	24	Belgium	128,319
10	West Germany	493,590	25	Yugoslavia	119,608
11	Poland	360,629	26	Netherlands	115,305
12	UK	352,292	27	Pakistan	111,237
13	Turkey	320,611	28	Nigeria [h]	108,100
14	Spain	318,022	29	Austria	107,099
15	Italy	301,846	30	Colombia	106,218

Densest road networks
Km road per km² land area 1985-88

1	Singapore	4.33	16	Puerto Rico	1.06
2	Belgium	3.91	17	Hungary	1.03
3	Japan	2.93		Italy	1.03
4	Netherlands	2.14	18	Trinidad & Tobago	1.01
5	West Germany	2.02	19	Mauritius	0.98
6	Switzerland	1.79	20	USA	0.68
7	Denmark	1.67		Lebanon[d]	0.68
8	Jamaica[c]	1.53	21	Bangladesh[b]	0.66
9	UK	1.46	23	Spain	0.64
	France	1.46	24	El Salvador	0.59
11	Hong Kong	1.45	25	Czechoslovakia	0.58
12	Ireland	1.34	26	Costa Rica	0.57
13	Cyprus	1.32	27	South Korea	0.56
14	Austria	1.29		Portugal	0.56
15	Poland	1.18	28	Philippines	0.53

Highest car ownership
No. cars per 100 people 1988

1	USA	74	11	Switzerland	45
2	Iceland	60		Sweden	45
3	Canada	59	13	Italy	44
4	New Zealand	57	14	Neth Antilles[b]	43
5	Australia	56		Japan	43
6	West Germany	51		UK	43
7	France	48	17	Finland	41
	Luxembourg	48		Puerto Rico	41
9	Bermuda[d]	47	19	Belgium	40
10	Norway	46		Austria	40

a 1983.
b Estimate.
c 1984.
d 1982.

Most crowded road networks

No. vehicles per km road network 1985-88

1	Hong Kong	226	16	Japan	47
2	Israel[a]	195	17	Czechoslovakia[a]	43
3	Singapore[a]	149	18	Switzerland	42
4	Puerto Rico	148	19	Jordan	40
5	Kuwait	140	20	Spain	39
6	Italy	84	21	Portugal	36
7	Taiwan[a]	73		South Korea	36
8	UK	70	23	Luxembourg	35
9	Malaysia	67		Venezuela	35
10	Lebanon[a]	64	25	France	34
11	West Germany	63		Thailand	34
	Trinidad & Tobago	63	27	Mexico[a]	33
13	Greece	61	28	Yugoslavia[a]	32
14	Netherlands	50	29	Belgium	31
15	Saudi Arabia	47		Bulgaria[a]	31

Most used road networks

'000 vehicle km per year per km road network 1985-88

1	Hong Kong	4,705.7	16	South Korea	458.2
2	Kuwait	3,433.4	17	Sweden	450.2
3	Jordan	1,321.4	18	South Africa	438.5
4	UK	929.6	19	Thailand	408.7
5	Italy	923.4	20	Belgium	373.3
6	West Germany	843.8	21	Bulgaria	310.3
7	Netherlands	761.4	22	Spain	291.9
8	Tunisia	726.4	23	Yugoslavia	290.8
9	Iraq	657.2	24	Argentina	236.6
10	Luxembourg	581.3	25	Colombia	193.3
11	Japan	497.0	26	North Yemen	189.9
12	USA	494.2	27	Chile	183.2
13	Denmark	491.0	28	Canada[b]	168.8
14	Austria	464.9	29	Poland	152.6
15	France	459.6	30	Turkey	69.6

Most accidents

No. people injured per 100m vehicle km 1985-88

1	South Korea	1,126.0	11	Japan	137.2
2	Cameroon	400.0	12	South Africa	130.5
3	Turkey	329.9	13	UK	116.0
4	Hong Kong	317.0	14	USA	112.9
5	Canada	206.8	15	West Germany	10.40
6	Chile	190.3	16	Iraq	70.9
7	Spain	178.4	17	Italy	69.3
8	Belgium	167.0	18	Switzerland	68.9
9	Portugal	147.0	19	North Yemen	68.0
10	Austria[c]	138.0	20	Poland	66.0

a Estimate.
b Excluding buses.
c 1984.

Transport: *planes and trains*

Most air passenger km
M passenger km[a] per year 1988

1	USA	674,629	21	Indonesia	14,428
2	USSR	213,169	22	New Zealand	10,850
3	Japan	84,054	23	Philippines	10,375
4	UK	83,042	24	Argentina	8,862
5	France	47,799	25	Pakistan	8,743
6	Canada	46,259	26	Malaysia	8,658
7	Australia	40,363	27	Sweden	7,830
8	W.Germany	34,097	28	South Africa	7,632
9	Singapore	28,062	29	Greece	7,531
10	China	25,615	30	Venezuela	6,907
11	Netherlands	24,144	31	Belgium	6,528
12	Brazil	23,712	32	Portugal	5,673
13	Spain	22,272	33	Yugoslavia	5,667
14	Italy	19,168	34	Norway	5,632
15	India	18,010	35	Egypt	5,512
16	Thailand	16,682	36	Iran	4,417
17	Mexico	14,946	37	Colombia	4,294
18	Saudi Arabia	14,935	38	Finland	4,034
19	South Korea	14,682	39	Denmark	3,935
20	Switzerland	14,525	40	Jordan	3,927

Busiest airports
No. passengers '000 1988

1	Chicago	O'Hare	56,679
2	Atlanta	Hartsfield	45,900
3	Los Angeles	Los Angeles Intl	44,399
4	Dallas	Dallas/Ft Worth	44,271
5	London	Heathrow	37,510
6	Tokyo	Narita	32,177
7	Denver	Stapleton	31,798
8	New York	Kennedy	31,166
9	San Francisco	San Francisco Intl	30,507
10	Miami	Miami Intl	24,525

Busiest international airports
No. international passengers '000 1988

1	London	Heathrow	30,659
2	London	Gatwick	19,619
3	Frankfurt	Frankfurt / Main	18,398
4	Paris	Charles de Gaulle	16,172
	New York	Kennedy	16,172
6	Hong Kong	Hong Kong Intl	15,277
7	Amsterdam	Schiphol	14,397
8	Tokyo	Narita	13,893
9	Singapore	Changi	11,381
10	Switzerland	Zurich	10,194

a Air passenger km data refer to the distance travelled by each aircraft of national origin.

Longest railway network
'000 km 1986-88

1	USSR[d]	247.2			Romania[a]	11.2
2	USA[d]	225.4	22	Yugoslavia	9.3
3	Canada[b]	65.8	23	Pakistan	8.8
4	India	61.8	24	Turkey	8.2
5	China	52.6	25	Hungary	7.6
6	Australia[a]	39.3	26	Indonesia	6.4
7	France	34.6	27	Chile	6.2
8	Argentina[a]	34.1	28	Finland	5.9
9	West Germany	27.4	29	Austria	5.7
10	Poland	24.2	30	Egypt	4.9
11	South Africa[a]	23.8	31	Sudan	4.8
12	Brazil	22.1		Zaire	4.8
13	Mexico	20.0	33	North Korea[e]	4.6
14	Japan	19.9		Iran	4.6
15	UK	16.6	35	New Zealand[c]	4.3
16	Italy	16.0	36	Norway	4.2
17	East Germany	14.0		Bulgaria	4.2
18	Czechoslovakia	13.1	38	Algeria	3.8
19	Spain	12.7	39	Thailand	3.7
20	Sweden	11.2	40	Portugal	3.6

Most rail passengers
Km per year per person 1986-88

1	Japan	2,745	13	Italy	722
2	Switzerland	1,523	12	South Africa[a]	873
3	East Germany	1,353	11	Bulgaria	897
4	Czechoslovakia	1,286	14	Sweden	716
5	Poland	1,282	15	West Germany	640
6	USSR[d]	1,276	16	Netherlands	639
7	France	1,074	17	Finland	633
8	Austria	971		Belgium	633
9	Denmark	937	19	South Korea	588
10	Hungary	906	20	Luxembourg	584

Most rail freight
M tonnes km per year 1986-88

1	USSR[df]	3,600,000	11	France	52,521
2	USA[a]	1,328,702	12	Mexico	45,444
3	China	945,565	13	Australia[a]	39,444
4	Canada[b]	235,524	14	Brazil	37,843
5	India	223,097	15	Yugoslavia	26,071
6	Poland	121,425	16	Hungary	21,387
7	South Africa[a]	90,576	17	Japan	20,928
8	Czechoslovakia	67,985	18	Italy	19,490
9	West Germany	59,331	19	Bulgaria	18,324
10	East Germany	58,841	20	Sweden	17,761

a	1984.	d	1985.
b	1982.	e	1981.
c	Class 1 railways only (about 96%).	f	Estimate.

Transport: *sail away*

Largest fleets

No. vessels over 100 GRT [a]

1	Japan	9,804		21	France	811
2	USSR	6,741		22	India	797
3	USA	6,428		23	Brazil	719
4	Panama	5,022		24	Singapore	715
5	Spain	2,343		25	Poland	714
6	UK	2,142		26	Australia	709
7	Norway	2,078		27	Mexico	659
8	South Korea	1,930		28	Sweden	633
9	Greece	1,874		29	Peru	621
10	China	1,841		30	Taiwan	617
11	Indonesia	1,736		31	Honduras	587
12	Italy	1,583		32	Bahamas	572
13	Liberia	1,507		33	Malaysia	499
14	Philippines	1,483			Yugoslavia	499
15	Cyprus	1,352		35	Romania	462
16	Denmark	1,240		36	Argentina	451
17	West Germany	1,233		37	Egypt	431
18	Canada	1,225		38	Cuba	412
19	Netherlands	1,173		39	Iceland	396
20	Turkey	872		40	Hong Kong	394

Largest ports

Total cargo traffic '000 tons 1987 [b]

1	Kobe	157,926		21	Le Havre	51,874
2	Singapore	129,459		22	Corpus Christi	51,713
3	Shanghai	128,320		23	Houston[c]	51,418
4	Nagoya	109,596		24	Los Angeles	48,613
5	Yokohama	108,602		25	Hampton Roads	48,423
6	Marseilles	91,266		26	Richards Bay	47,709
7	Antwerp	91,101		27	Genoa	45,027
8	Kitakyushu	88,639		28	Inchon	43,037
9	Osaka	81,764		29	Hedland Port	42,880
10	Hong Kong	70,538		30	New Orleans[e]	40,702
11	Kaohsiung	67,938		31	Tampa	40,090
12	Tokyo	66,403		32	Newcastle	39,087
13	Vancouver	63,957		33	Sydney Ports	35,875
14	Philadelphia[c]	62,258		34	Baltimore	33,837
15	Tubarao	62,023		35	Tees/Hartlepool	33,502
16	Hamburg	56,726		36	Milford Haven	32,815
17	New York/New Jersey[e]	54,654		37	Sao Sebastian	32,745
18	Pusan	54,072		38	Dunkirk	32,365
19	London	53,667		39	Bombay	30,091
20	Long Beach	52,122		40	Bremen Ports	29,981

a Gross Tonnage (GRT) = total volume within the hull and above deck. 1 GRT=100 cu ft.
  Data refer to latest available year, 1985-88.
b Total cargo loaded and discharged
c Foreign traffic only.

Tourism

Most tourist arrivals
No. arrivals 1987

1	France[b]	36,818	21	Thailand	3,483
2	Spain	32,900	22	Singapore	3,373
3	USA	28,787	23	Netherlands	3,189
4	Italy[c]	25,749	24	Malaysia[d]	3,146
5	Austria	15,761	25	Poland	3,100
6	UK	15,445	26	Ireland	2,662
7	Canada	15,043	27	Belgium[a]	2,516
8	West Germany	12,780	28	Turkey	2,468
9	Hungary	11,826	29	Morocco	2,248
10	Switzerland	11,600	30	Japan	1,939
11	China	10,760	31	Brazil	1,929
12	Yugoslavia[c]	8,907	32	Jordan	1,898
13	Bulgaria	7,594	33	South Korea	1,875
14	Greece	7,564		Tunisia	1,875
15	Czechoslovakia[c]	6,126	35	Puerto Rico[e]	1,872
16	Portugal	6,102	36	Egypt	1,795
17	Mexico	5,407	37	Australia	1,785
18	USSR	5,246	38	Norway	1,782
19	Romania	5,142	39	Argentina	1,763
20	Hong Kong	4,502	40	East Germany	1,500

Biggest tourist spending
$m 1987

1	West Germany	23,551	11	Belgium	3,886
2	USA	20,785	12	Sweden	3,781
3	UK	11,898	13	Norway	3,056
4	Japan	10,760	14	Denmark	2,860
5	France	8,618	15	Kuwait	2,505
6	Netherlands	6,362	16	Mexico	2,361
7	Canada	5,840	17	Australia	2,351
8	Italy	4,536	18	Saudi Arabia	2,000
9	Austria	4,516	19	Spain	1,938
10	Switzerland	4,339	20	New Zealand	1,784

Largest tourist receipts
$m 1987

1	USA	15,374	11	Belgium	2,980
2	Spain	14,760	12	Netherlands	2,666
3	Italy	12,174	13	Saudi Arabia	2,600
4	France	12,008	14	South Korea	2,299
5	UK	10,229	15	Denmark	2,219
6	West Germany	7,716	16	Singapore	2,216
7	Austria	7,604	17	Greece	2,192
8	Switzerland	5,352	18	Portugal	2,148
9	Canada	3,939	19	Japan	2,097
10	Mexico	3,497	20	Sweden	2,033

a World Tourism Organization estimate.
b Arrivals in hotels and holiday villages.
c Excluding nationals returning from abroad.
d Departures.
e Arrivals by air only.

Education

Highest primary enrolment
No. enrolled as % relevant age group

1	Angola	134		Lesotho	113
2	China	132	22	Laos	111
3	Fiji	129	23	Uruguay	110
4	Zimbabwe	128		Argentina	110
5	Portugal	124		Syria	110
6	Peru	122		Barbados	110
7	Qatar	121		Bahrain	110
8	Mexico	118	28	Cameroon	109
	Madagascar	118	29	Malta	107
	Indonesia	118		New Zealand	107
11	Ecuador	117		Venezuela	107
	Turkey	117	32	Cyprus	106
13	Tunisia	116		Honduras	106
14	Netherlands	115		Panama	106
	Singapore	115		Australia	106
16	Colombia	114		Mauritius	106
	Iran	114		UK	106
	Botswana	114		East Germany	106
19	Spain	113		Philippines	106
	France	113		Hong Kong	106

Lowest primary enrolment
No. enrolled as % relevant age group

1	Somalia	15	22	Rwanda	67
2	Afghanistan	21	23	Mozambique	68
3	Mali	23	24	Papua New Guinea	70
4	Bhutan	26		Bangladesh	70
5	Niger	29		Côte d'Ivoire	70
6	Guinea	30		Uganda	70
7	Burkina Faso	32	28	Morocco	71
8	Liberia	35		Ghana	71
9	Ethiopia	37		Saudi Arabia	71
10	Pakistan	40	31	Zaire	76
11	Sudan	49	32	Guatemala	77
12	Chad	51		Nigeria	77
13	Mauritania	52	34	El Salvador	79
14	Sierra Leone	54	35	Nepal	82
15	Burundi	59	36	Guyana	90
16	Senegal	60		Egypt	90
17	Benin	63	38	North Yemen	91
18	Tanzania	66		Bolivia	91
	South Yemen	66	40	Kuwait	94
	Malawi	66		Puerto Rico	94
	CAR	66			

Notes: The gross enrolment ratios shown are the actual number enrolled as a percentage of the number of children in the official primary age group. They may exceed 100 when children outside the primary age group are receiving primary education either because they have not moved on to secondary education or because they have started primary education early.

Most literate
% adult literacy rate

1	Australia	99		West Germany	99
	Austria	99		Switzerland	99
	Belgium	99		Ireland	99
	Canada	99	20	Czechoslovakia	98
	Denmark	99		Poland	98
	Netherlands	99		Chile	98
	New Zealand	99	23	Italy	97
	Norway	99	24	Cuba	96
	Finland	99		Argentina	96
	Luxembourg	99		Trinidad & Tobago	96
	Japan	99		Romania	96
	East Germany	99	28	Uruguay	95
	Sweden	99		South Korea	95
	France	99		Israel	95
	USSR	99		Spain	95
	UK	99			

Least literate
% adult literacy rate

1	Somalia	12	13	Senegal	28
2	Niger	14	14	Guinea	29
	Burkina Faso	14	15	Oman	30
4	Mali	17		Namibia	30
	Mauritania	17		Sierra Leone	30
6	Sudan	23		Pakistan	30
7	Afghanistan	24	20	Bangladesh	33
8	North Yemen	25	21	Morocco	34
	Bhutan	25	22	Liberia	35
10	Nepal	26		Burundi	35
	Chad	26	24	Haiti	38
12	Benin	27	25	Mozambique	39

Highest tertiary[b] enrolment
Students per 100 pop.

1	USA	5.14	11	Israel	2.76
2	Canada[a]	4.95	12	Netherlands	2.74
3	Bermuda	4.76	13	Norway	2.73
4	Puerto Rico	4.10	14	East Germany	2.64
5	South Korea	3.67	15	Lebanon	2.63
6	Philippines	3.58	16	West Germany	2.59
7	Argentina	2.93		Cuba	2.59
8	Finland	2.83	18	Costa Rica	2.57
9	Panama	2.79	19	Belgium	2.56
10	Ecuador	2.77		Venezuela	2.56

a Full time students only.
b Tertiary education includes all levels of post-secondary education including courses leading to awards not equivalent to a university degree, courses leading to a first university degree and postgraduate courses.

Life: *the chances*

Highest life expectancy
Years 1987-88

1	Japan	78		Barbados	74
2	Australia	77	32	Malta	73
	Iceland	77		Singapore	73
	Switzerland	77		East Germany	73
	Sweden	77	35	Yugoslavia	72
	Canada	77		Panama	72
	Netherlands	77		Chile	72
	Spain	77		Kuwait	72
	Norway	77		Bulgaria	72
10	France	76		Czechoslovakia	72
	Denmark	76		Poland	72
	Greece	76	42	Hungary	71
	Cyprus	76		Uruguay	71
	Israel	76		Romania	71
	Italy	76		Albania	71
	Hong Kong	76		Trinidad & Tobago	71
	USA	76		Argentina	71
	New Zealand	76	49	Fiji	70
19	West Germany	75		Sri Lanka	70
	Luxembourg	75		Venezuela	70
	UK	75		Bahrain	70
	Finland	75		North Korea	70
	Belgium	75		USSR	70
	Austria	75		Malaysia	70
25	Costa Rica	74	55	Mexico	69
	Cuba	74		UAE	69
	Portugal	74		Guyana	69
	Puerto Rico	74		China	69
	Jamaica	74		Mauritius	69
	Ireland	74		South Korea	69

Highest male life expectancy
Years 1987-88

1	Japan	75		Sweden	74
	Iceland	75		Switzerland	74
3	Greece	74	10	Cyprus	73
	Israel	74		Australia	73
	Netherlands	74		Hong Kong	73
	Norway	74		Denmark	73
	Spain	74		Canada	73

Highest female life expectancy
Years 1987-88

1	Japan	81		
2	Australia	80	New Zealand	80
	Spain	80	Netherlands	80
	Sweden	80	Iceland	80
	Norway	80	France	80
	Canada	80	Switzerland	80

Lowest life expectancy
Years 1987-88

1	Ethiopia	41		Togo	53
	Afghanistan	41		Zaire	53
	Sierra Leone	41		Cambodia	53
4	Guinea	43		Tanzania	53
5	Mali	44	37	Zambia	54
6	Niger	45		Papua New Guinea	54
	Angola	45		Madagascar	54
	Somalia	45		Ghana	54
9	CAR	46		Liberia	54
	Chad	46	42	Haiti	55
	Mauritania	46		Oman	55
	Senegal	46	44	Indonesia	56
	Bhutan	46	45	Lesotho	57
14	Malawi	47		Namibia	57
	Mozambique	47		Pakistan	57
	Benin	47	48	India	58
17	Burkina Faso	48	49	Zimbabwe	59
	Laos	48		Kenya	59
19	Sudan	49		Botswana	59
	Burundi	49	52	Burma	60
	Rwanda	49		Egypt	60
	Congo	49	54	South Africa	61
23	Nepal	51		Libya	61
	Cameroon	51		Morocco	61
	Uganda	51		Peru	61
	Nigeria	51	58	Guatemala	62
	North Yemen	51		Algeria	62
	Bangladesh	51	60	El Salvador	63
	South Yemen	51		Saudi Arabia	63
30	Gabon	52		Nicaragua	63
	Côte d'Ivoire	52		Vietnam	63
32	Bolivia	53		Philippines	63

Lowest male life expectancy
Years 1987-88

1	Ethiopia	39	6	Niger	43
	Sierra Leone	39		Angola	43
3	Guinea	41		Somalia	43
	Afghanistan	41	9	Chad	44
5	Mali	42		CAR	44

Lowest female life expectancy
Years 1987-88

1	Afghanistan	42		Mali	46
2	Ethiopia	43	8	Chad	47
	Sierra Leone	43		Senegal	47
4	Guinea	44		CAR	47
5	Angola	46		Bhutan	47
	Niger	46		Somalia	47

Death: *the chances*

Highest death rates[b]
No. deaths per 1,000 pop.

1	Ethiopia	23.6	51	Kenya	11.9
2	Sierra Leone	23.4		UK	11.9
3	Afghanistan	23.0		Czechoslovakia	11.9
4	Guinea	21.9		Austria	11.9
5	Niger	20.9	55	Botswana	11.7
6	Mali	20.8	56	Luxembourg	11.6
7	Angola	20.2		Bulgaria	11.6
	Somalia	20.2	58	Belgium	11.5
9	Malawi	20.0	59	Denmark	11.3
10	CAR	19.7		India	11.3
11	Chad	19.5	61	Indonesia	11.2
12	Benin	19.0	62	Romania	10.8
	Mauritania	19.0	63	USSR	10.6
14	Senegal	18.9		Norway	10.6
15	Mozambique	18.5	65	France	10.4
	Burkina Faso	18.5	66	Zimbabwe	10.2
17	Congo	17.2		Finland	10.2
18	Rwanda	17.1		Italy	10.2
19	Burundi	17.0		Uruguay	10.2
20	Bhutan	16.8		Switzerland	10.2
21	Cambodia	16.6	71	Egypt	10.1
22	Laos	16.4		Portugal	10.1
	Gabon	16.4	73	Poland	9.9
24	Sudan	15.8	74	Malta	9.8
	South Yemen	15.8		South Africa	9.8
26	North Yemen	15.7	76	Burma	9.7
27	Cameroon	15.6		Morocco	9.7
	Nigeria	15.6		Greece	9.7
29	Bangladesh	15.5	79	Vietnam	9.5
30	Uganda	15.4	80	Libya	9.4
31	Nepal	14.8	81	Peru	9.2
32	Côte d'Ivoire	14.2	82	Spain	9.1
33	Bolivia	14.1		Algeria	9.1
	Togo	14.1	84	Guatemala	9.0
35	Madagascar	14.0	85	USA	8.8
	Tanzania	14.0		Ireland	8.8
37	Zaire	13.9		Yugoslavia	8.8
38	Zambia	13.7	88	Netherlands	8.7
39	Hungary	13.4	89	Argentina	8.6
40	Liberia	13.3	90	El Salvador	8.5
41	Ghana	13.1	91	Turkey	8.4
42	East Germany	12.8		New Zealand	8.4
43	Oman	12.7		Barbados	8.4
	Haiti	12.7	94	Cyprus	8.2
45	Pakistan	12.6	95	Honduras	8.1
46	Lesotho	12.4	96	Nicaragua	8.0
47	Sweden	12.2		Iran	8.0
	Namibia	12.2		Mongolia	8.0
49	Papua New Guinea	12.1	99	Brazil	7.9
50	West Germany	12.0	100	Iraq	7.8

Highest infant mortality[a]
No. deaths per 1,000 live births

1	Mozambique	172	2	New Zealand	109
	Angola	172		Laos	109
3	Afghanistan	171	28	Pakistan	108
4	Mali	168	29	Sudan	107
5	Sierra Leone	153	30	Tanzania	105
	Ethiopia	153	31	Nigeria	104
7	Malawi	149	32	Gabon	102
8	Guinea	146		Uganda	102
9	Burkina Faso	137	34	Lesotho	99
10	Niger	134	35	India	98
11	CAR	131	36	Côte d'Ivoire	95
	Chad	131	37	Cameroon	93
	Somalia	131		Togo	93
14	Bhutan	127	39	Ghana	89
	Nepal	127	40	Peru	87
	Cambodia	127	41	Liberia	86
17	Mauritania	126	42	Indonesia	84
18	Rwanda	121	43	Egypt	83
19	Madagascar	119		Zaire	83
20	South Yemen	118	45	Libya	80
	Bangladesh	118		Morocco	80
22	Haiti	116		Senegal	80
23	North Yemen	115	48	Zambia	79
24	Burundi	111	49	Turkey	74
25	Bolivia	109	50	Algeria	73

Lowest death rates[b]
No. deaths per 1,000 pop.

1	Kuwait	2.8
2	UAE	3.6
3	Bahrain	3.9
4	Costa Rica	4.0
5	Qatar	4.3
6	Fiji	5.0
7	Panama	5.2
8	North Korea	5.4
	Guyana	5.4
	Venezuela	5.4

Lowest infant mortality[a]
No. deaths per 1,000 live births

1	Japan	5
2	Sweden	6
	Finland	6
4	Switzerland	7
	Ireland	7
	Canada	7
7	Norway	8
	Netherlands	8
	East Germany	8
	West Germany	8

a   Infant mortality rates refer to 1988.
b   Death rate data refer to 1985-90.

Notes: The data for the number of deaths per 1,000 population are crude rates, i.e. not adjusted for differences in age structure. Thus a country with a high proportion of older people will have a higher rate than one with a younger population. This explains why a number of developed countries have apparently high death rates.

Both death and, in particular, infant mortality rates can be underestimated in certain countries where not all deaths are officially recorded.

Death: *the causes*

Cancer
%

1	New Zealand	37.2
2	Netherlands	26.8
3	Switzerland	24.8
4	Denmark	24.4
5	UK	24.0
	France	24.0
7	West Germany	23.7
	Canada	23.7
	Luxembourg	23.7
10	Belgium	23.5
11	Iceland	23.2
12	Costa Rica	22.7
13	Uruguay	22.3
14	Austria	22.2
	Italy	22.2
16	Australia	21.8
17	Ireland	21.6
18	Japan	21.2
19	USA	21.1
20	Czechoslovakia	20.7

Heart attack
%

1	Malta	40.9
2	Sweden	38.3
3	USA	37.2
4	USSR	37.1
5	Finland	35.8
6	Australia	35.2
7	Argentina	34.7
8	Yugoslavia	34.5
9	Ireland	34.4
10	Israel	34.1
11	Austria	33.5
	Iceland	33.5
13	West Germany	33.2
14	Denmark	33.0
	Canada	33.0
16	Mauritius	32.8
17	Norway	32.7
18	Cuba	32.2
19	Switzerland	31.5
20	UK	31.2

Infectious disease
%

1	Guatemala	16.5
2	Mexico	6.7
3	Ecuador	6.2
4	Venezuela	5.6
5	Sri Lanka	5.3
6	Kuwait	3.4
7	Singapore	3.3
	Bahamas	3.3
9	Chile	3.0
10	Argentina	2.4
	Costa Rica	2.4
12	South Korea	2.3
	Barbados	2.3
14	Guyana	2.2
15	Israel	2.1
16	Trinidad & Tobago	2.0
17	Uruguay	1.9
18	Puerto Rico	1.8
19	Mauritius	1.6
20	Bahrain	1.5

Motor accident
%

1	Bahrain	3.5
2	Kuwait	3.4
3	Venezuela	2.7
4	Portugal	2.0
5	Ecuador	1.9
6	South Korea	1.7
	Luxembourg	1.7
8	Mexico	1.6
	New Zealand	1.6
10	Puerto Rico	1.5
	Greece	1.5
	Belgium	1.5
13	USA	1.4
	Costa Rica	1.4
	Austria	1.4
16	Trinidad & Tobago	1.3
	Bahamas	1.3
	Australia	1.3
	France	1.3

Notes: Data refer to the chances a newborn baby has of eventually dying from one of the causes shown. Statistics are only available for a limited number of countries and many less developed countries are excluded.

Stroke
%

1	Portugal	26.4
2	USSR	21.5
3	Bulgaria	21.1
4	Greece	20.6
5	Japan	17.9
6	Barbados	17.3
7	Czechoslovakia	17.0
8	Spain	16.8
9	Luxembourg	16.4
10	Romania	15.9
11	Hungary	15.5
12	Italy	15.4
	Mauritius	15.4
14	Austria	15.3
15	Trinidad & Tobago	14.9
16	Guyana	14.8
17	Yugoslavia	14.5
	South Korea	14.5
19	Uruguay	14.3
20	Bahamas	13.7

Injury and poisoning
%

1	Mexico	8.5
2	Hungary	8.4
3	France	7.7
4	Cuba	7.3
5	Switzerland	7.0
	Venezuela	7.0
7	Finland	6.9
	Ecuador	6.9
9	Sri Lanka	6.8
10	Denmark	6.4
	USSR	6.4
12	Chile	6.3
	Austria	6.3
14	Costa Rica	6.2
	Czechoslovakia	6.2
16	Luxembourg	5.9
17	Puerto Rico	5.8
18	Belgium	5.6
19	Israel	5.5
	Norway	5.5
	South Korea	5.5

AIDS
Cases per 100,000 inhabitants[a]

1	Bermuda	210.34	21	Canada	12.06
2	Bahamas	145.83	22	Spain	10.15
3	Congo	66.14	23	Denmark	9.63
4	USA	45.96	24	Australia	9.45
5	Burundi	45.73	25	Côte d'Ivoire	8.70
6	Uganda	42.90	26	Italy	8.12
7	Haiti	40.13	27	Honduras	7.17
8	Barbados	37.20	28	Netherlands	7.07
9	Trinidad & Tobago	36.77	29	Qatar	6.97
10	Malawi	33.37	30	Guyana	6.93
11	Rwanda	26.76	31	West Germany	6.90
12	Kenya	25.14	32	Burkina Faso	6.53
13	Zambia	25.13	33	Ghana	6.52
14	CAR	22.95	34	Belgium	5.68
15	Tanzania	17.92	35	Brazil	5.58
16	Switzerland	15.80	36	Luxembourg	5.41
17	Dominican Republic	14.96	37	Iceland	5.20
18	France	14.36	38	Jamaica	4.94
19	Zaire	13.86	39	UK	4.76
20	Zimbabwe	12.93	40	New Zealand	4.68

a AIDS data refer to the total number of cases reported to the World Health
Organisation up to the end of 1989. The number of cases diagnosed and reported
depends on the quality of medical practice and administration and is likely to be
under-recorded in a number of countries.

Till death us do part

Highest marriage rates
No. marriages per 1,000 inhabitants

1	Bermuda[a]	11.9		Mexico[a]	7.2
2	Mauritius	11.2	32	Australia	7.1
3	USSR[a]	9.8		Romania	7.1
4	USA	9.7		Canada	7.1
5	Fiji[a]	9.5	35	Portugal	7.0
6	Syria	9.4		Israel	7.0
7	Egypt	9.1		Philippines	7.0
8	Singapore	9.0	38	Switzerland	6.8
	Puerto Rico	9.0		Yugoslavia	6.8
	Bangladesh[a]	9.0	40	UK	6.7
11	Iran	8.9	41	Trinidad & Tobago	6.6
	South Korea	8.9	42	West Germany	6.5
13	Albania[a]	8.5		Uruguay[a]	6.5
	Costa Rica	8.5		Poland	6.5
15	Bahamas	8.4	45	Bahrain	6.4
16	Cuba	8.2	46	Denmark	6.3
	East Germany	8.2		Thailand	6.3
18	Cyprus	8.0		Nicaragua[a]	6.3
19	Sri Lanka	7.9	49	Hungary	6.2
20	Brazil	7.8	50	Netherlands	6.1
	Mongolia	7.8	51	Tunisia	6.0
	Hong Kong	7.8		Argentina[a]	6.0
23	Czechoslovakia	7.6		Ecuador	6.0
	Turkey	7.6		Peru[a]	6.0
	Chile	7.6	55	Japan	5.8
26	Taiwan	7.5		Belgium	5.8
	New Zealand	7.5	57	Algeria	5.7
28	Brunei	7.4		Macao	5.7
29	Indonesia	7.2		Jordan	5.7
	Bulgaria[a]	7.2	60	Italy	5.5

Youngest brides
Av. age years

1	Egypt	17
2	Guatemala	18
	Jordan	18
4	Algeria	19
	Bahrain	19
6	Mexico	20
	Kuwait	20
	Qatar	20
	Romania	20
10	USSR	21

Oldest brides
Av. age years

1	Bermuda	27
	Barbados	27
	USA	27
4	Dominican Republic	26
	Denmark	26
	Macao	26
	Mauritius	26
	Sweden	26
9	Hong Kong	25
10	UK	24

a 1985.

Notes: Marriage rates refer to registered marriages only and, therefore reflect the customs surrounding registry and efficiency of administration. The data are based on 1987 figures (except where specified) and hence will be affected by the population age structure at that date.

Highest divorce rates[c]
No. divorces per 1,000 inhabitants

1	Bermuda[a]	4.9	31	Poland	1.3
2	USA	4.8		Japan	1.3
3	Puerto Rico	4.2	33	Barbados	1.2
4	USSR	3.4		Israel	1.2
5	East Germany	3.1	35	Libya[b]	1.1
6	UK	2.9		Indonesia	1.1
	Bahrain[a]	2.9	37	Uruguay[a]	1.0
	Cuba	2.9		Costa Rica[b]	1.0
9	Denmark	2.8		Singapore	1.0
10	Hungary	2.7		Qatar	1.0
11	Australia	2.5	41	Tunisia[b]	0.9
	Czechoslovakia	2.5		Yugoslavia	0.9
	New Zealand	2.5		Portugal	0.9
14	Canada	2.4		Jordan	0.9
15	Sweden	2.3		Greece	0.9
16	Iceland	2.2	46	Trinidad & Tobago[a]	0.8
17	West Germany	2.1		Albania	0.8
18	Austria	2.0		Iran	0.8
	Belgium	2.0	49	Syria	0.7
	Finland	2.0		Panama	0.7
	France	2.0		Brunei	0.7
	Luxembourg	2.0	52	South Korea	0.6
23	Norway	1.9		Hong Kong	0.6
	Netherlands	1.9		Thailand	0.6
25	Switzerland	1.8	55	Italy	0.5
26	Bulgaria	1.7		Spain	0.5
27	Egypt	1.6	57	Ecuador	0.4
28	Romania	1.5		Mexico[b]	0.4
	Bahamas	1.5		Mauritius	0.4
30	Kuwait	1.4		Turkey	0.4

Youngest grooms
Av. age years

1	Poland	23
	East Germany	23
	Guatemala	23
	Honduras	23
	Mexico	23
	Bahrain	23
	Puerto Rico	23
	Uruguay	23
	Venezuela	23
10	Philippines	24

Oldest grooms
Av. age years

1	Bermuda	28
	Barbados	28
	Sweden	28
	Macao	28
	Switzerland	28
	Denmark	28
7	Finland	27
	South Korea	27
	Mauritius	27
	Singapore	27

a 1985.
b 1984.
c Divorce rates are based on 1987 figures (except where specified) and, therefore, will reflect the proportion of the population presently married.

Households and prices

Biggest households
Pop. per dwelling 1980-88

1	North Yemen	8.7	27	Rwanda	5.7
2	UAE	7.9		Bahrain	5.7
3	South Yemen	7.3		Singapore	5.7
	Iran	7.3	30	Fiji	5.6
	Cameroon	7.3		Nepal	5.6
6	Chad	7.2		Libya	5.6
7	Saudi Arabia	6.9		Philippines	5.6
8	Oman	6.8	34	Côte d'Ivoire	5.5
	Somalia	6.8	35	Guinea	5.4
10	Benin	6.7		Burundi	5.4
11	Mauritania	6.6	37	Sri Lanka	5.3
12	Iraq	6.5		Egypt	5.3
13	Syria	6.4		Laos	5.3
	Morocco	6.4		Congo	5.3
15	Burkina Faso	6.3		Turkey	5.3
16	Togo	6.2	42	Costa Rica	5.2
17	Kenya	6.1		Sierra Leone	5.2
	Haiti	6.1		Mexico	5.2
	India	6.1		Pakistan	5.2
20	Algeria	6.0		Ghana	5.2
	Ethiopia	6.0	47	El Salvador	5.1
	Bangladesh	6.0		Angola	5.1
23	Zaire	5.9		Thailand	5.1
	Sudan	5.9		Vietnam	5.1
25	Qatar	5.8		Uganda	5.1
26	Papua New Guinea	5.8			

Highest cost of living[a]
1989 index USA = 100

1	Iran	229	16	USSR	115
2	Japan	186	17	Israel	112
3	Gabon	170	18	France	111
4	Congo	164	19	South Korea	110
5	Togo	162	20	Sweden	109
6	Cameroon	152		Italy	109
7	Côte d'Ivoire	147	22	West Germany	108
8	Libya	145	23	Papua New Guinea	106
9	Taiwan	145		China	106
10	Norway	144	25	Spain	104
11	Finland	138		UK	104
12	Senegal	128		Ireland	104
13	Denmark	118	28	Canada	102
14	Austria	117	29	USA	100
15	Switzerland	116	30	Australia	97

a The cost of living index shown is compiled by Business International for use by companies in determining expatriate compensation: it is a comparison of the cost of maintaining a typical Western lifestyle in the country rather than a comparison of the purchasing power of a citizen of the country. The index is based on typical urban prices an international executive and family will face abroad. The prices are for products of international comparable quality found in a supermarket or

Smallest households

Pop. per dwelling 1980-88

1	Bahamas	1.9		Romania	3.0
2	Sweden	2.2		Uruguay	3.0
	West Germany	2.2		Japan	3.0
	Denmark	2.2		Italy	3.0
5	Iceland	2.3		Yugoslavia	3.0
	Finland	2.3	33	Albania	3.1
	Switzerland	2.3	34	Israel	3.3
8	East Germany	2.4		Lebanon	3.3
	Norway	2.4	36	Malta	3.4
10	Netherlands	2.5		Malaysia	3.4
	France	2.5	38	Argentina	3.5
	Austria	2.5	39	China	3.6
13	Spain	2.6	40	Puerto Rico	3.7
	UK	2.6	41	Brazil	3.8
	Hungary	2.6	42	Ireland	3.9
	Belgium	2.6		Jamaica	3.9
	New Zealand	2.6		Botswana	3.9
18	Luxembourg	2.6		Neth Antilles	3.9
19	Czechoslovakia	2.7	46	USSR	4.0
	USA	2.7		South Africa	4.0
	Canada	2.7		Nigeria	4.0
	Greece	2.7		Dominican Republic	4.0
23	Australia	2.8		Bolivia	4.0
24	Bulgaria	2.9	51	Hong Kong	4.1
	Poland	2.9		Indonesia	4.1
	Portugal	2.9		Jordan	4.1
27	Cyprus	3.0			

Lowest cost of living[a]

1989 index USA = 100

1	Ecuador	37		South Africa	58
2	Brazil	42	17	Tunisia	61
3	Paraguay	45	18	Thailand	65
4	Hungary	46	19	Guatemala	66
5	Venezuela	49	20	Costa Rica	68
6	Argentina	50	21	Jordan	70
	Zimbabwe	50	22	Philippines	71
	Yugoslavia	50	23	Turkey	73
9	India	53		Bangladesh	73
	Nigeria	53	25	Morocco	74
11	Colombia	54	26	Portugal	76
	Pakistan	54	27	Malaysia	79
13	Kenya	57	28	Panama	81
	Uruguay	57	29	Bahrain	82
15	Chile	58		Indonesia	82

department store. Prices found in local markets and bazaars are not used unless the available merchandise is of the specified quality and the shopping area itself is safe for executive and family members. New York City prices are used as the base, so USA = 100. Iran and Francophone countries in Sub-Saharan Africa using the CFA franc appear expensive since their currencies are over-valued.

Consumer goods: *ownership*

TV
No. people per TV 1988

1	Bermuda	1.2		Italy		3.4
	USA	1.2	27	Sweden		3.5
3	Japan	1.7		Trinidad & Tobago		3.5
4	Canada	1.8	29	Portugal		3.7
5	Australia	2.1	30	Israel		3.8
6	Yugoslavia	2.2		Barbados		3.8
7	Bahrain	2.4	32	Kuwait		3.9
	West Germany	2.4		Puerto Rico		3.9
	Denmark	2.4	34	Romania		4.0
10	Norway	2.6	35	Hong Kong		4.2
11	France	2.7	36	Ireland		4.3
	Netherlands	2.7	37	Poland		4.4
	New Zealand	2.7	38	Neth Antilles		4.5
14	Austria	2.8	39	Argentina		4.6
	Spain	2.8		Bahamas		4.6
	Switzerland	2.8	41	Singapore		4.7
	UK	2.8	42	Cuba		5.0
18	Qatar	2.9	43	South Korea		5.2
19	Belgium	2.9		Brazil		5.2
20	Czechoslovakia	3.0	45	East Germany		5.8
	Greece	3.0		Uruguay		5.8
22	Bulgaria	3.3	47	Brunei		6.1
	Lebanon	3.3		Panama		6.1
	Finland	3.3		Chile		6.1
25	Saudi Arabia	3.4	50	Venezuela		7.2

Telephone
No. people per telephone 1986

1	Sweden	1.0	23	Israel		2.6
2	Switzerland	1.2		Czechoslovakia		2.6
	Denmark	1.2	25	Qatar		3.2
4	USA	1.3		Taiwan		3.2
	Norway	1.3	27	Barbados		3.3
	Canada	1.3	28	Bahrain		3.4
7	Luxembourg	1.4	29	Ireland		3.7
	Finland	1.4		UK		3.7
9	New Zealand	1.5	31	Neth Antilles		4.0
	Italy	1.5	32	Spain		4.1
11	Netherlands	1.6	33	East Germany		4.3
	France	1.6	34	Bulgaria		4.5
	West Germany	1.6	35	UAE		4.7
14	Iceland	1.7	36	Portugal		4.8
15	Japan	1.8	37	South Korea		5.4
	Australia	1.8	38	Kuwait		5.8
17	Austria	1.9	39	Brunei		6.5
18	Bahamas	2.2	40	South Africa		6.9
	Hong Kong	2.2	41	Yugoslavia		7.6
	Belgium	2.2		Uruguay		7.6
21	Singapore	2.3	43	Costa Rica		7.9
22	Greece	2.5	44	Saudi Arabia		8.0

Fridge
% households owning 1988

1	Canada	100	14	UK	93
	USA	100	15	Ireland	92
3	East Germany	99	16	West Germany	91
4	Japan	98		Poland	91
	Netherlands	98	18	Hungary	90
6	Austria	97		Czechoslovakia	90
	Finland	97	20	Italy	88
	France	97	21	Norway	85
9	Sweden	96	22	Denmark	84
	Switzerland	96	23	Greece	74
	Bulgaria	96		Portugal	74
12	Belgium	94	25	Romania	30
	Spain	94			

Video cassette recorder
% households owning 1988

1	Japan	53	9	Switzerland	14
2	UK	49	10	Belgium	13
3	Netherlands	32	11	Sweden	10
4	West Germany	30		France	10
5	Norway	22	13	Italy	9
6	Spain	19	14	Austria	6
7	Ireland	18	15	Finland	5
8	Denmark	15		Greece	5

Dishwasher
% households owning 1988

1	USA	38	9	Italy	24
2	West Germany	34		Norway	24
3	Switzerland	32	11	Finland	15
4	Sweden	30	12	Spain	13
5	Austria	27	13	Ireland	10
	Belgium	27	14	Netherlands	9
	Denmark	27	15	UK	9
	France	27			

Microwave
% households owning 1988

1	Japan	57	9	Norway	18
2	UK	35	10	France	17
3	USA	34	11	Switzerland	15
4	Finland	28	12	Canada	13
5	Sweden	25	13	Austria	12
6	Netherlands	22	14	Italy	10
7	West Germany	20	15	Denmark	9
	Ireland	20			

Notes: A number of difficulties arise when dealing with household penetration data. Definitions of articles can vary (for example fridges may include fridge freezers in some countries and exclude them in others). Ownership levels of newer products, such as microwaves, can increase rapidly from one year to the next.

Culture and crime

Books published[a]

Per year

1	USSR	83,011
2	West Germany	65,670
3	UK	52,861
4	USA	48,793
5	Japan	44,686
6	South Korea	44,288
7	France	43,505
8	China	40,265
9	Spain	38,302
10	Canada	18,373
11	Brazil	17,648
12	Italy	17,109
13	Colombia	15,041
14	India	14,965
15	Netherlands	13,329
16	Switzerland	12,410
17	Sweden	11,516
18	Denmark	11,129
19	Yugoslavia	10,619
20	Czechoslovakia	10,565

Library book loans[a]

'000 per year

1	Japan	228,708
2	West Germany	212,900
3	USA	197,328
4	Netherlands	168,604
5	Canada	167,011
6	China	162,060
7	Poland	158,645
8	France	107,115
9	East Germany	105,178
10	Czechoslovakia	100,126
11	Denmark	84,514
12	Finland	80,800
13	Sweden	71,946
14	Romania	56,752
15	Hungary	48,766
16	Bulgaria	34,095
17	New Zealand	29,366
18	Norway	17,919
19	Ireland	13,819
20	Mexico	13,040

Cinema attendances[a]

'000 per year

1	USSR	14.8
2	Singapore	12.5
3	Hong Kong	12.3
4	Bulgaria	9.5
5	North Korea	9.2
6	Romania	9.1
7	Cuba	7.7
8	Taiwan	6.4
9	India	5.9
10	Vietnam	5.8
11	Hungary	5.3
12	Czechoslovakia	4.8
13	USA	4.6
14	East Germany	4.2
15	Ireland	3.3
16	Norway	3.0
	Canada	3.0
	Yugoslavia	3.0
19	Bangladesh	2.8
20	Poland	2.5

Most translated authors[b]

1983

		No. translations
1	V. I. Lenin	287
2	W. Disney Productions	284
3	A. Christie	264
4	J. Verne	206
5	Pope John Paul II	199
6	E. Blyton	184
7	B. Cartland	171
8	J. Grimm	162
9	H. C. Andersen	149
10	W. Shakespeare	123
	K. Marx	123
12	F. Engels	103
13	C. Perrault	99
	L. N. Tolstoy	99
15	A. C. Doyle	95
16	R. Goscinny	90
17	J. V. Andropov	89
18	G. Simenon	87
19	F. M. Dostoevsky	86
20	I. Asimov	82

a Data for books, libraries and cinemas are for the latest available year in the 1980s.
b The world's most translated book is the Bible with 228 translations in 1983.

Biggest drinkers[a]
Av. ann. consumption of alcohol per head, litres 1986-88

1	France	13.0
2	Spain	12.7
3	Switzerland	11.0
4	Belgium	10.7
	Hungary	10.7
6	West Germany	10.6
7	Portugal	10.5
	East Germany	10.5
9	Italy	10.0
10	Austria	9.9
11	Denmark	9.6
12	Bulgaria	8.9
	Argentina	8.9
14	Australia	8.8
15	Czechoslovakia	8.6
16	New Zealand	8.3
	Netherlands	8.3
18	Canada	8.0
19	UK	7.7
20	USA	7.6

Biggest smokers
Av. ann. consumption of cigarettes per head 1986-88

1	Cyprus	3,737
2	Greece	3,217
3	Malta	2,933
4	Kuwait	2,773
5	Poland	2,652
6	Hungary	2,550
7	Japan	2,537
8	Yugoslavia	2,454
9	Colombia	2,265
10	China	2,265
11	USA	2,100
12	Canada	2,055
13	Switzerland	1,997
14	Spain	1,982
15	South Korea	1,960
	South Africa	1,960
17	Austria	1,914
18	West Germany	1,906
19	Australia	1,900
20	New Zealand	1,815

Murders[b]
No. per 100,000 pop. 1986

1	Philippines	38.70
2	Lesotho	36.40
3	Sri Lanka	18.90
4	Jamaica	17.96
5	Guyana	15.60
6	Lebanon	13.17
7	Zimbabwe	12.60
8	Thailand	12.36
9	Bahamas	12.20
10	Botswana	11.00
11	Rwanda	9.70
12	Honduras	9.40
13	Tanzania	8.77
14	USA	8.60
15	Venezuela	8.44
16	Zambia	7.63
17	Mexico	7.42
18	Angola	7.40
19	Ethiopia	7.36
20	Luxembourg	7.00

Drug offences[b]
No. per 100,000 pop. 1986

1	Bahamas	528.9
2	New Zealand	524.0
3	Sweden	471.7
4	Australia	388.2
5	Switzerland	242.5
6	Canada	219.8
7	Mauritius	202.8
8	Trinidad & Tobago	175.3
9	Denmark	172.6
10	Jamaica	164.9
11	Philippines	126.3
12	Israel	118.8
13	Luxembourg	116.8
14	West Germany	110.8
15	Norway	109.8
16	Barbados	108.3
17	Panama	96.9
18	France	88.8
19	Zimbabwe	78.5
20	Thailand	75.3

a Alcohol consumption is based on 100% alcohol.
b Crime statistics are based on offences recorded by the police. The number will therefore depend partly on the efficiency of police administration systems, the definition of offences, and the proportion of crimes reported.

Environment: *trees and disasters*

Top deforesters
Km² per year 1982-87

1	Brazil	-22,325	21	Malawi	-995
2	China	-9,699	22	Cameroon	-987
3	Paraguay	-5,888	23	Nicaragua	-957
4	Mexico	-4,829	24	Guinea	-907
5	Côte d'Ivoire	-3,562	25	Laos	-905
6	Zaire	-3,492	26	Zambia	-867
7	Colombia	-3,054	27	Chad	-756
8	Sudan	-2,851	28	Guatemala	-722
9	Venezuela	-2,778	29	India	-684
10	Nigeria	-2,769	30	Ghana	-662
11	Peru	-2,765	31	Honduras	-659
12	Ecuador	-2,738	32	Argentina	-602
13	Malaysia	-2,366	33	Niger	-557
14	Thailand	-2,289	34	Bolivia	-553
15	Philippines	-1,875	35	Burkina Faso	-548
16	Madagascar	-1,454	36	Somalia	-527
17	Tanzania	-1,276	37	Vietnam	-521
18	Indonesia	-1,214	38	Benin	-475
19	Mozambique	-1,192	39	Uganda	-463
20	Angola	-1,072	40	Mali	-427

Top reafforesters
Km² per year 1982-87

1	Canada	21,024	6	UK	411
2	USSR	18,708	7	Spain	320
3	Italy	812	8	New Zealand	290
4	Algeria	667	9	Yugoslavia	189
5	Burma	664	10	Pakistan	185

Fastest forest depletion
% av. ann. decrease in forested area 1982-87

1	Côte d'Ivoire	-5.6	18	Mexico	-1.1
2	Paraguay	-3.8	19	Madagascar	-1.0
3	El Salvador	-3.7	20	Venezuela	-0.9
4	Togo	-3.1		Guinea	-0.9
5	Nicaragua	-2.6	22	Mozambique	-0.8
6	Malawi	-2.3		Uganda	-0.8
7	Ecuador	-2.3		Kenya	-0.8
8	Niger	-2.2		China	-0.8
9	Honduras	-1.9		Ghana	-0.8
10	Nigeria	-1.9		Burkina Faso	-0.8
11	Haiti	-1.8	28	Panama	-0.7
12	Guatemala	-1.8		Laos	-0.7
13	Philippines	-1.7	30	South Yemen	-0.6
14	Thailand	-1.6		Somalia	-0.6
15	Benin	-1.3		Sudan	-0.6
16	Malaysia	-1.2		Colombia	-0.6
17	Lebanon	-1.2		Chad	-0.6

Most forested countries
% total area covered with forest 1988

1	Papua New Guinea	85		11	Indonesia	67
2	Guyana	83		12	Brazil	66
3	Gabon	78		13	Fiji	65
4	Zaire	77		14	Malaysia	60
5	Cambodia	76		15	CAR	58
	Finland	76		16	Laos	56
7	North Korea	75		17	Peru	54
8	Bhutan	70		18	Cameroon	53
9	Sweden	68		19	Panama	52
10	Japan	67			Zimbabwe	52

Oil tanker spills

	Country affected	Oil spilled ('000 tonnes)	Name	Flag	Year
1	Trinidad & Tobago	276	Atlantic Express	Greece	1979
2	South Africa	255	Castello de Belver	Spain	1983
3	France	228	Amoco Cadiz	Liberia	1978
4	UK	121	Torrey Canyon	Liberia	1967
5	Oman	120	Sea Star	South Korea	1972
6	Greece	102	Irenes Serenade	Greece	1980
7	Spain	101	Urquiola	Spain	1976
8	USA	99	Hawaiian Patriot	Liberia	1977
9	Turkey	94	Independenta	Romania	1979
10	Portugal	84	Jakob Maersk	Denmark	1975

Industrial disasters[a]

	Location	Origin of accident	Deaths
1978	San Carlos, Spain	transport accident	216
1979	Three Mile Island, USA	reactor failure	...
1979	Missisauga, Canada	chemical explosion	...
1979	Novosibirsk, USSR	chemical plant accident	300
1980	A. Kjelland, Norway	platform collapse	123
1981	San Juan, Brazil	chlorine leakage	...
1981	Tacoa, Venezuela	oil explosion	145
1981	Montanas, Mexico	rail accident	28
1983	Nile, Egypt	gas explosion	317
1984	Sao Paolo, Brazil	pipeline explosion	508
1984	St J Ixhautepec, Mexico	gas explosion	503
1984	Bhopal, India	chemical leakage	2,800
1986	Chernobyl, USSR	reactor explosion	31
1987	Bhopal, India	chemical leakage	...
1987	Shangsi, China	fertilizer misuse	...
1987	Miamisburg, USA	rail accident	...
1988	North Sea, UK	oil platform explosion	167
1988	Tours, France	chemical leakage	...
1988	Islamabad, Pakistan	explosions	100
1988	Arzamas, USSR	explosives	73

a The industrial disasters include some of the major accidents, 1987-88. They have not been ranked due to difficulties in comparing the effects of each.

Environment: *pollution and waste*

Nitrogen oxide emissions/population
Kg per head

1	USA	82	11	Sweden	38
2	Canada	75	12	Netherlands	37
3	Luxembourg	62	13	Belgium	32
4	Finland	57	14	Switzerland	30
5	Australia	55	15	Italy[b]	28
6	Norway	48	16	New Zealand[a]	27
	Denmark	48	17	Austria	26
	West Germany	48	18	Spain[a]	24
9	France[a]	46	19	Greece[a]	22
10	UK	40	20	Ireland	20

Sulphur oxide emissions/population
Kg per head

1	Canada	179	11	Ireland	61
2	Finland	119	12	Sweden	59
3	USA	97	13	Italy[b]	56
4	Australia	89	14	Greece[a]	55
5	Denmark	88	15	West Germany	52
6	Belgium	86	16	Austria	43
7	UK	85	17	Norway	36
8	Spain[a]	65	18	Netherlands	31
	Luxembourg	65	19	New Zealand[a]	27
10	France	63	20	Portugal	26

Glass recycling
Recovery rates %

1	Netherlands	62.0	11	Spain	22.0
2	Japan	54.4	12	Sweden	20.0
3	New Zealand[c]	53.0		Finland	20.0
4	Switzerland	47.0	14	Australia	17.0
5	Austria	44.0	15	Portugal	14.0
6	Belgium	39.0	16	UK	13.0
7	Italy	38.0	17	Canada[a]	12.0
8	West Germany	37.0	18	Ireland	8.0
9	Denmark	32.0		USA	8.0
10	France	26.0			

Paper recycling
Recovery rates %

1	Netherlands[d]	50.3	11	Denmark	31.0
2	Japan	49.6	12	Finland	30.0
3	Spain	44.1	13	UK	27.0
4	West Germany	41.2	14	Norway	21.1
5	Sweden	40.0	15	USA	20.0
6	Portugal[a]	38.0	16	New Zealand	19.0
	Switzerland[a]	38.0	17	Canada[a]	18.0
8	Austria	36.8	18	Ireland	15.0
9	France	33.0	19	Belgium	14.7
10	Australia	31.8			

Solid hazardous waste generated
Kg per head

1	USA	1,076	11	Norway	29
2	Canada[a]	127	12	Austria	26
3	Netherlands	102	13	Finland	25
4	Portugal	101	14	Denmark	24
5	Belgium	92	15	Australia	18
6	West Germany	82		Switzerland	18
7	UK	68	17	New Zealand[a]	15
8	Sweden	59	18	Luxembourg	11
9	Spain	44	19	Ireland	6
10	France	36	20	Japan	5

Solid industrial waste generated
Kg per head

1	Austria[a]	4,074	11	Belgium	806
2	Finland	3,030	12	Italy[a]	609
3	USA	2,549	13	Norway[g]	520
4	Japan	2,545	14	Sweden	474
5	Canada	2,351	15	Ireland	446
6	Australia[a]	1,210	16	Greece	390
7	Portugal	1,076	17	Luxembourg	365
8	West Germany	914	18	Netherlands[f]	267
9	France	895	19	Denmark	257
10	UK[e]	876	20	Spain	131

Solid municipal waste generated
Kg per head

1	USA[a]	723	11	Luxembourg	354
2	New Zealand	657	12	Japan	339
3	Canada	617	13	West Germany	317
4	Australia	605	14	Sweden	314
5	Norway	469	15	Ireland	311
6	Netherlands	441		Belgium	311
7	Denmark	421	17	Spain	271
8	Finland	404	18	France	268
9	Switzerland	378	19	Italy	261
10	UK[e]	355	20	Greece	250

a Estimate for 1980.
b Excluding emissions from industrial processes.
c Refillable glass bottles only.
d Re-utilisation in the paper industry only.
e England and Wales only.
f Non-chemical waste only.
g Wastes from the chemical industry only.

Notes: The statistics cover OECD countries only. They normally refer to various years in the mid to late 1980s, though some refer to an earlier period.

Part II
COUNTRY PROFILES

ALGERIA

Area	2,382,000 sq km	Currency	Algerian dinar (AD)
Capital	Algiers		

People

Population	23.8m	Life expectancy: men		61 yrs
Pop. per sq km	10		women	64 yrs
Av. ann. growth		Adult literacy		45%
in pop. 1983-88	3.0%	Fertility rate (per woman)		6.1
Pop. under 15	44.4%			
Pop. over 65	3.4%		*per 1,000 pop.*	
No. men per 100 women	100	Crude birth rate		40.2
Human Development Index	61	Crude death rate		9.1

The economy

GDP	AD320bn	GDP per head	$2,269
GDP	$54bn	GDP per head in purchasing	
Av. ann. growth in real		power parity (USA=100)	15
GDP 1980-88	2.9%		

Origins of GDP

	% of total
Agriculture	13.9
Industry, of which:	42.3
manufacturing	12.0
Services	43.8

Components of GDP

	% of total
Private consumption	49.6
Public consumption	18.8
Investment	30.7
Exports	15.3
Imports	-14.4

Structure of manufacturing

	% of total		*% of total*
Agric. & food processing	26	Other	43
Textiles & clothing	20	Av. ann. increase in industrial	
Metal products & machinery	11	output 1980-88	3.1%

Energy

	'000 TCE		
Total output	123,759	% output exported	66.9
Total consumption	33,287	% consumption imported	3.6
Consumption per head,			
kg coal equivalent	1,441		

Inflation and finance

		av. ann. increase 1983-88	
Consumer price			
inflation 1989	9.2%	Narrow money (M1)	10.5%
Av. ann. inflation 1984-89	9.1%	Broad money	12.0%

Exchange rates

	end 1989		*av. 1989*
AD per $	8.03	Effective rates	*1985 = 100*
AD per SDR	10.56	– nominal	...
AD per Ecu	9.61	– real	...

Principal exports

	$m fob		$m fob
Energy & products	7,709	Agric. products &	
Semi-finished products	179	foodstuffs	30
Machinery & industrial			
equipment	93	Total incl. others	**8,128**

Main export destinations[a]

	% of total		% of total
Italy	21.0	Belgium	7.7
USA	19.2	Netherlands	6.2
France	19.0		

Principal imports

	$m cif		$m cif
Machinery & industrial		Agric. products & foodstuffs	1,793
equipment	2,001	Consumer goods	874
Semi-finished products	1,942	Total incl. others	**9,130**

Main origins of imports[a]

	% of total		% of total
France	18.0	West Germany	9.5
Italy	13.8	Japan	4.3
USA	10.5		

Balance of payments,[b] reserves and debt $m

Visible exports fob	9,029	Overall balance	-40
Visible imports fob	-6,616	Change in reserves	-20
Trade balance	2,413	Level of reserves	
Invisibles inflows	675	end Dec.	1,917
Invisibles outflows	-3464	No. months import cover	2.3
Net transfers	517	Foreign debt	24,850
Current account balance	141	– as % of GDP	45.9
– as % of GDP	0.3	Debt service	6,444
Capital balance	-352	Debt service ratio	66.4%

Family life

No. households	3.7m	Divorces per 1,000 pop.	...
Av. no. per household	6.0	Cost of living end 1989	
Marriages per 1,000 pop.	5.7	New York = 100	83

a 1989; January–June.
b 1987.

ARGENTINA

Area	2,777,000 sq km	Currency	Austral (A)
Capital	Buenos Aires		

People

Population	32.0m	Life expectancy: men	67yrs
Pop. per sq km	12	women	74yrs
Av. ann. growth		Adult literacy	94%
in pop. 1983-88	1.5%	Fertility rate (per woman)	3.0
Pop. under 15	29.9%		
Pop. over 65	9.1%		*per 1,000 pop.*
No men per 100 women	98	Crude birth rate	21.4
Human Development Index	91	Crude death rate	8.6

The economy

GDP[a]	A74.3bn	GDP per head	$2,759
GDP[a]	$88bn	GDP per head in purchasing	
Av. ann. growth in real		power parity (USA=100)	26
GDP 1980-88	-0.9%		

Origins of GDP

	% of total
Agriculture	14.7
Industry, of which:	29.8
manufacturing	22.4
Services	55.5

Components of GDP

	% of total
Private consumption[b]	84.6
Public consumption	...
Invesyment	13.2
Exports	13.3
Imports	-11.1

Structure of manufacturing

	% of total		% of total
Food & agric.	24	Other	50
Textiles & clothing	10	Av. ann. increase in industrial	
Machinery & transport	16	output 1980-88	-1.5%

Energy

	'000 TCE		
Total output	59,224	% output exported	1.4
Total consumption	60,228	% consumption imported	11.2
Consumption per head			
kg coal equivalent	1,912		

Inflation and finance

Consumer price		*av. ann. increase 1983-88*	
inflation 1989	3,079.2%	Narrow money (M1)	279.4%
Av. ann. inflation 1984-89	444.0%	Broad money	302.2%

Exchange rates

	end 1989		av.1989
A per $	625.50	Effective rates,	1985 = 100
A per SDR	840.20	– nominal	...
A per Ecu	748.70	– real	...

Principal exports

	$m fob		$m fob
Meat	607	Wheat	355
Maize	382	Wool	184
Hides & skins	368	Total incl. others	**9,135**

Main export destinations

	% of total		% of total
USA	15.3	Brazil	7.2
West Germany	8.8	Netherlands	5.1
USSR	8.3		

Principal imports

	$m cif		$m cif
Machinery & industrial		Minerals	651
equipment	1,514	Agric. products &	
Chemicals	1,114	foodstuffs	160
Metals	659	Total incl. others	**5,322**

Main origins of imports

	% of total		% of total
USA	18.8	Italy	6.1
Brazil	17.3	Bolivia	5.9
West Germany	10.7		

Balance of payments, reserves and debt $bn

Visible exports fob	9.1	Overall balance	-1.3
Visible imports fob	-4.9	Change in reserves	-1.9
Trade balance	4.2	Level of reserves	
Invisibles inflows	2.2	end Dec.[c]	3.4
Invisibles outflows	-8.0	No. months import cover	5.7
Net transfers	-	Foreign debt	58.9
Current account balance	-1.6	– as % of GDP	66.9
– as % of GDP	-1.8	Debt service	5.8
Capital balance	0.4	Debt service ratio	51.2%

Family life

No. households	8.8m	Divorces per 1,000 pop.	...
Av. no. per household	3.5	Cost of living end 1989	
Marriages per 1,000 pop.	6.0	New York = 100	50

a 1986.
b Including public consumption.
c Excluding gold.

AUSTRALIA

Area	7,682,000 sq km	Currency	Australian dollar (A$)
Capital	Canberra		

People

Population	16.53m	Life expectancy: men	73 yrs
Pop. per sq km	2	women	80 yrs
Av. ann. growth		Adult literacy	99%
in pop. 1983-88	1.4%	Fertility rate (per woman)	1.85
Pop. under 15	22.2%		
Pop. over 65	11.0%		*per 1,000 pop.*
No. men per 100 women	100	Crude birth rate	15.0
Human Development Index	98	Crude death rate	7.4

The economy

GDP	A$297bn	GDP per head	$14,083
GDP	$233bn	GDP per head in purchasing	
Av. ann. growth in real		power parity (USA=100)	71
GDP 1980-88	3.4%		

Origins of GDP

	% of total		*% of total*
		Components of GDP	
Agriculture	4.0	Private consumption	57.4
Industry, of which:	31.2	Public consumption	18.5
manufacturing	17.2	Investment	26.7
Services	64.8	Exports	17.5
		Imports	-21.5

Structure of manufacturing

	% of total		*% of total*
Agric. & food processing	18	Other	54
Textiles & clothing	7	Av. ann. increase in industrial	
Machinery & transport	21	output 1980-88	2.7%

Energy

	'000 TCE		
Total output	193,494	% output exported	45.7
Total consumption	111,231	% consumption imported	12.4
Consumption per head,			
kg coal equivalent	6,845		

Inflation and finance

			av. ann. increase 1983-88
Consumer price			
inflation 1989	7.1%	Narrow money (M1)	14.2%
Av. ann. inflation 1984-89	7.7%	Broad money	15.3%

Exchange rates

	end 1989		*av. 1989*
A$ per $	1.26	Effective rates	*1985 = 100*
A$ per SDR	1.66	– nominal	...
A$ per Ecu	1.51	– real	...

Principal exports[a]

	$bn fob		$bn fob
Wool	4.86	Iron	1.86
Coal & coke	3.87	Wheat & flour	1.72
Non-ferrous ores	3.31	Total incl. others	35.42

Main export destinations

	% of total		% of total
Japan	21.3	EC[b]	10.3
USA	10.2	Asean	8.9
New Zealand	5.1		

Principal imports[a]

	$bn cif		$bn cif
Capital goods	10.61	Consumer goods	5.90
Processed industrial supplies	10.53	Energy & products	1.56
Motor vehicles & other transport equipment	6.57	Total incl. others	38.41

Main origins of imports

	% of total		% of total
USA	21.5	EC[b]	28.1
Japan	20.7	Asean	6.0
UK	7.3		

Balance of payments, reserves and aid $bn

Visible exports fob	32.8	Capital balance	14.7
Visible imports fob	-33.9	Overall balance	5.3
Trade balance	-1.1	Change in reserves	4.9
Invisibles inflows	11.2	Level of reserves	
Invisibles outflows	-21.7	end Dec.	16.9
Net transfers	1.5	No. months import cover	3.6
Current account balance	-10.1	Aid given	1.1
– as % of GDP	-4.3	– as % of GDP	0.47

Family life

No. households	5.7m	Divorces per 1,000 pop.	2.5
Av. no. per household	2.8	Cost of living end 1989	
Marriages per 1,000 pop.	7.1	New York = 100	97

a Year ending June 30, 1989.
b Excluding UK.

AUSTRIA

Area	84,000 sq km	Currency	Schilling (Sch)
Capital	Vienna		

People

Population	7.61m	Life expectancy: men	71 yrs
Pop. per sq km	91	women	78 yrs
Av. ann. growth		Adult literacy	99%
in pop. 1983-88	0.1%	Fertility rate (per woman)	1.5
Pop. under 15	17.6%		
Pop. over 65	15.0%		*per 1,000 pop.*
No. men per 100 women	92	Crude birth rate	11.6
Human Development Index	96	Crude death rate	11.9

The economy

GDP	Sch1,567bn	GDP per head	$16,675
GDP	$127bn	GDP per head in purchasing	
Av. ann. growth in real		power parity (USA=100)	66
GDP 1980-88	1.8%		

Origins of GDP

	% of total		% of total
		Components of GDP	
Agriculture	4.7	Private consumption	56.4
Industry, of which:	39.9	Public consumption	17.4
manufacturing	26.0	Investment	28.2
Services	55.4	Exports	43.2
		Imports	-45.2

Structure of manufacturing

	% of total		% of total
Agric. & food processing	17	Other	50
Textiles & clothing	8	Av. ann. increase in industrial	
Machinery & transport	25	output 1980-88	1.3%

Energy

	'000 TCE		
Total output	8,406	% output exported	20.1
Total consumption	30,456	% consumption imported	77.1
Consumption per head,			
kg coal equivalent	4,018		

Inflation and finance

		av. ann. increase 1983-88	
Consumer price			
inflation 1989	2.6%	Narrow money (M1)	6.4%
Av. ann. inflation 1984-89	2.2%	Broad money	6.9%

Exchange rates

	end 1989		av. 1989
Sch per $	11.82	Effective rates	1985 = 100
Sch per SDR	15.53	– nominal	110
Sch per Ecu	14.14	– real	108

Principal exports

	$bn fob		$bn fob
Machinery & transport		Raw materials excl. fuels	1.67
equipment	10.59	Agric. products & foodstuffs	1.05
Manufactured products	10.17	Energy & products	0.34
Chemicals	3.01	Total incl. others	31.03

Main export destinations

	% of total		% of total
West Germany	35.0	France	4.6
Italy	10.4	EC	64.0
Switzerland	7.2	Efta	11.0
UK	4.7	Eastern Europe[a]	9.0

Principal imports

	$bn cif		$bn cif
Machinery & transport		Energy & products	2.60
equipment	13.42	Raw materials excl. fuels	1.99
Manufactured products	6.98	Agric. products & foodstuffs	1.98
Chemicals	3.84	Total incl. others	36.55

Main origins of imports

	% of total		% of total
West Germany	44.5	France	3.9
Italy	8.9	EC	68.0
Japan	5.1	Efta	7.0
Switzerland	4.4	Eastern Europe[a]	6.0

Balance of payments, reserves and aid $bn

Visible exports fob	30.1	Capital balance	1.2
Visible imports fob	-36.3	Overall balance	0.4
Trade balance	-6.2	Change in reserves	-0.2
Invisibles inflows	21.4	Level of reserves	
Invisibles outflows	-15.9	end Dec.	10.5
Net transfers[b]	-36	No. months import cover	2.4
Current account balance	-0.7	Aid given	0.3
– as % of GDP	-0.5	– as % of GDP	0.24

Family life

No. households	3.3m	Divorces per 1,000 pop.	2.0
Av. no. per household	2.5	Cost of living end 1989	
Marriages per 1,000 pop.	4.7	New York = 100	117

a Excluding Yugoslavia.
b $m.

BANGLADESH

Area	144,000 sq km	Currency	Taka (Tk)
Capital	Dacca		

People

Population	104.5m	Life expectancy: men	51 yrs
Pop. per sq km	726	women	50 yrs
Av. ann. growth		Adult literacy	49%
in pop. 1983-88	2.0%	Fertility rate (per woman)	5.5
Pop. under 15	43.9%		
Pop. over 65	2.9%		per 1,000 pop.
No. men per 100 women	106	Crude birth rate	42.2
Human Development Index	32	Crude death rate	15.5

The economy

GDP	Tk594bn	GDP per head	$179
GDP	$19bn	GDP per head in purchasing	
Av. ann. growth in real		power parity (USA=100)	5
GDP 1980-88	2.9%		

Origins of GDP

	% of total	Components of GDP	% of total
Agriculture	46.8	Private consumption[a]	96.9
Industry, of which:	12.7	Public consumption	...
manufacturing	7.4	Investment	11.0
Services	40.5	Exports	5.5
		Imports	-13.3

Structure of manufacturing

	% of total		% of total
Agric. & food processing	26	Other	32
Textiles & clothing	36	Av. ann. increase in industrial	
Metal products & machinery	6	output 1980-88	4.3%

Energy

	'000 TCE		
Total output	4,906	% output exported	...
Total consumption	6,564	% consumption imported	41.4
Consumption per head,			
kg coal equivalent	64		

Inflation and finance

Consumer price			av. ann. increase 1983-88
inflation 1989	10.0%	Narrow money (M1)	10.9%
Av. ann. inflation 1984-89	10.1%	Broad money	19.4%

Exchange rates

	end 1989		av. 1989
Tk[b] per $	32.27	Effective rates	1985 = 100
Tk[b] per SDR	42.41	– nominal	...
Tk[b] per Ecu	38.63	– real	...

Principal exports

	$m fob		$m fob
Raw jute	753.0	Fish & fish products	159.1
Textiles & clothing	437.4		
Jute goods	292.3	Total incl. others	**1,030.3**

Main export destinations

	% of total		% of total
USA	31.9	UK	5.4
Italy	8.6	Singapore	4.3
Japan	5.5		

Principal imports

	$m cif		$m cif
Agric. products & foodstuffs	554.3	Energy products	282.2
		Chemicals	211.8
Machinery & transport equipment	391.8	Total incl. others	**2,466.8**

Main origins of imports

	% of total		% of total
Japan	12.0	Singapore	7.6
USA	9.0	EC	13.0
UAE	7.6		

Balance of payments, reserves and debt $bn

Visible exports fob	1.3	Overall balance	0.2
Visible imports fob	-2.7	Change in reserves	0.2
Trade balance	-1.4	Level of reserves	
Invisibles inflows	0.3	end Dec.	1.1
Invisibles outflows	-0.8	No. months import cover	3.6
Net transfers	1.6	Foreign debt	10.2
Current account balance	-0.3	– as % of GDP	53.8
– as % of GDP	-1.5	Debt service	0.32
Capital balance	0.5	Debt service ratio	19.8%

Family life

No. households	16.8m	Divorces per 1,000 pop.	...
Av. no. per household	6.0	Cost of living end 1989	
Marriages per 1,000 pop.	9.0	New York = 100	73

a Including public consumption.
b Principal rate.

BELGIUM

Area	33,000 sq km	Currency	Belgian franc (Bfr)
Capital	Brussels		

People

Population	9.9m	Life expectancy: men	72 yrs
Pop. per sq km	300	women	78 yrs
Av. ann. growth		Adult literacy	99%
in pop. 1983-88	0.1%	Fertility rate (per woman)	1.6
Pop. under 15	18.1%		
Pop. over 65	14.7%		*per 1,000 pop.*
No. men per 100 women	96	Crude birth rate	11.7
Human Development Index	97	Crude death rate	11.5

The economy

GDP	Bfr5,604bn	GDP per head	$15,394
GDP	$153bn	GDP per head in purchasing	
Av. ann. growth in real		power parity (USA=100)	65
GDP 1980-88	1.5%		

Origins of GDP

	% of total		% of total
Agriculture	2.0	**Components of GDP**	
Industry, of which:	30.7	Private consumption	64.0
manufacturing	21.9	Public consumption	16.0
Services	67.3	Investment	18.0
		Exports	81.8
		Imports	-79.9

Structure of manufacturing

	% of total		% of total
Agric. & food processing	19	Other	50
Textiles & clothing	8	Av. ann. increase in industrial	
Machinery & transport	23	output 1980-88	1.2%

Energy

	'000 TCE		
Total output	9,232	% output exported[a]	266.9
Total consumption	55,155	% consumption imported[a]	135.7
Consumption per head,			
kg coal equivalent	5,560		

Inflation and finance

			av. ann. increase 1983-88
Consumer price			
inflation 1989	3.1%	Narrow money (M1)	4.3%
Av. ann. inflation 1984-89	2.4%	Broad money	6.9%

Exchange rates

	end 1989		av. 1989
Bfr per $	35.76	Effective rates	1985 = 100
Bfr per SDR	46.99	– nominal	109
Bfr per Ecu	42.59	– real	92

Principal exports

	$bn fob		$bn fob
Machinery & transport		Precious stones & jewellery	6.5
equipment	27.4	Textiles & clothing	6.3
Chemicals	14.5	Petroleum & products	3.4
Metals & products	12.5		
Agric. products &			
foodstuffs	6.8	Total incl. others	**91.9**

Main export destinations

	% of total		% of total
France	20.0	Italy	6.2
West Germany	19.5	USA	5.0
Netherlands	14.7	EC	82.2
UK	9.3		

Principal imports

	$bn cif		$bn cif
Machinery & transport		Metals & products	7.7
equipment	30.3	Energy & products	6.0
Chemicals	11.7	Precious stones & jewellery	5.7
Agric. products &		Textiles & clothing	5.2
foodstuffs	10.4	Total incl. others	**92.0**

Main origins of imports

	% of total		% of total
West Germany	24.5	USA	4.3
Netherlands	17.8	Italy	4.3
France	15.4	Japan	2.3
UK	7.6	EC	73.1

Balance of payments, reserves and aid $bn

Visible exports fob	84.8	Capital balance	-2.4
Visible imports fob	-83.7	Overall balance	0.9
Trade balance	1.1	Change in reserves	-0.3
Invisibles inflows	56.0	Level of reserves	
Invisibles outflows	-52.0	end Dec.	10.8
Net transfers	-1.8	No. months import cover	1.0
Current account balance	3.4	Aid given	0.6
– as % of GDP	2.2	– as % of GDP	0.39

Family life

No. households	4.1m	Divorces per 1,000 pop.	2.0
Av. no. per household	2.6	Cost of living end 1989	
Marriages per 1,000 pop.	5.8	New York = 100	97

a Energy trade data are distorted by transitory and oil refining activities.

BRAZIL

Area	8,512,000 sq km	Currency[a]	Cruzeiro (Cr)
Capital	Brasília		

People

Population	144.4m	Life expectancy: men		62 yrs
Pop. per sq km	17		women	68 yrs
Av. ann. growth		Adult literacy		78%
in pop. 1983-88	2.2%	Fertility rate (per woman)		3.5
Pop. under 15	35.2%			
Pop. over 65	4.7%			*per 1,000 pop.*
No. men per 100 women	100	Crude birth rate		28.6
Human Development Index	78	Crude death rate		7.9

The economy

GDP	Cr92bn	GDP per head	$2,451
GDP	$354bn	GDP per head in purchasing	
Av. ann. growth in real		power parity (USA=100)	25
GDP 1980-88	2.4%		

Origins of GDP
% of total

		Components of GDP	
			% of total
Agriculture	9.7	Private consumption	61.1
Industry, of which:	32.8	Public consumption	12.1
manufacturing	26.1	Investment	21.7
Services	57.5	Exports	10.2
		Imports	-5.1

Structure of manufacturing
% of total

Agric. & food processing	15	Other	49
Textiles & clothing	12	Av. ann. increase in industrial	
Machinery & transport	24	output 1980-88	1.3%

Energy
'000 TCE

Total output	73,427	% output exported	13.0
Total consumption	108,492	% consumption imported	53.8
Consumption per head,			
kg coal equivalent	767		

Inflation and finance

Consumer price		*av. ann. increase 1983-88*	
inflation 1989	286.9%	Narrow money (M1)	...
Av. ann. inflation 1984-89	390.2%	Broad money	...

Exchange rates

	end 1989		av. 1989
Cr per $	11.36	Effective rates,	1985 = 100
Cr per SDR	14.93	– Nominal	...
Cr per Ecu	13.60	– Real	...

Principal exports

	$bn fob		$bn fob
Metallurgical products	5.70	Iron ore	1.80
Transport equipment		Machines & mechanical	
& parts	3.89	instruments	1.46
Soya beans	3.05		
Chemical products	2.26	Total incl. others	**33.78**

Main export destinations

	% of total		% of total
USA	22.6	West Germany	3.8
Japan	6.3	Argentina	3.2
Netherlands	6.2	UK	2.8
Italy	4.2	France	2.5

Principal imports

	$bn cif		$bn cif
Fuel & lubricants	4.14	Cereals	0.19
Chemicals	1.50		
Iron & steel	0.26	Total incl. others	**14.71**

Main origins of imports

	% of total		% of total
USA	34.3	France	3.7
West Germany	9.1	Canada	2.7
Japan	9.1	UK	2.3
Argentina	4.6	Opec	20.4

Balance of payments, reserves and debt $bn

Visible exports fob	33.8	Overall balance	2.0
Visible imports fob	-14.6	Change in reserves	0.4
Trade balance	19.2	Level of reserves	
Invisibles inflows	3.1	end Dec.	7.4
Invisibles outflows	-17.4	No. months import cover	2.8
Net transfers	0.1	Foreign debt	114.6
Current account balance	4.9	– as % of GDP	32.3
– as % of GDP	1.4	Debt service	16.6
Capital balance	2.9	Debt service ratio	44.4%

Family life

No. households	31.1m	Divorces per 1,000 pop.	0.2
Av. no. per household	3.8	Cost of living end 1989	
Marriages per 1,000 pop.	7.8	New York = 100	42

a On January 15, 1989 the new cruzado replaced the previous currency, the cruzado, at a rate of 1 = 1,000. In March 1990 the new cruzado was renamed the cruzeiro.

CAMEROON

Area	475,000 sq km	Currency	CFA franc (CFAfr)
Capital	Yaoundé		

People

Population	11.1m	Life expectancy: men		49 yrs
Pop. per sq km	23		women	53 yrs
Av. ann. growth		Adult literacy		47%
in pop. 1983-88	3.0%	Fertility rate (per woman)		5.8
Pop. under 15	43.5%			
Pop. over 65	3.9%			per 1,000 pop.
No. men per 100 women	97	Crude birth rate		41.6
Human Development Index	47	Crude death rate		15.6

The economy

GDP	CFAfr3,768bn	GDP per head	$1,135
GDP	$12.6bn	GDP per head in purchasing	
Av. ann. growth in real		power parity (USA=100)	14
GDP 1980-88	4.2%		

Origins of GDP

	% of total		% of total
		Components of GDP	
Agriculture	20.8	Private consumption	74.3
Industry, of which:	31.3	Public consumption	11.1
manufacturing	10.8	Investment	18.2
Services	47.9	Exports	16.4
		Imports	-19.9

Structure of manufacturing

	% of total		% of total
Agric. & food processing	50	Other	30
Textiles & clothing	13	Av. ann. increase in industrial	
Metal products & machinery	7	output 1980-88	7.2%

Energy

	'000 TCE		
Total output	12,575	% output exported	73.4
Total consumption	3,024	% consumption imported	-
Consumption per head,			
kg coal equivalent	280		

Inflation and finance

Consumer price			av. ann. increase 1983-88
inflation 1988	8.6%	Narrow money (M1)	0.6%
Av. ann. inflation 1983-88	6.9%	Broad money	2.6%

Exchange rates

	end 1989		av. 1989
CFAfr per $	289.4	Effective rates	1985 = 100
CFAfr per SDR	380.3	– nominal	133
CFAfr per Ecu	346.4	– real	...

Principal exports

	$m fob		$m fob
Crude oil	802	Cocoa	189
Coffee	192	Total incl. others	**1,639**

Main export destinations

	% of total		% of total
France	28.2	USA	13.3
Netherlands	15.3	West Germany	7.6

Principal imports[a]

	$m fob		$m fob
Machinery & industrial equipment	291	Agric. products & foodstuffs	155
Consumer goods	231		
Motor vehicles & other transport equipment	170	Total incl. others	**1,484**

Main origins of imports

	% of total		% of total
France	40.1	Italy	5.7
West Germany	7.1	Bel/Lux	4.3

Balance of payments,[b] reserves and debt $bn

Visible exports fob	1.7	Overall balance	-0.4
Visible imports fob	-1.4	Change in reserves	-0.4
Trade balance	0.2	Level of reserves	
Invisibles inflows	0.4	end Dec.	0.16
Invisibles outflows	-1.5	No. months import cover	0.7
Net transfers	-0.1	Foreign debt	4.2
Current account balance	-0.9	– as % of GDP	33.4
– as % of GDP	-7.1	Debt service	0.64
Capital balance	0.4	Debt service ratio	31.2%

Family life

No. households	1.4m	Divorces per 1,000 pop.	...
Av. no. per household	7.3	Cost of living end 1989	
Marriages per 1,000 pop.	...	New York = 100	152

a 1986/87; year starting July 1.
b 1987.

CANADA

Area	9,221,000 sq km	Currency	Canadian dollar (C$)
Capital	Ottawa		

People

Population	26.0m	Life expectancy: men	73 yrs
Pop. per sq km	3	women	80 yrs
Av. ann. growth		Adult literacy	99%
in pop. 1983-88	0.9%	Fertility rate (per woman)	1.7
Pop. under 15	20.9%		
Pop. over 65	11.4%		*per 1,000 pop.*
No. men per 100 women	98	Crude birth rate	14.1
Human Development Index	98	Crude death rate	7.4

The economy

GDP	C$602bn	GDP per head	$18,834
GDP	$489bn	GDP per head in purchasing	
Av. ann. growth in real		power parity (USA=100)	93
GDP 1980-88	3.5%		

Origins of GDP

	% of total		*% of total*
		Components of GDP	
Agriculture	3.0	Private consumption	56.0
Industry, of which:	35.0	Public consumption	17.7
manufacturing	19.0	Investment	24.6
Services	62.0	Exports	34.0
		Imports	-32.5

Structure of manufacturing

	% of total		*% of total*
Agric. & food processing	15	Other	53
Textiles & clothing	7	Av. ann. increase in industrial	
Machinery & transport	25	output 1980-88	3.1%

Energy

	'000 TCE		
Total output	332,315	% output exported	37.8
Total consumption	254,022	% consumption imported	19.3
Consumption per head,			
kg coal equivalent	9,915		

Inflation and finance

			av. ann. increase 1983-88
Consumer price			
inflation 1989	4.0%	Narrow money (M1)	15.5%
Av. ann. inflation 1984-89	4.2%	Broad money	7.7%

Exchange rates

	end 1989		*av. 1989*
C$ per $	1.16	Effective rates	1985 = 100
C$ per SDR	1.52	– nominal	105
C$ per Ecu	1.39	– real	114

Principal exports

	$bn fob		$bn fob
Motor vehicles & other transport equipment	28.9	Agric. products & foodstuffs	10.7
Industrial supplies	24.3	Energy products	9.6
Forest products	17.4		
Machinery & industrial equipment	17.3	Total incl. others	**117.8**

Main export destinations

	% of total		% of total
USA	73.9	China	1.8
Japan	6.3	West Germany	1.3
UK	2.6	EC	8.0

Principal imports

	$bn cif		$bn cif
Motor vehicles & other transport equipment	27.0	Consumer goods	11.1
Machinery & industrial equipment	26.9	Agric. products & foodstuffs	6.1
		Energy products	4.2
Industrial supplies	19.9	Total incl. others	**112.2**

Main origins of imports

	% of total		% of total
USA	65.9	Taiwan	1.7
Japan	7.0	South Korea	1.7
UK	3.5	EC	12.2
West Germany	2.9		

Balance of payments, reserves and aid $bn

Visible exports fob	114.8	Capital balance	17.5
Visible imports fob	-106.0	Overall balance	7.6
Trade balance	8.9	Change in reserves	7.5
Invisibles inflows	21.9	Level of reserves	
Invisibles outflows	-42.6	end Dec.	16.2
Net transfers	3.5	No. months import cover	1.3
Current account balance	-8.3	Aid given	2.34
– as % of GDP	-1.7	– as % of GDP	0.49

Family life

No. households	8.9m	Divorces per 1,000 pop.	2.4
Av. no. per household	2.7	Cost of living end 1989	
Marriages per 1,000 pop.	7.1	New York = 100	102

CHILE

Area	757,000 sq km	Currency	Chilean peso (peso)
Capital	Santiago		

People

Population	12.8m	Life expectancy: men	68 yrs
Pop. per sq km	17	women	75 yrs
Av. ann. growth		Adult literacy	91%
in pop. 1983-88	1.7%	Fertility rate (per woman)	2.7
Pop. under 15	30.6%		
Pop. over 65	6.0%		*per 1,000 pop.*
No. men per 100 women	98	Crude birth rate	23.8
Human Development Index	93	Crude death rate	6.4

The economy

GDP	5,411bn pesos	GDP per head	$1,732
GDP	$22bn	GDP per head in purchasing	
Av. ann. growth in real		power parity (USA=100)	28
GDP 1980-88	2.1%		

Origins of GDP

		Components of GDP	
	% of total		*% of total*
Agriculture	9.4	Private consumption	67.9
Industry, of which:	37.1	Public consumption	10.1
manufacturing	20.6	Investment	18.1
Services	53.5	Exports	27.9
		Imports	-24.1

Structure of manufacturing

	% of total		*% of total*
Agric. & food processing	27	Other	62
Textiles & clothing	7	Av. ann. increase in industrial	
Metal products & machinery	4	output 1980-88	2.5%

Energy

		'000 TCE	
Total output	6,736	% output exported	0.1
Total consumption	11,763	% consumption imported	53.9
Consumption per head,			
kg coal equivalent	938		

Inflation and finance

Consumer price		*av. ann. increase 1983-88*	
inflation 1989	17.0%	Narrow money (M1)	...
Av. ann. inflation 1984-89	20.2%	Broad money	...

Exchange rates

	end 1989		*av. 1989*
Peso per $	297.4	Effective rates	*1985 = 100*
Peso per SDR	370.8	– nominal	126
Peso per Ecu	356.0	– real	72

Principal exports

	$bn fob		$bn fob
Copper	3.42	Agric. products &	
Industrial products incl.		foodstuffs	0.93
other mining prods.	2.71	Total incl. others	**7.05**

Main export destinations

	% of total		% of total
USA	19.8	UK	5.2
Japan	12.5	Brazil	4.8
West Germany	11.6	Argentina	2.4
Italy	6.4		

Principal imports

	$bn cif		$bn cif
Industrial supplies	2.83	Agric. products &	
Capital goods	1.37	foodstuffs	0.26
Consumer goods	1.09	Total incl. others	**5.29**

Main origins of imports

	% of total		% of total
USA	20.4	Argentina	5.7
Brazil	11.3	Venezuela	3.4
Japan	8.0	France	3.0
West Germany	7.4		

Balance of payments, reserves and debt $bn

Visible exports fob	7.1	Overall balance	0.8
Visible imports fob	-4.8	Change in reserves	0.8
Trade balance	2.2	Level of reserves	
Invisibles inflows	1.4	end Dec.[a]	3.2
Invisibles outflows	-4.0	No. months import cover	4.3
Net transfers	0.2	Foreign debt	19.7
Current account balance	-0.2	– as % of GDP	89.0
– as % of GDP	-0.8	Debt service	1.86
Capital balance	0.2	Debt service ratio	22.0%

Family life

No. households	2.6m	Divorces per 1,000 pop.	...
Av. no. per household	4.7	Cost of living end 1989	
Marriages per 1,000 pop.	7.6	New York = 100	58

a Excluding gold.

CHINA

Area	9,561,000 sq km	Currency	Yuan/Renminbi (Rmb)
Capital	Beijing		

People

Population	1,104.0m	Life expectancy: men		68 yrs
Pop. per sq km	115		women	71 yrs
Av. ann. growth		Adult literacy		65%
in pop. 1983-88	1.3%	Fertility rate (per woman)		2.4
Pop. under 15	26.2%			
Pop. over 65	5.8%			*per 1,000 pop.*
No. men per 100 women	106	Crude birth rate		20.5
Human Development Index	72	Crude death rate		6.7

The economy

GNP	Rmb1,402bn	GNP per head	$301
GNP	$333bn	GNP per head in purchasing	
Av. ann. growth in real		power parity (USA=100)	12
GDP 1980-88	11.4%		

Origins of GNP		Components of GNP	
	% of total		*% of total*
Agriculture	33.8	Private consumption	61.1
Industry, of which:	52.3	Public consumption	8.7
manufacturing	36.3	Investment	37.0
Services	13.8	Exports	12.4
		Imports	-19.2

Structure of manufacturing

	% of total		*% of total*
Agric. & food processing	13	Other	48
Textiles & clothing	13	Av. ann. increase in industrial	
Metal products & machinery	26	output 1980-88	13.4%

Energy

	'000 TCE		
Total output	884,742	% output exported	6.2
Total consumption	815,339	% consumption imported	0.1
Consumption per head,			
kg coal equivalent	749		

Inflation and finance

			av. ann. increase 1983-88
Consumer price			
inflation 1989	20.7%	Narrow money (M1)	25.7%
Av. ann. inflation 1984-89	12.8%	Broad money	28.8%

Exchange rates

	end 1989		*av. 1989*
Rmb per $	4.72	Effective rates	1985 = 100
Rmb per SDR	6.21	– nominal	...
Rmb per Ecu	5.65	– real	...

Principal exports

	$bn fob		$bn fob
Textiles & clothing	11.3	Agric. products & foodstuffs	1.7
Petroleum & products	3.4	Metal products	1.0
Machinery & transport		Iron & steel	1.0
equipment	2.8	Total incl. others	**41.1**

Main export destinations

	% of total		% of total
Hong Kong & Macao	38.4	Singapore	3.1
Japan	16.7	USSR	3.1
USA	7.1	West Germany	3.1

Principal imports

	$bn fob		$bn fob
Machinery & transport		Plastic products	3.6
equipment	16.7		
Iron & steel	4.6	Total incl. others	**46.4**

Main origins of imports

	% of total		% of total
Hong Kong & Macao	21.7	West Germany	6.2
Japan	20.0	Canada	3.4
USA	12.0	USSR	3.2

Balance of payments, reserves and debt $bn

Visible exports fob	41.1	Overall balance	2.7
Visible imports fob	-46.4	Change in reserves	2.4
Trade balance	-5.3	Level of reserves	
Invisibles inflows	6.0	end Dec.	19.1
Invisibles outflows	-5.0	No. months import cover	4.5
Net transfers	0.4	Foreign debt	42.0
Current account balance	-3.9	- as % of GNP	12.6
- as % of GNP	-1.2	Debt service	4.6
Capital balance	7.6	Debt service ratio	9.7%

Family life

No. households	290.5m	Divorces per 1,000 pop.	...
Av. no. per household	3.6	Cost of living end 1989	
Marriages per 1,000 pop.	...	New York = 100	106

COLOMBIA

Area	1,142,000 sq km	Currency	Colombian peso (peso)
Capital	Bogotá		

People

Population	30.2m	Life expectancy: men	63 yrs
Pop. per sq km	26	women	67 yrs
Av. ann. growth		Adult literacy	85%
in pop. 1983-88	1.9%	Fertility rate (per woman)	3.6
Pop. under 15	36.2%		
Pop. over 65	4.0%		*per 1,000 pop.*
No. men per 100 women	101	Crude birth rate	29.2
Human Development Index	80	Crude death rate	7.4

The economy

GDP	11,910bn pesos	GDP per head	$1,316
GDP	$40bn	GDP per head in purchasing	
Av. ann. growth in real		power parity (USA=100)	20
GDP 1980-88	3.3%		

Origins of GDP

	% of total
Agriculture	17.1
Industry, of which:	37.0
manufacturing	23.6
Services	45.9

Components of GDP

	% of total
Private consumption	64.6
Public consumption	9.6
Investment	19.0
Exports	19.2
Imports	-12.4

Structure of manufacturing

	% of total
Agric. & food processing	34
Textiles & clothing	14
Machinery & transport	8

	% of total
Other	44
Av. ann. increase in industrial	
output 1980-88	5.3%

Energy

	'000 TCE		
Total output	50,473	% output exported	50.1
Total consumption	24,289	% consumption imported	3.4
Consumption per head,			
kg coal equivalent	817		

Inflation and finance

Consumer price			*av. ann. increase 1983-88*
inflation 1988	28.1%	Narrow money (M1)	26.4%
Av. ann. inflation 1983-88	22.0%	Broad money	27.2%

Exchange rates

	end 1989		av. 1989
Peso per $	433.9	Effective rates	1985 = 100
Peso per SDR	570.2	– nominal	54
Peso per Ecu	519.4	– real	59

Principal exports

	$bn fob		$bn fob
Coffee	1.61	Coal	0.33
Gold	1.41	Ferro-nickel	0.18
Petroleum & products	0.95	Total incl. others	**5.31**

Main export destinations

	% of total		% of total
USA	40.4	Latin America	13.1
West Germany	11.8	EC	28.6
Netherlands	4.7		

Principal imports

	$bn fob		$bn fob
Industrial supplies	2.19	Energy & others	0.14
Capital goods	1.52	Total incl. others	**4.53**
Consumer goods	0.55		

Main origins of imports

	% of total		% of total
USA	36.7	Latin America	16.5
West Germany	7.5	EC	20.5
France	3.7		

Balance of payments, reserves and debt $bn

Visible exports fob	5.2	Overall balance	0.2
Visible imports fob	-4.5	Change in reserves	0.3
Trade balance	0.6	Level of reserves	
Invisibles inflows	1.6	end Dec.	3.7
Invisibles outflows	-3.6	No. months import cover	5.5
Net transfers	1.0	Foreign debt	17.0
Current account balance	-0.5	– as % of GDP	43.5
– as % of GDP	-1.2	Debt service	3.1
Capital balance	1.1	Debt service ratio	46.0%

Family life

No. households	5.9m	Divorces per 1,000 pop.	...
Av. no. per household	4.9	Cost of living end 1989	
Marriages per 1,000 pop.	3.3	New York = 100	54

CÔTE D'IVOIRE

Area	322,000 sq km	Currency	CFA franc (CFAfr)
Capital	Abidjan		

People

Population	11.6m	Life expectancy: men	51 yrs
Pop. per sq km	36	women	54 yrs
Av. ann. growth		Adult literacy	42%
in pop. 1983-88	4.5%	Fertility rate (per woman)	7.4
Pop. under 15	49.4%		
Pop. over 65	2.2%		*per 1,000 pop.*
No. men per 100 women	103	Crude birth rate	50.9
Human Development Index	39	Crude death rate	14.2

The economy

GDP	CFAfr3,308bn	GDP per head	$856
GDP	$10bn	GDP per head in purchasing	
Av. ann. growth in real		power parity (USA=100)	10
GDP 1980-88	0.6%		

Origins of GDP

	% of total
Agriculture	31.1
Industry, of which:	20.2
manufacturing	10.2
Services	48.7

Components of GDP

	% of total
Private consumption	66.2
Public consumption	16.5
Investment	11.3
Exports	32.7
Imports	-26.7

Structure of manufacturing

	% of total		*% of total*
Agric. & food processing	...	Other	...
Textiles & clothing	...	Av. ann. increase in industrial	
Metal products & machinery	...	output 1980-88	-2.4%

Energy

	'000 TCE		
Total output	1,416	% output exported	42.4
Total consumption	2,384	% consumption imported	80.9
Consumption per head,			
kg coal equivalent	214		

Inflation and finance

			av. ann. increase 1983-88
Consumer price			
inflation 1989	6.0%	Narrow money (M1)	3.4%
Av. ann. inflation 1984-89	5.6%	Broad money	6.4%

Exchange rates

	end 1989		*av. 1989*
CFAfr per $	289.4	Effective rates	1985 = 100
CFAfr per SDR	380.3	– nominal	186
CFAfr per Ecu	346.4	– real	118

Principal exports

	$m fob		$m fob
Cocoa beans & products	1,192	Sawn timber	178
Coffee & products	366	Raw cotton	97
Petroleum & products	291	Total incl. others	**2,369**

Main export destinations

	% of total		% of total
Netherlands	16.9	USA	7.8
France	14.8	Italy	7.2

Principal imports

	$m cif		$m cif
Agric. products & foodstuffs	428	Energy & products	289
Motor vehicles & other transport equipment	342	Total incl. others	**1,853**

Main origins of imports

	% of total		% of total
France	30.6	West Germany	5.4
Nigeria	10.8	Italy	5.3

Balance of payments, reserves and debt $bn

Visible exports fob	2.4	Overall balance	-1.1
Visible imports fob	-1.5	Change in reserves	0.06
Trade balance	0.8	Level of reserves	
Invisibles inflows	0.6	end Dec.	0.03
Invisibles outflows	-2.3	No. months import cover	0.1
Net transfers	-0.4	Foreign debt	14.1
Current account balance	-1.3	– as % of GDP	142.0
– as % of GDP	-12.9	Debt service	1.1
Capital balance	-0.3	Debt service ratio	36.2%

Family life

No. households	1.8m	Divorces per 1,000 pop.	...
Av. no. per household	5.5	Cost of living end 1989	
Marriages per 1,000 pop.	...	New York = 100	147

CZECHOSLOVAKIA

Area	128,000 sq km	Currency	Koruna (Kcs)
Capital	Prague		

People

Population	15.6m	Life expectancy:	men	68 yrs
Pop. per sq km	122		women	75 yrs
Av. ann. growth		Adult literacy		98%
in pop. 1983-88	0.3%	Fertility rate (per woman)		2.0
Pop. under 15	23.3%			
Pop. over 65	11.6%			*per 1,000 pop.*
No. men per 100 women	95	Crude birth rate		14.0
Human Development Index	93	Crude death rate		11.9

The economy

NMP	Kcs606bn	GDP per head	$2,737
GDP	$43bn	GDP per head in purchasing	
Av. ann. growth in real		power parity (USA=100)	...
GDP 1980-86	2.1%		

Origins of GDP[a]		Components of GDP[a]	
	% of total		*% of total*
Agriculture	7.6	Private consumption[b]	70.2
Industry, of which:	70.6	Public consumption	8.7
manufacturing	...	Investment	21.1
Services	21.8	Exports	...
		Imports	...

Structure of manufacturing

	% of total		*% of total*
Agric. & food processing	...	Other	...
Textiles & clothing	...	Av. ann. increase in industrial	
Metal products & machinery	...	output 1980-88	2.7%

Energy

	'000 TCE		
Total output	67,914	% output exported	10.9
Total consumption	98,262	% consumption imported	44.4
Consumption per head,			
kg coal equivalent	6,311		

Inflation and finance

Consumer price			*av. ann. increase 1983-88*
inflation 1989	1.4%	Narrow money (M1)	...
Av. ann. inflation 1984-89	...	Broad money	...

Exchange rates

	end 1989		av. 1989
Kcs[c] per $	16.48	Effective rates	1985 = 100
Kcs[c] per SDR	21.66	– nominal	...
Kcs[c] per Ecu	19.73	– real	...

Principal exports[d]

	$bn fob		$bn fob
Machinery & industrial		Chemicals & products	0.72
equipment	1.24	Organic raw materials	
Raw materials	1.08	(excl. food)	0.60
Consumer goods	1.08	Total incl. others	5.33

Main export destinations

	% of total		% of total
USSR	43.1	Austria	2.5
Poland	10.3	EC	9.9
East Germany	8.8	Socialist countries	79.0
West Germany	4.6		

Principal imports[d]

	$bn fob		$bn fob
Machinery & industrial		Agric. products & foodstuffs	0.58
equipment	2.25	Raw materials	0.48
Chemicals & products	0.90		
Organic raw materials			
(excl. food)	0.79	Total incl. others	5.49

Main origins of imports

	% of total		% of total
USSR	40.3	Austria	3.2
East Germany	10.6	EC	10.9
Poland	10.6	Socialist countries	77.9
West Germany	5.6		

Balance of payments, reserves and debt[e] $bn

Visible exports fob	24.9	Capital balance	...
Visible imports fob	-24.2	Overall balance	...
Trade balance	0.7	Change in reserves	...
Invisibles inflows	...	Level of reserves	
Invisibles outflows	...	end Dec.	...
Net transfers	...	Foreign debt	6.0
Current account balance	0.3	– as % of GDP	14.0
– as % of GDP	0.7	Debt service	0.9
No. months import cover	...	Debt service ratio	18.7%

Family life

No. households	5.9m	Divorces per 1,000 pop.	2.5
Av. no. per household	2.7	Cost of living end 1989	
Marriages per 1,000 pop.	7.6	New York = 100	...

a   As % of NMP.
b   Includes net trade.
c   Official rate.
d   1987; for non-socialist countries.
e   Convertible currency debt only. The debt service ratio is calculated as a % of
    convertible currency exports only.

DENMARK

Area	43,000 sq km	Currency	Danish krone (Dkr)
Capital	Copenhagen		

People

Population	5.13m	Life expectancy: men	73 yrs
Pop. per sq km	119	women	78 yrs
Av. ann. growth		Adult literacy	99%
in pop. 1983-88	0.1%	Fertility rate (per woman)	1.5
Pop. under 15	17.0%		
Pop. over 65	15.5%		*per 1,000 pop.*
No. men per 100 women	97	Crude birth rate	10.7
Human Development Index	97	Crude death rate	11.3

The economy

GDP	Dkr724bn	GDP per head	$20,988
GDP	$108bn	GDP per head in purchasing	
Av. ann. growth in real		power parity (USA=100)	74
GDP 1980-88	1.9%		

Origins of GDP

	% of total		*% of total*
		Components of GDP	
Agriculture	4.5	Private consumption	53.6
Industry, of which:	28.5	Public consumption	25.9
manufacturing	20.0	Investment	17.5
Services	66.9	Exports	32.3
		Imports	-29.3

Structure of manufacturing

	% of total		*% of total*
Agric. & food processing	22	Other	49
Textiles & clothing	6	Av. ann. increase in industrial	
Machinery & transport	23	output 1980-88	1.9%

Energy

	'000 TCE		
Total output	9,971	% output exported	70.2
Total consumption	27,425	% consumption imported	96.1
Consumption per head,			
kg coal equivalent	5,346		

Inflation and finance

Consumer price		*av. ann. increase 1983-88*	
inflation 1989	4.8%	Narrow money (M1)	15.6%
Av. ann. inflation 1984-89	4.3%	Broad money	11.0%

Exchange rates

	end 1989		*av. 1989*
Dkr per $	6.60	Effective rates	*1985 = 100*
Dkr per SDR	8.68	– nominal	108
Dkr per Ecu	7.91	– real	115

Principal exports

	$bn fob		$bn fob
Agric. products & foodstuffs	5.65	Furniture	1.04
		Transport equipment	0.67
Machinery & electrical products	6.52	Energy & products	0.67
Chemicals	2.72	Total incl. others	27.10

Main export destinations

	% of total		% of total
West Germany	17.6	USA	5.8
UK	11.7	EC	49.2
Sweden	11.5	Efta	24.8
Norway	7.0		

Principal imports

	$bn cif		$bn cif
Machinery & electrical products	4.81	Energy & products	1.62
		Iron & steel	1.04
Chemicals	2.92	Textiles & clothing	0.69
Transport equipment	2.04	Total incl. others	25.91

Main origins of imports

	% of total		% of total
West Germany	23.2	Netherlands	6.0
Sweden	12.3	EC	51.3
UK	7.1	Efta	23.4
USA	6.0		

Balance of payments, reserves and aid $bn

Visible exports fob	27.6	Capital balance	3.8
Visible imports fob	-25.7	Overall balance	1.3
Trade balance	1.9	Change in reserves	0.7
Invisibles inflows	12.5	Level of reserves	
Invisibles outflows	-16.0	end Dec.	11.5
Net transfers	-0.2	No. months import cover	3.3
Current account balance	-1.8	Aid given	0.92
– as % of GDP	-1.7	– as % of GDP	0.89

Family life

No. households	2.3m	Divorces per 1,000 pop.	2.8
Av. no. per household	2.2	Cost of living end 1989	
Marriages per 1,000 pop.	6.3	New York = 100	118

EGYPT

Area	998,000 sq km	Currency	Egyptian pound (£E)
Capital	Cairo		

People

Population	51.9m	Life expectancy: men		59 yrs
Pop. per sq km	52	women		62 yrs
Av. ann. growth		Adult literacy		43%
in pop. 1983-88	2.5%	Fertility rate (per woman)		4.8
Pop. under 15	40.9%			
Pop. over 65	3.9%			*per 1,000 pop.*
No. men per 100 women	103	Crude birth rate		36.0
Human Development Index	50	Crude death rate		10.1

The economy

GDP[a]	£E52bn	GDP per head	$568
GDP[b]	$30bn	GDP per head in purchasing	
Av. ann. growth in real		power parity (USA=100)	16
GDP 1980-88	5.4%		

Origins of GDP

	% of total		% of total
	% of total		*% of total*
Agriculture	16.7	Private consumption	76.8
Industry, of which:	27.8	Public consumption	14.2
manufacturing	14.0	Investment	17.7
Services	55.5	Exports	14.6
		Imports	-23.4

Components of GDP

Structure of manufacturing

	% of total		% of total
	% of total		*% of total*
Agric. & food processing	20	Other	40
Textiles & clothing	27	Av. ann. increase in industrial	
Machinery & transport	13	output 1980-88	4.5%

Energy

	'000 TCE		
	'000 TCE		
Total output	72,749	% output exported	49.6
Total consumption	34,549	% consumption imported	8.0
Consumption per head,			
kg coal equivalent	674		

Inflation and finance

Consumer price		*av. ann. increase 1983-88*	
inflation 1989	21.3%	Narrow money (M1)	13.5%
Av. ann. inflation 1984-89	18.9%	Broad money	20.1%

Exchange rates

	end 1989		av. 1989
	end 1989		*av. 1989*
£E[c] per $	1.10	Effective rates	1985 = 100
£E[c] per SDR	1.45	– nominal	...
£E[c] per Ecu	1.32	– real	...

Principal exports[d]

	$bn fob		$bn fob
Petroleum & products	1.56	Raw cotton	0.36
Industrial goods	0.49	Other agric. products	0.12
Cotton yarn & textiles	0.45	Total incl. others	...

Main export destinations

	% of total		% of total
Italy	21.4	USSR	5.8
Romania	11.6	France	5.2
UK	6.1	USA	5.2

Principal imports[d]

	$bn cif		$bn cif
Agric. products & foodstuffs	4.09	Chemicals & rubber	1.24
		Wood, paper & textiles	1.04
Machinery & transport equipment	2.08	Raw materials	0.50
		Total incl. others	...

Main origins of imports

	% of total		% of total
USA	18.9	Italy	6.2
West Germany	9.0	Romania	6.0
France	7.3	UK	4.2

Balance of payments, reserves and debt $bn

Visible exports fob	2.6	Overall balance	-0.1
Visible imports fob	-9.4	Change in reserves[e]	-42
Trade balance	-6.8	Level of reserves	
Invisibles inflows	5.0	end Dec.	2.1
Invisibles outflows	-3.9	No. months import cover	1.9
Net transfers	4.4	Foreign debt	50.0
Current account balance	-1.2	– as % of GDP	169.4
– as % of GDP	-4.0	Debt service	1.8
Capital balance	1.3	Debt service ratio	24.0%

Family life

No. households	9.5m	Divorces per 1,000 pop.	1.6
Av. no. per household	5.3	Cost of living end 1989	
Marriages per 1,000 pop.	9.1	New York = 100	89

a Year ended June 30, 1988.
b Estimate for calendar year 1988 calculated using commercial exchange rate.
c Central Bank rate.
d Because of this multiple exchange rate system it is difficult to convert trade data in Egyptian pounds to dollars. Hence the Central Bank rate has been used to convert exports of petroleum and raw cotton and imports of agricultural products and foodstuffs. The commercial rate has been used for the remainder.
e $m.

FINLAND

Area	338,000 sq km	Currency	Markka (Fmk)
Capital	Helsinki		

People

Population	4.95m	Life expectancy: men		71 yrs
Pop. per sq km	15	women		79 yrs
Av. ann. growth		Adult literacy		99%
in pop. 1983-88	0.4%	Fertility rate (per woman)		1.7
Pop. under 15	19.3%			
Pop. over 65	13.2%			per 1,000 pop.
No. men per 100 women	94	Crude birth rate		12.5
Human Development Index	97	Crude death rate		10.2

The economy

GDP	Fmk438bn	GDP per head	$21,156
GDP	$105bn	GDP per head in purchasing	
Av. ann. growth in real		power parity (USA=100)	70
GDP 1980-88	3.2%		

Origins of GDP

	% of total
Agriculture	6.6
Industry, of which:	33.9
manufacturing	24.0
Services	59.5

Components of GDP

	% of total
Private consumption	53.4
Public consumption	20.5
Investment	26.4
Exports	24.7
Imports	-25.1

Structure of manufacturing

	% of total		% of total
Agric. & food processing	13	Other	67
Textiles & clothing	6	Av. ann. increase in industrial	
Machinery & transport	24	output 1980-88	2.9%

Energy

	'000 TCE		
Total output	4,850	% output exported[a]	70.9
Total consumption	28,062	% consumption imported[a]	102.0
Consumption per head,			
kg coal equivalent	5,692		

Inflation and finance

			av. ann. increase 1983-88
Consumer price			
inflation 1989	4.8%	Narrow money (M1)	10.9%
Av. ann. inflation 1984-89	6.6%	Broad money	15.2%

Exchange rates

	end 1989		av. 1989
Fmk per $	4.06	Effective rates	1985 = 100
Fmk per SDR	5.33	– nominal	105
Fmk per Ecu	4.86	– real	106

Principal exports

	$bn fob		$bn fob
Paper & products	7.36	Chemicals	2.00
Metals & engineering		Wood & products	1.81
equipment	6.95	Total incl. others	**22.17**

Main export destinations

	% of total		% of total
USSR	14.9	France	5.3
Sweden	14.1	Norway	3.5
UK	13.0	EC	44.2
West Germany	10.8	Efta	20.5
USA	5.8	CMEA	16.6

Principal imports

	$bn cif		$bn cif
Raw materials	10.92	Energy & products	1.77
Consumer goods	5.07		
Capital goods	4.06	Total incl. others	**21.99**

Main origins of imports

	% of total		% of total
West Germany	16.9	USA	6.3
Sweden	13.3	France	4.1
USSR	12.1	EC	43.5
Japan	7.4	Efta	18.9
UK	6.8	CMEA	14.7

Balance of payments, reserves and aid $bn

Visible exports fob	21.8	Capital balance	1.9
Visible imports fob	-20.7	Overall balance	0.3
Trade balance	1.1	Change in reserves[b]	-48
Invisibles inflows	6.1	Level of reserves	
Invisibles outflows	-9.6	end Dec.	6.9
Net transfers	-0.7	No. months import cover	2.7
Current account balance	-3.0	Aid given	0.6
– as % of GDP	-2.9	– as % of GDP	0.59

Family life

No. households	2.1m	Divorces per 1,000 pop.	2.0
Av. no. per household	2.3	Cost of living end 1989	
Marriages per 1,000 pop.	5.3	New York = 100	138

a Energy trade data are distorted by transitory and oil refinery activities.
b $m.

FRANCE

Area	547,000 sq km	Currency	Franc (Fr)
Capital	Paris		

People

Population	55.9m	Life expectancy: men	72 yrs
Pop. per sq km	102	women	80 yrs
Av. ann. growth		Adult literacy	99%
in pop. 1983-88	0.4%	Fertility rate (per woman)	1.9
Pop. under 15	20.2%		
Pop. over 65	15.6%		*per 1,000 pop.*
No. men per 100 women	95	Crude birth rate	14.0
Human Development Index	97	Crude death rate	10.4

The economy

GDP	Fr5,159bn	GDP per head	$17,004
GDP	$950bn	GDP per head in purchasing	
Av. ann. growth in real		power parity (USA=100)	68
GDP, 1980-88	1.9%		

Origins of GDP		Components of GDP	
	% of total		*% of total*
Agriculture	3.6	Private consumption	60.1
Industry, of which:	32.1	Public consumption	18.8
manufacturing	22.0	Investment	20.9
Services	64.3	Exports	21.5
		Imports	-21.4

Structure of manufacturing

	% of total		*% of total*
Agric. & food processing	18	Other	42
Textiles & clothing	7	Av. ann. increase in industrial	
Metal products & machinery	33	output 1980-88	2.4%

Energy

	'000 TCE		
Total output	67,111	% output exported	29.0
Total consumption	206,944	% consumption imported	82.6
Consumption per head,			
kg coal equivalent	3,704		

Inflation and finance

Consumer price			*av. ann. increase 1983–88*
inflation 1989	3.5%	Narrow money (M1)	9.6%
Av. ann. inflation 1983–89	3.5%	Broad money	8.7%

Exchange rates

	end 1989		*av. 1989*
Fr per $	5.78	Effective rates	*1985 = 100*
Fr per SDR	7.61	– nominal	95
Fr per Ecu	6.92	– real	102

Principal exports

	$bn fob		$bn fob
Capital equipment	43.05	Motor vehicles & other	
Agric. products		transport equipment	21.55
& foodstuffs	28.29	Steel & other metals	17.08
Chemicals	26.38		
Non-durable consumer			
goods	24.01	Total incl. others	**167.47**

Main export destinations

	% of total		% of total
West Germany	16.4	USA	7.3
Italy	12.2	Netherlands	5.3
UK	9.8	EC	61.5
Bel/Lux	9.0		

Principal imports

	$bn cif		$bn cif
Capital equipment	43.07	Steel & other metals	17.83
Non-durable consumer		Motor vehicles & other	
goods	28.56	transport equipment	17.56
Chemicals	28.31	Energy products	14.38
Agric. products			
& foodstuffs	21.68	Total incl. others	**178.49**

Main origins of imports

	% of total		% of total
West Germany	19.7	UK	7.3
Italy	11.7	Netherlands	5.3
Bel/Lux	9.1	EC	60.4
USA	7.7		

Balance of payments, reserves and aid $bn

Visible exports fob	160.6	Capital balance	3.4
Visible imports fob	-168.7	Overall balance	-0.1
Trade balance	-8.1	Change in reserves	-7.7
Invisibles inflows	87.3	Level of reserves	
Invisibles outflows	-76.0	end Dec.	59.1
Net transfers	-6.7	No. months import cover	2.9
Current account balance	-3.5	Aid given[a]	6.9
– as % of GDP	-0.4	– as % of GDP	0.72

Family life

No. households	25.5m	Divorces per 1,000 pop.	2.0
Av. no. per household	2.5	Cost of living end 1989	
Marriages per 1,000 pop.	4.9	New York = 100	111

a Including aid to French overseas territories.

EAST GERMANY

Area	108,000 sq km	Currency	Deutschemark (DM)
Capital	Berlin		Mark[a] (EM)

People

Population	16.7m	Life expectancy: men		70 yrs
Pop. per sq km	154		women	76 yrs
Av. ann. growth		Adult literacy		...
in pop. 1983-88	-	Fertility rate		1.7
Pop. under 15	19.8%			
Pop. over 65	13.1%			*per 1,000 pop.*
No. men per 100 women	92	Crude birth rate		12.9
Human Development Index	95	Crude death rate		12.8

The economy

NMP[b]	EM268bn	GDP per head	$5,526
GDP[c]	$88bn	GDP per head in purchasing	
Av. ann. growth in real		power parity (USA=100)	...
NMP 1980-88	4.0%		

Origins of NMP[b]

	% of total
Agriculture	12.9
Industry, of which:	73.8
manufacturing	...
Services	13.3

Components of NMP[b]

	% of total
Private consumption[d]	72.1
Public consumption	6.4
Investment	21.5
Exports	...
Imports	...

Structure of manufacturing

	% of total		% of total
Agric. & food processing	...	Other	...
Textiles & clothing	...	Av. ann. increase in industrial	
Metal products & machinery	...	output 1980-88	3.8%

Energy

	'000 TCE		
Total output	95,931	% output exported	10.5
Total consumption	131,306	% consumption imported	36.4
Consumption per head,			
kg coal equivalent	7,891		

Inflation and finance

			av. ann. increase 1983-88
Consumer price			
inflation 1989	...	Narrow money (M1)	...
Av. ann. inflation 1984-89	...	Broad money	...

Exchange rates

	end 1989		*av. 1989*
EM[e] per $	1.68	Effective rates	*1985 = 100*
EM[e] per SDR	2.21	– nominal	...
EM[e] per Ecu	2.01	– real	...

Principal exports

	$bn fob		$bn fob
Machinery & transport equipment	24.2	Chemicals, building materials etc	7.1
Consumer goods	8.4	Other industrial supplies	3.6
Raw materials	7.7	Total incl. others	**51.2**

Main export destinations

	% of total		% of total
Socialist countries	69.5	Non-socialist countries	30.5

Principal imports

	$bn cif		$bn cif
Raw materials	18.3	Chemicals, building materials etc	4.8
Machinery & transport equipment	16.6	Consumer goods	2.8
Other industrial supplies	7.0	Total incl. others	**49.5**

Main origins of imports

	% of total		% of total
Socialist countries	68.7	Non-socialist countries	31.3

Balance of payments, reserves and debt $bn[f]

Visible exports fob	6.5	Capital balance	...
Visible imports fob	-7.1	Overall balance	...
Trade balance	-0.6	Change in reserves	...
Invisibles inflows	...	Level of reserves	
Invisibles outflows	...	end Dec.	...
Net transfers	...	Foreign debt	19.5
Current account balance	-0.5	– as % of GDP	22.2
– as % of GDP	...	Debt service	...
No. months import cover	...	Debt service ratio	72.0

Family life

No. households	7.1m	Divorces per 1,000 pop.	3.1
Av. no. per household	2.4	Cost of living end 1989	
Marriages per 1,000 pop.	8.2	New York = 100	...

a Prior to July 1990.
b At 1985 prices. Officially inflation was virtually non-existent between 1985 and 1988.
c Estimate using compromise exchange rate of $1 = EM3.5 (2EM = 1DM).
d Includes net trade.
e Official rate.
f Convertible currency only.

WEST GERMANY

Area	249,000sq km	Currency	Deutschemark (DM)
Capital	Bonn		

People

Population	61.2m	Life expectancy: men	72 yrs
Pop. per sq km	246	women	78 yrs
Av. ann. growth		Adult literacy	99%
in pop. 1983-88	-0.1%	Fertility rate (per woman)	1.4
Pop. under 15	14.9%		
Pop. over 65	15.4%		*per 1,000 pop.*
No. men per 100 women	93	Crude birth rate	10.4
Human Development Index	97	Crude death rate	12.0

The economy

GDP	DM2,122bn	GDP per head	$19,743
GDP	$1,208bn	GDP per head in purchasing	
Av. ann. growth in real		power parity (USA=100)	74
GDP 1980-88	1.7%		

Origins of GDP		Components of GDP	
	% of total		*% of total*
Agriculture	1.5	Private consumption	54.5
Industry, of which:	39.7	Public consumption	19.4
manufacturing	33.0	Investment	20.3
Services	58.8	Exports	32.4
		Imports	-26.7

Structure of manufacturing

	% of total		*% of total*
Agric. & food processing	12	Other	45
Textiles & clothing	5	Av. ann. increase in industrial	
Machinery & transport	38	output 1980-88	0.9%

Energy

	'000 TCE		
Total output	151,416	% output exported	12.2
Total consumption	344,020	% consumption imported	63.5
Consumption per head,			
kg coal equivalent	5,624		

Inflation and finance

Consumer price		*av. ann. increase 1983-88*	
inflation 1989	2.8%	Narrow money (M1)	8.0%
Av. ann. inflation 1984-89	1.3%	Broad money	6.4%

Exchange rates

	end 1989		*av. 1989*
DM per $	1.70	Effective rates	*1985 = 100*
DM per SDR	2.23	– nominal	118
DM per Ecu	2.02	– real	118

Principal exports

	$bn fob		$bn fob
Motor vehicles	58.35	Electrical engineering	
Mechanical engineering		products	36.25
products	49.72	Agric. products & foodstuffs	17.50
Chemicals	44.55	Iron & steel	12.54
		Total incl. others	**322.61**

Main export destinations[a]

	% of total		% of total
France	12.6	USA	8.0
UK	9.3	Bel/Lux	7.4
Italy	9.1	EC	54.3
Netherlands	8.7	CMEA	3.5

Principal imports

	$bn cif		$bn cif
Agric. products &		Motor vehicles	20.00
foodstuffs	32.78	Mechanical engineering	
Chemicals	25.91	products	14.49
Electrical engineering		Crude oil & natural gas	11.59
products	24.09	Total incl. others	**249.87**

Main origins of imports[a]

	% of total		% of total
France	12.1	UK	6.9
Netherlands	10.3	USA	6.6
Italy	9.1	EC	51.7
Bel/Lux	7.1	CMEA	3.6

Balance of payments, reserves and aid $bn

Visible exports fob	308.8	Capital balance	-67.9
Visible imports fob	-230.1	Overall balance	-18.4
Trade balance	78.7	Change in reserves	-19.4
Invisibles inflows	86.5	Level of reserves	
Invisibles outflows	-98.4	end Dec.	66.2
Net transfers	-18.2	No. months import cover	2.4
Current account balance	48.6	Aid given	4.73
– as % of GDP	4.0	– as % of GDP	0.39

Family life

No. households	28.3m	Divorces per 1,000 pop.	2.1
Av. no. per household	2.2	Cost of living end 1989	
Marriages per 1,000 pop.	6.5	New York = 100	108

a Excluding trade with East Germany.

GREECE

Area	132,000 sq km	Currency	Drachma (Dr)
Capital	Athens		

People

Population	10.0m	Life expectancy: men	74 yrs
Pop. per sq km	77.0	women	78 yrs
Av. ann. growth		Adult literacy	93%
in pop. 1983-88	0.3%	Fertility rate (per woman)	1.7
Pop. under 15	13.7%		
Pop. over 65	18.4%		*per 1,000 pop.*
No. men per 100 women	97.1	Crude birth rate	11.9
Human Development Index	94.9	Crude death rate	9.7

The economy

GDP	Dr7,446bn	GDP per head	$5,244
GDP	$52bn	GDP per head in purchasing	
Av. ann. growth in real		power parity (USA=100)	36
GDP 1980-88	1.4%		

Origins of GDP

	% of total
Agriculture	13.1
Industry, of which:	30.1
manufacturing	19.3
Services	56.8

Components of GDP

	% of total
Private consumption	67.2
Public consumption	20.7
Investment	19.0
Exports	22.9
Imports	-29.8

Structure of manufacturing

	% of total		*% of total*
Agric. & food processing	20	Other	44
Textiles & clothing	22	Av. ann. increase in industrial	
Metal products & machinery	14	output 1980-88	0.6%

Energy

	'000 TCE		
Total output	10,799	% output exported[a]	87.7
Total consumption	24,495	% consumption imported[a]	116.2
Consumption per head,			
kg coal equivalent	2,452		

Inflation and finance

Consumer price		*av. ann. increase 1982-87*	
inflation 1989	13.8%	Narrow money (M1)	16.8%
Av. ann. inflation 1984-85	17.1%	Broad money	22.4%

Exchange rates

	end 1989		*av. 1989*
Dr per $	157.8	Effective rates	*1985 = 100*
Dr per SDR	207.4	– nominal	62
Dr per Ecu	188.2	– real	101

Principal exports

	$bn fob		$bn fob
Manufactured products	3.11	Tobacco	0.18
Food & beverages	1.47	Raw materials & industrial	
Minerals	0.33	supplies	0.17
Petroleum products	0.49	Total incl. others	**5.47**

Main export destinations

	% of total		% of total
West Germany	25.1	UK	7.7
Italy	14.1	USA	6.3
France	8.6	EC	64.4

Principal imports

	$bn cif		$bn cif
Manufactured consumer		Petroleum	1.25
goods	3.05	Chemicals & products	0.70
Machinery equipment	2.56	Iron & steel	0.64
Foodstuffs	2.28	Total incl. others[b]	**12.39**

Main origins of imports

	% of total		% of total
West Germany	20.0	Netherlands	6.8
Italy	14.5	UK	5.0
France	8.0	EC	62.6

Balance of payments, reserves and debt $bn

Visible exports fob	5.9	Overall balance	0.9
Visible imports fob	-12.0	Change in reserves	1.0
Trade balance	-6.1	No. months import cover	3.5
Invisibles inflows	5.4	Level of reserves	
Invisibles outflows	-4.0	end Dec.	4.6
Net transfers	3.6	Foreign debt	23.5
Current account balance	-1.0	– as % of GDP	44.8
– as % of GDP	-1.8	Debt service	4.0
Capital balance	1.9	Debt service ratio	26.7%

Family life

No. households	3.2m	Divorces per 1,000 pop.	0.9
Av. no. per household	2.7	Cost of living end 1989	
Marriages per 1,000 pop.	5.2	New York = 100	90

a Energy trade figures are distorted by transitory and oil refining activities.
b 1987.

HONG KONG

Area	1,070 sq km	Currency	Hong Kong dollar (HK$)
Capital	Victoria		

People

Population	5.7m	Life expectancy:	men	73 yrs
Pop. per sq km	5,308		women	79 yrs
Av. ann. growth		Adult literacy		88%
in pop. 1983-88	1.2%	Fertility rate (per woman)		1.7
Pop. under 15	22.0%			
Pop. over 65	8.8%			*per 1,000 pop.*
No. men per 100 women	107	Crude birth rate		15.9
Human Development Index	94	Crude death rate		5.8

The economy

GDP	HK$429bn	GDP per head	$9,613
GDP	$55bn	GDP per head in purchasing	
Av. ann. growth in real		power parity (USA=100)	60
GDP 1980-88	7.6%		

Origins of GDP

	% of total
Agriculture	0.5
Industry, of which:	26.7
manufacturing	22.1
Services	72.8

Components of GDP

	% of total
Private consumption	59.9
Public consumption	7.1
Investment	27.8
Exports	115.8
Imports	-117.8

Structure of manufacturing

	% of total		% of total
Agric. & food processing	6	Other	34
Textiles & clothing	40	Av. ann. increase in industrial	
Machinery & transport	20	output 1980-88	6.5%

Energy

	'000 TCE		
Total output	...	% output exported	...
Total consumption	10,609	% consumption imported	133.9
Consumption per head,			
kg coal equivalent	1,891		

Inflation and finance

			av. ann. increase 1983-88
Consumer price			
inflation 1989	9.7%	Narrow money (M1)	...
Av. ann. inflation 1984-89	5.6%	Broad money	...

Exchange rates

	end 1989		av. 1989
HK$ per $	7.8	Effective rates	1985 = 100
HK$ per SDR	10.25	– nominal	...
HK$ per Ecu	9.34	– real	...

Principal exports[a]

	$bn fob		$bn fob
Clothing & textiles	11.51	Metal manufactures	0.79
Watches & clocks	2.14	Metal ores & scrap	0.21
Electronic components	1.40	Total incl. others	**28.73**

Main export destinations

	% of total		% of total
USA	32.2	Japan	5.8
China	19.3	Canada	2.8
West Germany	7.0	Singapore	2.6
UK	6.5		

Principal imports[b]

	$bn cif		$bn cif
Raw materials & semi-		Agric. products & foodstuffs	4.36
manufactured products	29.55	Fuels	1.60
Consumer goods	25.83		
Capital goods	10.82	Total incl. others	**72.15**

Main origins of imports

	% of total		% of total
China	34.9	South Korea	4.5
Japan	16.6	Singapore	4.0
Taiwan	9.2	West Germany	2.4
USA	8.2	UK	2.3

Balance of payments, reserves and debt $bn

Visible exports fob	63.2	Overall balance	...
Visible imports fob	-63.9	Change in reserves	...
Trade balance	-0.7	Level of reserves	
Invisibles inflows	...	end Dec.	...
Invisibles outflows	...	No. months import cover	...
Net transfers	...	Foreign debt	9.3
Current account balance		– as % of GDP	17.5
– as % of GDP	...	Debt service	1.6
Capital balance	...	Debt service ratio	1.1%

Family life

No. households	1.3m	Divorces per 1,000 pop.	0.6
Av. no. per household	4.1	Cost of living end 1989	
Marriages per 1,000 pop.	7.8	New York = 100	89

a Excluding re-exports.
b Including imports destined for re-export.

HUNGARY

Area	93,000 sq km	Currency	Forint (Ft)
Capital	Budapest		

People

Population	10.6m	Life expectancy: men	67 yrs
Pop. per sq km	114	women	74 yrs
Av. ann. growth		Adult literacy	98%
in pop. 1983-88	-0.2%	Fertility rate (per woman)	1.8
Pop. under 15	19.9%		
Pop. over 65	13.4%		*per 1,000 pop.*
No. men per 100 women	93	Crude birth rate	11.6
Human Development Index	92	Crude death rate	13.4

The economy

GDP	Ft1,411bn	GDP per head	$2,625
GDP	$28bn	GDP per head in purchasing	
Av. ann. growth in real		power parity (USA=100)	31
GDP 1980-88	1.8%		

Origins of GDP

	% of total		% of total
		Components of GDP	
Agriculture	10.4	Private consumption	61.0
Industry, of which:	47.5	Public consumption	11.3
manufacturing	...	Investment	24.9
Services	42.1	Exports	37.6
		Imports	-34.8

Structure of manufacturing

	% of total		% of total
Agric. & food processing	6	Other	46
Textiles & clothing	11	Av. ann. increase in industrial	
Machinery & transport	37	output 1980-88	1.8%

Energy

	'000 TCE		
Total output	22,012	% output exported	26.0
Total consumption	40,520	% consumption imported	60.0
Consumption per head,			
kg coal equivalent	3,819		

Inflation and finance

Consumer price		*av. ann. increase 1984-89*	
inflation 1989	15.6%	Narrow money (M1)	8.9%
Av. ann. inflation 1984-89	8.9%	Broad money	7.9%

Exchange rates

	end 1989		av. 1989
Ft per $	62.14	Effective rates	1985 = 100
Ft per SDR	81.66	– nominal	...
Ft per Ecu	74.38	– real	...

Principal exports[a]

	$m fob		$m fob
Semi-finished goods	2,489	Capital equipment	736
Food industry output	1,513	Fuels & electricity	227
Industrial consumer goods	910	Total incl. others	**5,875**

Main export destinations

	% of total		% of total
USSR	27.6	Italy	4.2
East Germany	5.3	Austria	5.7
Czechoslovakia	5.4	EC	22.6
West Germany	11.0	CMEA	45.5

Principal imports[a]

	$bn cif		$bn cif
Semi-finished goods	3,332	Industrial consumer goods	545
Capital equipment	732	Fuel & electricity	124
Food industry output	602	Total incl. others	**5,335**

Main origins of imports

	% of total		% of total
USSR	25.0	Italy	4.2
East Germany	5.3	Austria	5.7
Czechoslovakia	5.4	EC	22.6
West Germany	11.0	CMEA	45.5

Balance of payments, reserves and debt $bn[a]

Visible exports fob	5.8	Overall balance	-
Visible imports fob	-5.1	Change in reserves	0.1
Trade balance	0.7	Level of reserves	
Invisibles inflows	1.8	end Dec.	2.4
Invisibles outflows	-3.2	No. months import cover	3.5
Net transfers	0.1	Foreign debt	17.3
Current account balance	-0.6	– as % of GDP	62.3
– as % of GDP	-2.1	Debt service	3.7
Capital balance	0.7	Debt service ratio	40.6%

Family life

No. households	4.0m	Divorces per 1,000 pop.	2.7
Av. no. per household	2.6	Cost of living end 1989	
Marriages per 1,000 pop.	6.2	New York = 100	...

a Convertible currency debt only.

INDIA

Area	3,288,000 sq km	Currency	Indian rupee (Rs)
Capital	New Delhi		

People

Population	796.6m	Life expectancy: men	58 yrs
Pop. per sq km	242	women	58 yrs
Av. ann. growth		Adult literacy	41%
in pop. 1983-88	2.0%	Fertility rate (per woman)	4.3
Pop. under 15	36.5%		
Pop. over 65	4.5%		*per 1,000 pop.*
No. men per 100 women	107	Crude birth rate	32.0
Human Development Index	44	Crude death rate	11.3

The economy

GDP[a]	Rs3,838bn	GDP[a] per head	$333
GDP[a]	$265bn	GDP per head in purchasing	
Av. ann. growth in real		power parity (USA=100)	5
GDP 1980-88	5.7%		

Origins of GDP

	% of total		% of total
Agriculture	33.3	Private consumption	66.0
Industry, of which:	27.2	Public consumption	11.9
manufacturing	18.1	Investment	24.3
Services	39.5	Exports	6.2
		Imports	-8.4

Components of GDP

Structure of manufacturing

	% of total		% of total
Agric. & food processing	11	Other	47
Textiles & clothing	16	Av. ann. increase in industrial	
Machinery & transport	26	output 1980-88	6.5%

Energy

	'000 TCE		
Total output	208,630	% output exported	0.7
Total consumption	214,877	% consumption imported	15.3
Consumption per head,			
kg coal equivalent	275		

Inflation and finance

			av. ann. increase 1983-88
Consumer price			
inflation 1989	7.5%	Narrow money (M1)	15.4%
Av. ann. inflation 1984-89	8.5%	Broad money	17.5%

Exchange rates

	end 1989		av. 1989
Rs per $	17.04	Effective rates	1985 = 100
Rs per SDR	22.39	– nominal	...
Rs per Ecu	20.39	– real	...

Principal exports[a]

	$bn fob		$bn fob
Gems & jewellery	3.14	Textiles	1.42
Engineering products	1.66	Chemicals	1.09
Clothing	1.50	Total incl. others	**14.48**

Main export destination

	% of total		% of total
USA	18.6	West Germany	6.1
USSR	13.0	UK	5.8
Japan	10.8	EC	24.7

Principal imports[a]

	$bn cif		$bn cif
Capital goods	3.77	Chemicals	1.38
Crude oil & products	3.03	Iron & steel	1.25
Uncut gems & jewellery	2.05	Total incl. others	**19.77**

Main origins of imports

	% of total		% of total
Japan	11.1	West Germany	8.8
USA	9.5	UK	8.2
USSR	4.5		

Balance of payments, reserves and debt $bn

Visible exports fob	11.9	Overall balance	0.1
Visible imports fob	-17.7	Change in reserves	0.3
Trade balance	-5.8	Level of reserves	
Invisibles inflows	3.8	end Dec.	5.1
Invisibles outflows	-6.2	No. months import cover	2.6
Net transfers	3.0	Foreign debt	57.5
Current account balance	-5.2	– as % of GDP	21.3
– as % of GDP	-1.9	Debt service	3.4
Capital balance	5.7	Debt service ratio	21.7%

Family life

No. households	125.1m	Divorces per 1,000 pop.	...
Av. no. per household	6.1	Cost of living end 1989	
Marriages per 1,000 pop.	...	New York = 100	53

a Year ending 31 March, 1989.

INDONESIA

Area	1,919,000 sq km	Currency	Rupiah (Rp)
Capital	Djakarta		

People

Population	175.0m	Life expectancy: men	55 yrs
Pop. per sq km	91	women	57 yrs
Av. ann. growth		Adult literacy	67%
in pop. 1983-88	2.3%	Fertility rate (per woman)	3.3
Pop. under 15	35.0%		
Pop. over 65	3.9%		*per 1,000 pop.*
No. men per 100 women	99	Crude birth rate	27.4
Human Development Index	59	Crude death rate	11.2

The economy

GDP	Rp139,500bn	GDP per head	$473
GDP	$83bn	GDP per head in purchasing	
Av. ann. growth in real		power parity (USA=100)	9
GDP 1980-88	4.0%		

Origins of GDP

	% of total		% of total
		Components of GDP	
Agriculture	24.1	Private consumption	51.6
Industry, of which:	35.1	Public consumption	10.2
manufacturing	18.5	Investment	29.8
Services	40.8	Exports	40.8
		Imports	-32.3

Structure of manufacturing

	% of total		% of total
Agric. & food processing	23	Other	56
Textiles & clothing	11	Av. ann. increase in industrial	
Machinery & transport	10	output 1980-88	2.0%

Energy

	'000 TCE		
Total output	131,819	% output exported	72.0
Total consumption	46,629	% consumption imported	23.6
Consumption per head,			
kg coal equivalent	274		

Inflation and finance

			av. ann. increase 1983-88
Consumer price			
inflation 1989	6.1%	Narrow money (M1)	13.7%
Av. ann. inflation 1984-89	6.9%	Broad money	23.5%

Exchange rates

	end 1989		av. 1989
Rp per $	1,797	Effective rates	1985 = 100
Rp per SDR	2,362	– nominal	...
Rp per Ecu	2,151	– real	...

Principal exports

	$bn fob		$bn fob
Petroleum & products	5.04	Rubber & products	1.21
Food & products	2.68	Coffee	0.55
Natural gas	2.64		
Textiles & clothing	1.38	Total incl. others	**19.22**

Main export destinations[a]

	% of total		% of total
Japan	41.7	Netherlands	3.4
USA	16.0	Hong Kong	2.9
Singapore	8.6	China	2.6
South Korea	4.4		

Principal imports

	$bn cif		$bn cif
Raw materials & fuels	6.73	Food & beverages	0.70
Spare parts & accessories	2.79		
Capital goods	2.56	Total incl. others	**13.25**

Main origins of imports[a]

	% of total		% of total
Japan	25.6	Taiwan	4.7
USA	13.1	Australia	4.4
Singapore	6.8	Saudi Arabia	4.3
West Germany	6.7		

Balance of payments, reserves and debt $bn

Visible exports fob	19.4	Overall balance	-0.1
Visible imports fob	-13.7	Change in reserves	-0.5
Trade balance	5.7	Level of reserves	
Invisibles inflows	1.9	end Dec.	5.8
Invisibles outflows	-9.2	No. months import cover	3.1
Net transfers	0.4	Foreign debt	52.6
Current account balance	-1.2	– as % of GDP	63.6
– as % of GDP	-1.4	Debt service	9.1
Capital balance	2.2	Debt service ratio	43.0%

Family life

No. households	40.9m	Divorces per 1,000 pop.	1.1
Av. no. per household	4.1	Cost of living end 1989	
Marriages per 1,000 pop.	7.2	New York = 100	82

a Estimate.

IRAN

Area	1,648,000 sq km	Currency	Rial (IR)
Capital	Tehran		

People

Population	52.5m	Life expectancy: men	65 yrs
Pop. per sq km	32	women	66 yrs
Av. ann. growth		Adult literacy	51%
in pop. 1983-88	3.5%	Fertility rate (per woman)	5.6
Pop. under 15	43.9%		
Pop. over 65	3.2%		*per 1,000 pop.*
No. men per 100 women	104	Crude birth rate	42.4
Human Development Index	66	Crude death rate	8.0

The economy

GDP[a]	IR21,270bn	GDP per head	$1,222
GDP[b]	$64bn	GDP per head in purchasing	
Av. ann. growth in real		power parity (USA=100)	28
GDP 1980-88	2.3%		

Origins of GDP

	% of total		*% of total*
		Components of GDP[c]	
Agriculture	21.0	Private consumption	57.1
Industry, of which:	31.0	Public consumption	15.6
manufacturing[d]	23.0	Investment	28.6
Services	48.0	Exports	3.5
		Imports	-4.0

Structure of manufacturing

	% of total		*% of total*
Agric. & food processing	13	Other	43
Textiles & clothing	22	Av. ann. increase in industrial	
Metal products & machinery	22	output 1980-88	2.1%

Energy

	'000 TCE		
Total output	186,445	% output exported	49.6
Total consumption	65,638	% consumption imported	8.0
Consumption per head,			
kg coal equivalent	1,285		

Inflation and finance

Consumer price			*av. ann. increase 1984-89*
inflation 1989	37.5%	Narrow money (M1)	...
Av. ann. inflation 1984-89	...	Broad money	...

Exchange rates

	end 1989		*av. 1989*
IR per $	70.23	Effective rates	*1985 = 100*
IR per SDR	92.30	– nominal	...
IR per Ecu	84.07	– real	...

Principal exports[e]

	$bn fob		$bn fob
Crude oil	15.02	Others	0.47
Petroleum products	1.39	Total incl. others	**16.88**

Main export destinations

	% of total		% of total
Japan	12.7	Turkey	6.8
Netherlands	11.5	Bel/Lux	6.4
India	7.6	Italy	6.0
Romania	7.0	Spain	5.3
West Germany	7.0	Singapore	4.4

Principal imports[e]

	$bn cif		$bn cif
Motor vehicles & other transport	3.90	Agric. products & foodstuffs	1.54
Iron & steel products	3.36	Total incl. others	**11.99**

Main origins of imports

	% of total		% of total
West Germany	19.5	Italy	4.4
Japan	9.6	Brazil	3.5
USSR	5.7	Netherlands	3.1
Turkey	5.3	Romania	2.7
UK	5.2	China	2.6

Balance of payments,[f] reserves and debt $bn

Visible exports fob	17.1	Capital balance	-2.8
Visible imports fob	-14.7	Overall balance	-4.1
Trade balance	2.4	Change in reserves	-4.2
Invisibles inflows	1.1	Level of reserves	
Invisibles outflows	-3.8	end Dec.	...
Net transfers	-	Foreign debt	5.3
Current account balance	-0.4	– as % of GDP	8.3
– as % of GDP	-0.6	Debt service	0.8
No. months import cover	...	Debt service ratio	7.4%

Family life

No. households	6.6m	Divorces per 1,000 pop.	...
Av. no. per household	7.3	Cost of living end 1989	
Marriages per 1,000 pop.	...	New York = 100	229

a 1987-88. Iranian year beginning March 21.
b Estimate based on a compromise exchange rate of $1=IR313.3.
c Data do not add to 100 due to a statistical discrepancy.
d Including mining and quarrying other than oil and gas extraction.
e 1985-86. Iranian year beginning March 21.
f 1984-85. Iranian year beginning March 21.

IRAQ

Area	442,000 sq km	Currency	Iraqi dinar (ID)
Capital	Baghdad		

People

Population	17.3m	Life expectancy: men		63 yrs
Pop. per sq km	39		women	65 yrs
Av. ann. growth		Adult literacy		89%
in pop. 1983-88	3.4%	Fertility rate (per woman)		6.4
Pop. under 15	36.4%			
Pop. over 65	2.7%		*per 1,000 pop.*	
No. men per 100 women	104	Crude birth rate		42.6
Human Development Index	76	Crude death rate		7.8

The economy

GDP	ID28.3 bn	GDP per head	$3,090
GDP[a]	$52bn	GDP per head in purchasing	
Av. ann. growth in real		power parity (USA=100)	...
GDP 1980-88	-4.3%		

Origins of GDP		Components of GDP	
	% of total		*% of total*
Agriculture	11.9	Private consumption	...
Industry, of which:	56.8	Public consumption	...
manufacturing		Investment	...
Services	31.2	Exports	10.8
		Imports	-8.5

Structure of manufacturing

	% of total		*% of total*
Agric. & food processing	...	Other	...
Textiles & clothing		Av. ann. increase in industrial	
Machinery & transport	...	output 1980-88	-5.0%

Energy

	'000 TCE		
Total output	150,948	% output exported	86.7
Total consumption	12,003	% consumption imported	-
Consumption per head,			
kg coal equivalent	735		

Inflation and finance

Consumer price		*av. ann. increase 1983-88*	
inflation 1989[c]	45.0%	Narrow money (M1)	...
Av. ann. inflation 1984-89[c]	38%	Broad money	...

Exchange rates

	end 1989		*av. 1989*
ID per $	0.31	Effective rates	*1985 = 100*
ID per SDR	0.41	– nominal	...
ID per Ecu	0.37	– real	...

Principal exports[d]

	$bn fob		$bn fob
Crude oil	13.00	Total incl. others	**13.50**

Main export destinations[b]

	% of total		% of total
Turkey	8.8	France	3.5
USA	7.0	Japan	3.5
West Germany	4.4	Brazil	3.5
UK	4.4		

Principal imports[cd]

	$bn cif		$bn cif
Civilian goods	7.1		
Military goods	4.0	Total incl. others	11.1

Main origins of imports[b]

	% of total		% of total
Brazil	11.1	Japan	4.4
Italy	8.1	Yugoslavia	4.4
France	6.7	USA	3.7
Turkey	5.2	West Germany	3.0

Balance of payments,[d] reserves and debt $bn

Visible exports fob	10.6	Overall balance	...
Visible imports fob	-9.0	Change in reserves	...
Trade balance	1.7	Level of reserves	
Invisibles inflows	...	end Dec.	...
Invisibles outflows	...	No. months import cover	...
Net transfers	...	Foreign debt[e]	20.7
Current account balance	-1.1	– as % of GDP	39.8
– as % of GDP	-2.1	Debt service	3.5
Capital balance	...	Debt service ratio[c]	32.6%

Family life

No. households	2.5m	Divorces per 1,000 pop.	...
Av. no. per household	6.5	Cost of living end 1989	
Marriages per 1,000 pop.	...	New York = 100	...

a Estimate, using compromise exchange rate of $1 = ID0.544.
b 1987.
c Estimate.
d Trade and balance of payments data for Iraq are estimates based on limited and frequently inconsistent information.
e Excludes large sums lent by Arab states during the Iran-Iraq war; whether some of these sums were loans or gifts is disputed.

IRELAND

Area	69,000 sq km	Currency	Punt (I£)
Capital	Dublin		

People

Population	3.5m	Life expectancy: men	72 yrs
Pop. per sq km	51	women	77 yrs
Av. ann. growth		Adult literacy	99%
in pop. 1983-88	0.2%	Fertility rate (per woman)	2.5
Pop. under 15	27.7%		
Pop. over 65	10.3%		*per 1,000 pop.*
No. men per 100 women	101	Crude birth rate	18.1
Human Development Index	96.1	Crude death rate	8.8

The economy

GDP	I£21bn	GDP per head	$9,181
GDP	$33bn	GDP per head in purchasing	
Av. ann. growth in real		power parity (USA=100)	41
GDP 1980-88	1.7%		

Origins of GDP		**Components of GDP**	
	% of total		*% of total*
Agriculture	12.0	Private consumption	58.0
Industry, of which:	37.0	Public consumption	17.0
manufacturing	...	Investment	16.0
Services	51.0	Exports	63.0
		Imports	-54.0

Structure of manufacturing

	% of total		*% of total*
Agric. & food processing	28	Other	45
Textiles & clothing	7	Av. ann. increase in industrial	
Machinery & transport	20	output 1980-88	2.2%

Energy

	'000 TCE		
Total output	3,953	% output exported	21.0
Total consumption	12,255	% consumption imported	72.9
Consumption per head,			
kg coal equivalent	3,462		

Inflation and finance

Consumer price		*av. ann. increase 1983-88*	
inflation 1989	4.1%	Narrow money (M1)	6.7%
Av. ann. inflation 1984-89	3.7%	Broad money	9.0%

Exchange rates

	end 1989		*av. 1989*
I£ per $	0.64	Effective rates	1985 = 100
I£ per SDR	0.84	– nominal	106
I£ per Ecu	0.77	– real	...

Principal exports

	$bn fob		$bn fob
Machinery & transport equipment	5.87	Chemicals	2.47
		Other products	3.46
Agric. products & foodstuffs	4.44	Total incl. others	**18.82**

Main export destinations

	% of total		% of total
UK	35	Netherlands	7
West Germany	11	Bel/Lux	4
France	9	Japan	2
USA	8	EC	74

Principal imports

	$bn cif		$bn cif
Machinery & transport equipment	5.38	Chemicals	2.0
		Total incl. others	**15.62**

Main origins of imports

	% of total		% of total
UK	42	France	4
USA	16	Netherlands	4
West Germany	9	Italy	3
Japan	5	EC	66

Balance of payments, reserves and aid $bn

Visible exports fob	18.4	Capital balance	0.2
Visible imports fob	-14.6	Overall balance	0.6
Trade balance	3.8	Change in reserves	0.3
Invisibles inflows	3.5	Level of reserves	
Invisibles outflows	-8.3	end Dec.	5.2
Net transfers	1.5	No. months import cover	2.7
Current account balance	0.7	Aid given	0.06
– as % of GDP	2.0	– as % of GDP	0.20

Family life

No. households	1.0m	Divorces per 1,000 pop.	
Av. no. per household	3.9	Cost of living end 1989	
Marriages per 1,000 pop.	5.1	New York = 100	104

ISRAEL

Area	20,000 sq km	Currency	New Israeli Shekel (NIS)
Capital	Tel Aviv		

People

Population	4.4m	Life expectancy: men		74 yrs
Pop. per sq km	219	women		77 yrs
Av. ann. growth		Adult literacy		92%
in pop. 1983-88	3.0%	Fertility rate (per woman)		2.9
Pop. under 15	30.9%			
Pop. over 65	8.9%			*per 1,000 pop.*
No. men per 100 women	100	Crude birth rate		21.6
Human Development Index	96	Crude death rate		6.9

The economy

GDP	NIS67bn	GDP per head	$9,368
GDP	$42bn	GDP per head in purchasing	
Av. ann. growth in real		power parity (USA=100)	52
GDP 1980-88	2.6%		

Origins of GDP[a]		Components of GDP	
	% of total		*% of total*
Agriculture	9.8	Private consumption	63.2
Industry, of which:	58.2	Public consumption	33.3
manufacturing	...	Investment	18.3
Services	31.9	Exports	36.1
		Imports	-50.9

Structure of manufacturing

	% of total		*% of total*
Agric. & food processing	13	Other	49
Textiles & clothing	10	Av. ann. increase in industrial	
Machinery & transport	28	output 1980-88	...

Energy

	'000 TCE		
Total output	75	% output exported[b]	262.7
Total consumption	12,210	% consumption imported[b]	122.2
Consumption per head,			
kg coal equivalent	2,794		

Inflation and finance

		av. ann. increase 1983-88	
Consumer price			
inflation 1989	19.8%	Narrow money (M1)	122.7%
Av. ann. inflation 1984-89	58.2%	Broad money	98.4%

Exchange rates

	end 1989		*av. 1989*
NIS per $	1.96	Effective rates	1985 = 100
NIS per SDR	2.58	– nominal	...
NIS per Ecu	2.35	– real	...

Principal exports

	$bn fob		$bn fob
Metal, machinery &		Agric. products & foodstuffs	1.09
electronics	2.83	Textiles & clothing	0.64
Diamonds	2.55		
Chemicals	1.11	Total incl. others	**9.45**

Main export destinations

	% of total		% of total
USA	30.9	Bel/Lux	4.6
Japan	7.0	Netherlands	4.1
UK	6.8	France	4.0
West Germany	4.9		

Principal imports

	$bn cif		$bn cif
Diamonds	2.42	Non-durable consumer	
Investment goods	1.97	products	0.74
Energy & products	1.06	Durable consumer products	0.73
		Total incl. others	**12.29**

Main origins of imports

	% of total		% of total
USA	17.9	UK	8.8
Bel/Lux	15.2	Italy	5.8
West Germany	10.8	Netherlands	3.5
Switzerland	9.3		

Balance of payments, reserves and debt $bn

Visible exports fob	10.1	Overall balance	-1.2
Visible imports fob	-13.2	Change in reserves	1.2
Trade balance	-3.0	Level of reserves	
Invisibles inflows	5.2	end Dec.	4.1
Invisibles outflows	-7.3	No. months import cover	2.4
Net transfers	4.6	Foreign debt	25.1
Current account balance	-0.6	– as % of GDP	59.9
– as % of GDP	-1.5	Debt service	4.8
Capital balance	-0.6	Debt service ratio	31.9%

Family life

No. households	1.3m	Divorces per 1,000 pop.	1.2
Av. no. per household	3.3	Cost of living end 1989	
Marriages per 1,000 pop.	7.0	New York = 100	112

a   1986.
b   Energy trade data are distorted by transitory and oil refining activities.

ITALY

Area	294,000 sq km	Currency	Lira (L)
Capital	Rome		

People

Population	57.44m	Life expectancy: men	72 yrs
Pop. per sq km	195	women	79 yrs
Av. ann. growth		Adult literacy	97%
in pop. 1983-88	0.2%	Fertility rate (per woman)	1.5
Pop. under 15	17.1%		
Pop. over 65	14.2%		*per 1,000 pop.*
No. men per 100 women	95	Crude birth rate	10.8
Human Development Index	97	Crude death rate	10.2

The economy

GDP	L1,079,000bn	GDP per head	$14,432
GDP	$829bn	GDP per head in purchasing	
Av. ann. growth in real		power parity (USA=100)	66
GDP 1980-88	2.2%		

Origins of GDP

	% of total
Agriculture	3.8
Industry, of which:	34.5
manufacturing	23.0
Services	61.7

Components of GDP

	% of total
Private consumption	61.7
Public consumption	17.4
Investment	21.4
Exports	18.1
Imports	-18.5

Structure of manufacturing

	% of total		% of total
Agric. & food processing	7	Other	48
Textiles & clothing	13	Av. ann. increase in industrial	
Machinery & transport	32	output 1980-88	1.4%

Energy

	'000 TCE		
Total output	30,254	% output exported	62.6
Total consumption	204,704	% consumption imported	93.8
Consumption per head,			
kg coal equivalent	3,570		

Inflation and finance

Consumer price			*av. ann. increase 1983-88*
inflation 1989	6.6%	Narrow money (M1)	9.7%
Av. ann. inflation 1984-89	6.2%	Broad money	9.9%

Exchange rates

	end 1989		av. 1989
L per $	1,271.0	Effective rates	1985 = 100
L per SDR	1,670.0	– nominal	100
L per Ecu	1,518.0	– real	108

Principal exports

	$bn fob		$bn fob
Engineering products	42.5	Chemicals	11.1
Textiles & clothing	23.9	Agric. products & foodstuffs	8.9
Transport equipment	12.1		
Raw materials	11.5	Total incl. others	**128.5**

Main export destinations

	% of total		% of total
West Germany	17.0	Japan	2.3
France	16.3	EC	56.5
USA	8.6	Efta	9.4
UK	7.9	CMEA	3.2

Principal imports

	$bn cif		$bn cif
Engineering products	32.0	Raw materials	16.1
Agric. products &		Energy	14.7
foodstuffs	22.5	Transport equipment	14.2
Chemicals	17.7	Total incl. others	**138.6**

Main origins of imports

	% of total		% of total
West Germany	21.2	Japan	2.5
France	13.8	EC	56.7
Netherlands	5.5	Efta	9.1
USA	5.5	CMEA	4.1

Balance of payments, reserves and aid $bn

Visible exports fob	128.1	Capital balance	13.6
Visible imports fob	-128.8	Overall balance	7.4
Trade balance	-0.7	Change in reserves	5.0
Invisibles inflows	42.5	Level of reserves	
Invisibles outflows	-45.9	end Dec.	63.2
Net transfers	-1.2	No. months import cover	4.3
Current account balance	-5.4	Aid given	3.2
– as % of GDP	-0.7	– as % of GDP	0.39

Family life

No. households	25.3m	Divorces per 1,000 pop.	0.5
Av. no. per household	3.0	Cost of living end 1989	
Marriages per 1,000 pop.	5.5	New York = 100	109

JAPAN

Area	378,000 sq km	Currency	Yen (¥)
Capital	Tokyo		

People

Population	122.6m	Life expectancy: men	75 yrs
Pop. per sq km	325	women	81 yrs
Av. ann. growth		Adult literacy	99%
in pop. 1983-88	0.5%	Fertility rate (per woman)	1.7
Pop. under 15	18.5%		
Pop. over 65	11.7%		*per 1,000 pop.*
No. men per 100 women	97	Crude birth rate	11.4
Human Development Index	100	Crude death rate	7.0

The economy

GDP	¥366,500bn	GDP per head	$23,325
GDP	$2,860bn	GDP per head in purchasing	
Av. ann. growth in real		power parity (USA=100)	72
GDP 1980-88	4.1%		

Origins of GDP

	% of total	**Components of GDP**	*% of total*
Agriculture	2.8	Private consumption	55.4
Industry, of which:	40.4	Public consumption	16.4
manufacturing	29.0	Investment	27.9
Services	56.8	Exports	17.8
		Imports	-17.6

Structure of manufacturing

	% of total		*% of total*
Agric. & food processing	10	Other	46
Textiles & clothing	6	Av. ann. increase in industrial	
Machinery & transport	38	output 1980-88	4.7%

Energy

	'000 TCE		
Total output	...	% output exported	9.9
Total consumption	456,739	% consumption imported[a]	114.4
Consumption per head,			
kg coal equivalent	3,471		

Inflation and finance

Consumer price		*av. ann. increase 1983-88*	
inflation 1989	2.3%	Narrow money (M1)	6.7%
Av. ann. inflation 1984-89	1.1%	Broad money	9.2%

Exchange rates

	end 1989		*av. 1989*
¥ per $	143.5	Effective rates	1985 = 100
¥ per SDR	188.5	– nominal	132
¥ per Ecu	171.7	– real	117

Principal exports

	$bn fob		$bn fob
Motor vehicles	48.8	Electronic tubes	12.3
Office machinery	18.4	Scientific & optical	
Iron & steel products	15.3	equipment	10.8
Chemicals	14.0	Total incl. others	**264.9**

Main export destinations

	% of total		% of total
USA	33.8	Hong Kong	4.4
West Germany	6.0	China	3.6
Taiwan	5.4		

Principal imports

	$bn cif		$bn cif
Energy	38.5	Chemicals	14.8
Agric. products &		Textiles	10.6
foodstuffs	29.1	Metal ores & scrap	8.5
Machinery & equipment	26.6	Total incl. others	**187.4**

Main origins of imports

	% of total		% of total
USA	22.4	Indonesia	5.1
South Korea	6.3	Taiwan	4.7
Australia	5.5		

Balance of payments, reserves and aid $bn

Visible exports fob	259.8	Capital balance	-66.2
Visible imports fob	-164.8	Overall balance	16.5
Trade balance	95.0	Change in reserves	15.8
Invisibles inflows	111.9	Level of reserves	
Invisibles outflows	-123.1	end Dec.	97.9
Net transfers	-4.1	No. months import cover	4.1
Current account balance	79.6	Aid given	9.13
– as % of GDP	2.8	– as % of GDP	0.32

Family life

No. households	40.1m	Divorces per 1,000 pop.	1.3
Av. no. per household	3.0	Cost of living end 1989	
Marriages per 1,000 pop.	5.8	New York = 100	186.0

a Energy trade data are distorted by transitory and oil refining activities.

KENYA

Area	583,000 sq km	Currency	Kenya shilling (KSh)
Capital	Nairobi		

People

Population	23.9m	Life expectancy: men		57 yrs
Pop. per sq km	41	women		61 yrs
Av. ann. growth		Adult literacy		60%
in pop. 1983-88	4.9%	Fertility rate (per woman)		8.1%
Pop. under 15	52.1%			
Pop. over 65	2.8%			*per 1,000 pop.*
No. men per 100 women	100	Crude birth rate		53.9
Human Development Index	48	Crude death rate		11.9

The economy

GDP	K£6.5bn[a]	GDP per head	$309
GDP	$7.4bn	GDP per head in purchasing	5
Av. ann. growth in real		power parity (USA=100)	
GDP 1980-88	4.3%		

Origins of GDP

	% of total
Agriculture	30.7
Industry, of which:	19.6
manufacturing	12.2
Services	49.7

Components of GDP

	% of total
Private consumption	60.5
Public consumption	19.3
Investment	21.1
Exports	25.6
Imports	-26.5

Structure of manufacturing

	% of total		% of total
Agric. & food processing	35	Other	39
Textiles & clothing	12	Av. ann. increase in industrial	
Machinery & transport	14	output 1980-88	3.5%

Energy

	'000 TCE		
Total output	279	% output exported[b]	291.4
Total consumption	2,340	% consumption imported[b]	138.6
Consumption per head,			
kg coal equivalent	102		

Inflation and finance

			av. ann. increase 1983-88
Consumer price			
inflation 1989	10.4%	Narrow money (M1)	10.8%
Av. ann. inflation 1984-89	8.2%	Broad money	13.8%

Exchange rates

	end 1989		av. 1989
KSh per $	21.60	Effective rates	1985 = 100
KSh per SDR	28.39	− nominal	...
KSh per Ecu	25.86	− real	...

Principal exports

	$m fob		$m fob
Coffee	275	Hides & skins	29
Tea	209		
Petroleum products	124	Total incl. others	**1,073**

Main export destinations

	% of total		% of total
UK	19.6	Uganda	8.8
West Germany	12.0	EC	47.6

Principal imports

	$m cif		$m cif
Industrial machinery	446	Iron & steel	136
Petroleum & products	237		
Motor vehicles & chassis	155	Total incl. others	**1,989**

Main origins of imports

	% of total		% of total
UK	18.9	EC	47.7
Japan	12.2	Middle East	14.3

Balance of payments, reserves and debt $m

Visible exports fob	1,017	Overall balance	-44
Visible imports fob	-1,802	Change in reserves	-46
Trade balance	-785	Level of reserves	
Invisibles inflows	862	end Dec.	281
Invisibles outflows	-878	No. months import cover	1.3
Net transfers	344	Foreign debt	5,887
Current account balance	-455	– as % of GDP	79.7
– as % of GDP	-6.2	Debt service	510
Capital balance	379	Debt service ratio	27.1%

Family life

No. households	3.5m	Divorces per 1,000 pop.	...
Av. no. per household	6.1	Cost of living end 1989	
Marriages per 1,000 pop.	...	New York = 100	57

a K£1 = KSh20.
b Energy trade data are distorted by transitory and oil refining activities.

MALAYSIA

Area	330,000 sq km	Currency	Malaysian dollar (M$)
Capital	Kuala Lumpur		

People

Population	16.9m	Life expectancy: men		68 yrs
Pop. per sq km	51		women	72 yrs
Av. ann. growth		Adult literacy		70%
in pop. 1983-88	2.8%	Fertility rate (per woman)		3.5
Pop. under 15	36.2%			
Pop. over 65	3.8%		*per 1,000 pop.*	
No. men per 100 women	102	Crude birth rate		28.6
Human Development Index	80	Crude death rate		5.6

The economy

GDP	M$91bn	GDP per head	$2,045
GDP	$35bn	GDP per head in purchasing	
Av. ann. growth in real		power parity (USA=100)	22
GDP 1980-88	5.1%		

Origins of GDP

	% of total
Agriculture	21.2
Industry, of which:	37.6
manufacturing	24.0
Services	41.2

Components of GDP

	% of total
Private consumption	49.7
Public consumption	14.2
Investment	25.4
Exports	67.8
Imports	-57.2

Structure of manufacturing

	% of total		*% of total*
Agric. & food processing	21	Other	51
Textiles & clothing	5	Av. ann. increase in industrial	
Machinery & transport	23	output 1980-88	6.5%

Energy

	'000 TCE		
Total output	52,036	% output exported	77.4
Total consumption	21,208	% consumption imported	43.2
Consumption per head,			
kg coal equivalent	1,283		

Inflation and finance

Consumer price			*av. ann. increase 1983-88*
inflation 1989	2.8%	Narrow money (M1)	6.9%
Av. ann. inflation 1984-89	1.4%	Broad money	7.9%

Exchange rates

	end 1989		*av. 1989*
M$ per $	2.70	Effective rates	*1985 = 100*
M$ per SDR	3.55	– nominal	75
M$ per Ecu	3.24	– real	72

Principal exports

	$bn fob		$bn fob
Electronic components	3.25	Rubber	2.01
Petroleum & products	2.34	Palm oil	1.73
Timber & products	2.23	Total incl. others	**21.19**

Main export destinations

	% of total		% of total
Singapore	19.3	South Korea	5.0
USA	17.3	UK	3.5
Japan	17.2	Hong Kong	3.5

Principal imports

	$bn cif		$bn cif
Manufacturing supplies	5.78	Metal products	1.10
Machinery & transport equipment	2.02	Agric. products & foodstuffs	1.00
Durables & consumer goods	1.29	Total incl. others	**16.58**

Main origins of imports

	% of total		% of total
Japan	23.4	UK	4.9
USA	17.7	Taiwan	4.6
Singapore	13.2	Australia	4.1

Balance of payments, reserves and debt $bn

Visible exports fob	20.8	Overall balance	-0.4
Visible imports fob	-15.3	Change in reserves	-0.9
Trade balance	5.6	Level of reserves	
Invisibles inflows	3.5	end Dec.	6.6
Invisibles outflows	-7.4	No. months import cover	3.5
Net transfers	0.2	Foreign debt	20.5
Current account balance	1.8	as % of GDP	59.3
– as % of GDP	5.2	Debt service	5.6
Capital balance	-2.4	Debt service ratio	22.9%

Family life

No. households	2.9m	Divorces per 1,000 pop.	...
Av. no. per household	3.4	Cost of living end 1989	
Marriages per 1,000 pop.	...	New York = 100	79

MEXICO

Area	1,973,000 sq km	Currency	Mexican peso (peso)
Capital	Mexico City		

People

Population	82.7m	Life expectancy: men		66 yrs
Pop. per sq km	42		women	72 yrs
Av. ann. growth		Adult literacy		90%
in pop. 1983-88	2.1%	Fertility rate (per woman)		3.6
Pop. under 15	37.2%			
Pop. over 65	3.8%			*per 1,000 pop.*
No. men per 100 women	100	Crude birth rate		29.0
Human Development Index	88	Crude death rate		5.8

The economy

GDP	398,000bn pesos	GDP per head	$2,102
GDP	$174bn	GDP per head in purchasing	26
Av. ann. growth in real		power parity (USA=100)	
GDP 1980-88	1.0%		

Origins of GDP		Components of GDP	
	% of total		*% of total*
Agriculture	9.0	Private consumption	63.4
Industry, of which:	35.4	Public consumption	11.6
manufacturing	26.3	Investment	16.6
Services	55.6	Exports	17.8
		Imports	-9.3

Structure of manufacturing

	% of total		*% of total*
Agric. & food processing	24	Other	50
Machinery & transport	14	Av. ann. increase in industrial	
Textiles & clothing	12	output 1980-88	0.4%

Energy

	'000 TCE		
Total output	249,646	% output exported	42.5
Total consumption	137,729	% consumption imported	4.6
Consumption per head,			
kg coal equivalent	1,697		

Inflation and finance

Consumer price		*av. ann. increase 1983-88*	
inflation 1989	20.0%	Narrow money (M1)	71.1%
Av. ann. inflation 1984-89	77.3%	Broad money	54.4%

Exchange rates

	end 1989		*av. 1989*
Peso per $	2,641	Effective rates	*1985 = 100*
Peso per SDR	3,471	– nominal	...
Peso per Ecu	3,161	– real	...

Principal exports

	$bn fob		$bn fob
Manufactured products	13.04	Agric. products & foodstuffs	1.46
Petroleum & products	7.88	Total incl. others	**22.77**

Main export destinations

	% of total		% of total
USA	72.9	France	1.8
Japan	4.9	West Germany	1.3
Spain	3.4		

Principal imports

	$bn cif		$bn cif
Industrial supplies	15.14	Consumer goods	3.50
Capital goods	4.77	Total incl. others	**23.41**

Main origins of imports

	% of total		% of total
USA	74.9	France	2.0
Japan	6.4	UK	1.2
West Germany	3.5		

Balance of payments, reserves and debt $bn

Visible exports fob	20.7	Overall balance	-10.1
Visible imports fob	-18.9	Change in reserves	-6.8
Trade balance	1.8	Level of reserves	
Invisibles inflows	11.2	end Dec.	6.0
Invisibles outflows	-16.4	No. months import cover	2.0
Net transfers	0.6	Foreign debt	101.6
Current account balance	-2.9	– as % of GDP	58.3
– as % of GDP	-1.7	Debt service	14.7
Capital balance	-6.7	Debt service ratio	46.1%

Family life

No. households	15.3m	Divorces per 1,000 pop.	0.4
Av. no. per household	5.2	Cost of living end 1989	
Marriages per 1,000 pop.	7.2	New York = 100	95

MOROCCO

Area	711,000 sq km	Currency	Dirham (Dh)
Capital	Rabat		

People

Population	23.9m	Life expectancy: men	59 yrs
Pop. per sq km	34	women	63 yrs
Av. ann. growth		Adult literacy	34%
in pop. 1983-88	2.7%	Fertility rate (per woman)	4.8
Pop. under 15	40.7%		
Pop. over 65	3.6%		per 1,000 pop.
No. men per 100 women	100	Crude birth rate	35.3
Human Development Index	49	Crude death rate	9.7

The economy

GDP	Dh180bn	GDP per head	$775
GDP	$19bn	GDP per head in purchasing	
Av. ann. growth in real		power parity (USA=100)	13
GDP 1980-88	3.6%		

Origins of GDP		Components of GDP	
	% of total		% of total
Agriculture	16.5	Private consumption	68.6
Industry, of which:	29.1	Public consumption	14.6
manufacturing	17.6	Investment	23.5
Services	54.4	Exports	19.1
		Imports	-25.9

Structure of manufacturing

	% of total		% of total
Agric. & food processing	26	Other	48
Textiles & clothing	16	Av. ann. increase in industrial	
Machinery & transport	10	output 1980-88	3.4%

Energy

	'000 TCE		
Total output	985	% output exported	6.2
Total consumption	7,832	% consumption imported	101.5
Consumption per head,			
kg coal equivalent	336		

Inflation and finance

Consumer price		av. ann. increase 1983-88	
inflation 1989	4.0%	Narrow money (M1)	12.6%
Av. ann. inflation 1984-89	5.1%	Broad money	13.7%

Exchange rates

	end 1989		av. 1989
Dh per $	8.12	Effective rates	1985 = 100
Dh per SDR	10.67	– nominal	107
Dh per Ecu	9.72	– real	91

Principal exports[a]

	$m fob		$m fob
Agric. products & foodstuffs	855	Fertilisers	313
Consumer goods	798	Phosphoric acid	171
Phosphates	489	Total incl. others	**3,660**

Main export destinations

	% of total		% of total
France	26.4	Italy	5.8
India	11.4	West Germany	5.6
Spain	6.8		

Principal imports[a]

	$m cif		$m cif
Semi-manufactured goods	1,429	Agric. products & foodstuffs	588
Industrial equipment	1,355		
Energy & fuels	843	Total incl. others	**4,820**

Main origins of imports

	% of total		% of total
France	22.4	USA	7.0
Spain	7.9	Italy	5.5
West Germany	7.3		

Balance of payments, reserves and debt $bn

Visible exports fob	3.6	Overall balance	0.3
Visible imports fob	-4.4	Change in reserves	0.3
Trade balance	-0.8	Level of reserves	
Invisibles inflows	1.8	end Dec.	0.6
Invisibles outflows	-2.2	No. months import cover	1.0
Net transfers	1.6	Foreign debt	19.9
Current account balance	0.5	– as % of GDP	107.5
– as % of GDP	2.5	Debt service	1.5
Capital balance	-0.2	Debt service ratio	28.3%

Family life

No. households	3.8m	Divorces per 1,000 pop.	...
Av. no. per household	6.4	Cost of living end 1989	
Marriages per 1,000 pop.	...	New York = 100	74

a 1989.

NETHERLANDS

Area	37,000 sq km	Currency	Guilder (G)
Capital	Amsterdam		

People

Population	14.8m	Life expectancy: men	74 yrs
Pop. per sq km	396	women	80 yrs
Av. ann. growth		Adult literacy	99%
in pop. 1983-88	0.6%	Fertility rate (per woman)	1.5
Pop. under 15	17.8%		
Pop. over 65	12.9%		*per 1,000 pop.*
No. men per 100 women	98	Crude birth rate	11.8
Human Development Index	98	Crude death rate	8.7

The economy

GDP	G451bn	GDP per head	$15,421
GDP	$228bn	GDP per head in purchasing	
Av. ann. growth in real		power parity (USA=100)	68
GDP 1980-88	1.4%		

Origins of GDP		Components of GDP	
	% of total		*% of total*
Agriculture	4.3	Private consumption	60.1
Industry, of which:	33.6	Public consumption	15.6
manufacturing	19.0	Investment	20.8
Services	62.1	Exports	54.5
		Imports	-51.0

Structure of manufacturing

	% of total		*% of total*
Agric. & food processing	19	Other	49
Textiles & clothing	4	Av. ann. increase in industrial	
Machinery & transport	28	output 1980-88	0.7%

Energy

	'000 TCE		
Total output	96,235	% output exported[a]	112.4
Total consumption	100,476	% consumption imported[a]	113.0
Consumption per head,			
kg coal equivalent	7,263		

Inflation and finance

			av. ann. increase 1983-88
Consumer price			
inflation 1989	1.1%	Narrow money (M1)	6.9%
Av. ann. inflation 1984-89	0.7%	Broad money	5.6%

Exchange rates

	end 1989		*av. 1989*
G per $	1.92	Effective rates	*1985 = 100*
G per SDR	2.52	– nominal	114
G per Ecu	2.28	– real	100

Principal exports

	$bn fob		$bn fob
Machinery & transport equipment	22.78	Chemicals & plastics	19.49
		Fuels	8.79
Agric. products & foodstuffs	20.61	Raw materials, oils & fuels	7.08
		Total incl. others	103.19

Main export destinations

	% of total		% of total
West Germany	26.2	Italy	6.4
Bel/Lux	14.7	EC	74.7
France	10.8	Opec	2.4
UK	10.8		

Principal imports

	$bn cif		$bn cif
Machinery & transport equipment	28.79	Chemicals & plastics	10.76
		Fuels	9.33
Agric. products & foodstuffs	13.54	Raw materials, oils & fats	6.30
		Total incl. others	99.44

Main origins of imports

	% of total		% of total
West Germany	26.3	France	7.6
Bel/Lux	14.7	USA	7.6
UK	7.7	EC	64.4

Balance of payments, reserves and aid $bn

Visible exports fob	98.6	Capital balance	-0.7
Visible imports fob	-90.4	Overall balance	1.6
Trade balance	8.2	Change in reserves	0.1
Invisibles inflows	38.0	Level of reserves	
Invisibles outflows	-39.5	end Dec.	29.9
Net transfers	-1.4	No. months import cover	2.8
Current account balance	5.3	Aid given	2.2
– as % of GDP	2.3	– as % of GDP	0.98

Family life

No. households	5.7m	Divorces per 1,000 pop.	1.9
Av. no. per household	2.5	Cost of living end 1989	
Marriages per 1,000 pop.	6.1	New York = 100	95

a Energy trade data are distorted due to transitory and oil refining activities.

NEW ZEALAND

Area	268,000 sq km	Currency New Zealand dollar (NZ$)	
Capital	Wellington		

People

Population	3.29m	Life expectancy: men	72 yrs
Pop. per sq km	12	women	80 yrs
Av. ann. growth		Adult literacy	99%
in pop. 1983-88	2.81%	Fertility rate (per woman)	1.9
Pop. under 15	22.5%		
Pop. over 65	12.4%		*per 1,000 pop.*
No. men per 100 women	98.2	Crude birth rate	22.6
Human Development Index	96.6	Crude death rate	8.4

The economy

GDP	NZ$59.2bn	GDP per head	$11,544
GDP	$38.0bn	GDP per head in purchasing	
Av. ann. growth in real		power parity (USA=100)	60.9
GDP 1980-88	1.7%		

Origins of GDP*

	% of total	Components of GDP	% of total
Agriculture	8.4	Private consumption	62.3
Industry, of which:	28.0	Public consumption	17.1
manufacturing	19.6	Investment	19.1
Services	63.6	Exports	28.4
		Imports	-26.9

Structure of manufacturing

	% of total		% of total
Agric. & food processing	26	Other	48
Textiles & clothing	10	Av. ann. increase in industrial	
Machinery & transport	16	output 1980-88	...

Energy

	'000 TCE		
Total output	11,006	% output exported	6.1
Total consumption	12,654	% consumption imported	30.6
Consumption per head,			
kg coal equivalent	3,858		

Inflation and finance

Consumer price			*av. ann. increase 1982-87*
inflation 1989	5.7%	Narrow money (M1)	17.1%
Av. ann. inflation 1984-89	11.5%	Broad money	20.1%

Exchange rates

	end 1989		av. 1989
NZ$ per $	1.68	Effective rates	1985 = 100
NZ$ per SDR	2.20	– nominal	92.9
NZ$ per Ecu	2.00	– real	118.4

Principal exports

	$bn fob		$bn fob
Meat	1.51	Fruit & vegetables	0.51
Dairy produce	1.17	Fish	0.34
Wool	1.12		
Forest products	0.73	Total incl. others	**9.30**

Main export destinations

	% of total		% of total
Japan	17.8	USA	13.5
Australia	17.5	EC	18.3

Principal imports

	$bn cif		$bn cif
Machinery & mechanical		Mineral fuels	0.37
appliances	2.15	Plastic & products	0.34
Vehicles & aircraft	0.93		
Metals & manufactures	0.49	Total incl. others	**7.12**

Main origins of imports

	% of total		% of total
Australia	21.6	USA	16.7
Japan	18.5	EC	18.5

Balance of payments, reserves and aid $bn

Visible exports fob	8.8	Capital balance	-2.5
Visible imports fob	-6.8	Overall balance	-2.9
Trade balance	2.0	Change in reserves	-0.4
Invisibles inflows	2.9	Level of reserves	
Invisibles outflows	-5.9	end Dec.	2.8
Net transfers	0.3	No. months import cover	2.6
Current account balance	-0.8	Aid given	0.11
– as % of GDP	-2.0	– as % of GDP	0.27

Family life

No. households	1.25m	Divorces per 1,000 pop.	2.5
Av. no. per household	2.6	Cost of living end 1989	
Marriages per 1,000 pop.	7.5	New York = 100	97

a 1987.

NIGERIA

Area	924,000 sq km	Currency	Naira (N)
Capital	Lagos		

People

Population	105.0m	Life expectancy: men	49 yrs
Pop. per sq km	114	women	52 yrs
Av. ann. growth		Adult literacy	43%
in pop. 1983-88	3.3%	Fertility rate (per woman)	7.0
Pop. under 15	48.4%		
Pop. over 65	2.4%		*per 1,000 pop.*
No. men per 100 women	98	Crude birth rate	49.8
Human Development Index	32	Crude death rate	15.6

The economy

GDP	N137bn	GDP per head	$287
GDP	$30bn	GDP per head in purchasing	
Av. ann. growth in real		power parity (USA=100)	7
GDP 1980-88	-1.3%		

Origins of GDP

	% of total		% of total
		Components of GDP	
Agriculture	35.9	Private consumption	74.4
Industry, of which:	23.6	Public consumption	6.7
manufacturing	10.0	Investment	6.3
Services	40.5	Exports	27.1
		Imports	-14.5

Structure of manufacturing

	% of total		% of total
Agric. & food processing	...	Other	...
Textiles & clothing	...	Av. ann. increase in industrial	
Machinery & transport	...	output 1980-88	-3.6%

Energy

	'000 TCE		
Total output	94,053	% output exported	86.5
Total consumption	16,834	% consumption imported	24.9
Consumption per head,			
kg coal equivalent	166		

Inflation and finance

			av. ann. increase 1983-88
Consumer price			
inflation 1989	40.9%	Narrow money (M1)	13.7%
Av. ann. inflation 1984-89	20.0%	Broad money	15.1%

Exchange rates

	end 1989		av. 1989
N per $	7.65	Effective rates	1985 = 100
N per SDR	10.05	− nominal	...
N per Ecu	9.16	− real	...

Principal exports

	$bn fob		$bn fob
Petroleum	6.68	Palm & kernel oil	0.02
Cocoa beans & products	0.59		
Rubber	0.06	Total incl. others	**7.40**

Main export destinations

	% of total		% of total
UK	14.5	Japan	6.4
West Germany	10.7	Italy	6.3
France	9.8	Netherlands	3.8
USA	7.4		

Principal imports

	$bn cif		$bn cif
Machinery & transport		Agric products &	
equipment	2.30	foodstuffs	0.47
Manufactured goods	1.26	Crude materials excl. fuels	0.15
Chemicals	1.08	Mineral fuels	0.06
		Total incl. others	**5.56**

Main origins of imports

	% of total		% of total
USA	36.2	Netherlands	4.8
Spain	9.6	Canada	2.8
West Germany	7.1	UK	2.3
France	5.1		

Balance of payments, reserves and debt $bn

Visible exports fob	7.4	Overall balance	-4.9
Visible imports fob	-5.0	Change in reserves	-0.5
Trade balance	2.4	Level of reserves	
Invisibles inflows	0.4	end Dec.	0.6
Invisibles outflows	-3.8	No. months import cover	0.9
Net transfers	-	Foreign debt	30.7
Current account balance	-1.0	– as % of GDP	102.1
– as % of GDP	-3.3	Debt service	2.1
Capital balance	-3.9	Debt service ratio	26.5%

Family life

No. households	24.1m	Divorces per 1,000 pop.	...
Av. no. per household	4.0	Cost of living end 1989	
Marriages per 1,000 pop.	...	New York = 100	53

NORWAY

Area	387,000 sq km	Currency	Norwegian krone (Nkr)
Capital	Oslo		

People

Population	4.20m	Life expectancy: men		74 yrs
Pop. per sq km	11		women	80 yrs
Av. ann. growth		Adult literacy		99%
in pop. 1983-88	0.3%	Fertility rate (per woman)		1.7
Pop. under 15	18.8%			
Pop. over 65	16.4%			*per 1,000 pop.*
No. men per 100 women	98	Crude birth rate		12.4
Human Development Index	98	Crude death rate		10.6

The economy

GDP	Nkr594bn	GDP per head	$21,724
GDP	$91bn	GDP per head in purchasing	
Av. ann. growth in real		power parity (USA=100)	84
GDP 1980-88	2.7%		

Origins of GDP		Components of GDP	
	% of total		*% of total*
Agriculture	3.5	Private consumption	51.9
Industry, of which:	31.5	Public consumption	20.6
manufacturing	15.2	Investment	28.1
Services	65.0	Exports	35.8
		Imports	-36.6

Structure of manufacturing

	% of total		*% of total*
Agric. & food processing	21	Other	50
Textiles & clothing	3	Av. ann. increase in industrial	
Machinery & transport	26	output 1980-88	3.4%

Energy

	'000 TCE		
Total output	124,789	% output exported	82.9
Total consumption	28,417	% consumption imported	30.6
Consumption per head,			
kg coal equivalent	6,782		

Inflation and finance

			av. ann. increase 1983-88
Consumer price			
inflation 1989	4.6%	Narrow money (M1)	23.2%
Av. ann. inflation 1984-89	6.6%	Broad money	11.8%

Exchange rates

	end 1989		*av. 1989*
Nkr per $	6.62	Effective rates	*1985 = 100*
Nkr per SDR	8.69	– nominal	89
Nkr per Ecu	7.92	– real	103

Principal exports

	$bn fob		$bn fob
Oil, gas & products	8.15	Chemicals	1.85
Non-ferrous metals	2.86	Fish & fish products	1.54
Machinery incl.		Ships & oil platforms	0.80
electricals	1.91	Total incl. others	**22.42**

Main export destinations

	% of total		% of total
UK	26.0	USA	6.1
West Germany	12.4	EC	65.2
Sweden	11.7	Efta	16.3
Netherlands	6.9		

Principal imports

	$bn cif		$bn cif
Machinery incl.		Transport equipment	
electricals	5.22	excl.ships	1.77
Ships & oil platforms	2.20	Food, drink & tobacco	1.27
Chemicals	1.90	Clothing	1.14
		Total incl. others	**23.18**

Main origins of imports

	% of total		% of total
Sweden	17.6	USA	6.6
West Germany	13.6	EC	46.2
UK	7.8	Efta	23.9
Denmark	7.6		

Balance of payments, reserves and aid $bn

Visible exports fob	23.0	Capital balance	5.4
Visible imports fob	-23.1	Overall balance	-0.1
Trade balance	-0.1	Change in reserves	-1.0
Invisibles inflows	12.9	Level of reserves	
Invisibles outflows	-15.5	end Dec.	13.3
Net transfers	-1.0	No. months import cover	4.1
Current account balance	-3.7	Aid given	0.99
– as % of GDP	-4.0	– as % of GDP	1.08

Family life

No. households	1.8m	Divorces per 1,000 pop.	1.9
Av. no. per household	2.4	Cost of living end 1989	
Marriages per 1,000 pop.	5.2	New York = 100	144

PAKISTAN

Area	796,000 sq km	Currency	Pakistan rupee (PRs)
Capital	Islamabad		

People

Population	105.4m	Life expectancy: men		57 yrs
Pop. per sq km	132	women		57 yrs
Av. ann. growth		Adult literacy		26%
in pop. 1983-88	3.1%	Fertility rate (per woman)		6.5
Pop. under 15	45.7%			
Pop. over 65	2.7%		*per 1,000 pop.*	
No. men per 100 women	109	Crude birth rate		47.0
Human Development Index	42	Crude death rate		12.6

The economy

GDP[a]	PRs67bn	GDP[a] per head	$365
GDP[a]	$39bn	GDP per head in purchasing	
Av. ann. growth in real		power parity (USA=100)	9
GDP 1980-88	6.3%		

Origins of GDP[a]		Components of GDP[a]	
	% of total		*% of total*
Agriculture	26.0	Private consumption	72.0
Industry, of which:	22.0	Public consumption	15.1
manufacturing	16.9	Investment	17.4
Services	52.0	Exports	13.2
		Imports	-17.8

Structure of manufacturing

	% of total		*% of total*
Agric. & food processing	34	Other	37
Textiles & clothing	21	Av. ann. increase in industrial	
Machinery & transport	8	output 1980-88	6.3%

Energy

	'000 TCE		
Total output	18,478	% output exported	-
Total consumption	25,500	% consumption imported	41.9
Consumption per head,			
kg coal equivalent	250		

Inflation and finance

Consumer price		*av. ann. increase 1984-89*	
inflation 1989	10.4%	Narrow money (M1)	13.5%
Av. ann. inflation 1984-89	6.6%	Broad money	11.8%

Exchange rates

	end 1989		*av. 1989*
PRs per $	21.42	Effective rates	*1985 = 100*
PRs per SDR	28.15	– nominal	...
PRs per Ecu	25.64	– real	...

Principal exports[b]

	$m fob		$m fob
Raw cotton	845	Cotton fabrics	442
Clothing	668	Rice	300
Cotton yarn	593	Total incl. others	**4,520**

Main export destinations[a]

	% of total		% of total
USA	11.5	UK	6.8
Japan	10.8	Italy	6.1
West Germany	7.2	Saudi Arabia	5.3

Principal imports[b]

	$m cif		$m cif
Non-electrical machinery	739	Transport equipment	385
Petroleum & products	738	Edible oils	281
Chemicals	415	Total incl. others	**6,590**

Main origins of imports[a]

	% of total		% of total
Japan	15.1	Kuwait	7.5
USA	10.7	UK	6.8
West Germany	7.6	Saudi Arabia	5.3

Balance of payments, reserves and debt $bn

Visible exports fob	4.4	Overall balance	0.1
Visible imports fob	-7.0	Change in reserves	0.3
Trade balance	-2.6	Level of reserves	
Invisibles inflows	0.9	end Dec.	1.2
Invisibles outflows	-2.4	No. months import cover	1.6
Net transfers	2.7	Foreign debt	17.0
Current account balance	-1.4	– as % of GDP	43.6
– as % of GDP[b]	-3.6	Debt service	1.5
Capital balance	1.5	Debt service ratio	28.7%

Family life

No. households	19.2m	Divorces per 1,000 pop.	...
Av. no. per household	5.2	Cost of living end 1989	
Marriages per 1,000 pop.	...	New York = 100	54

a Fiscal year ending June 30, 1988.
b Fiscal year ending June 30, 1989.

PERU

Area	1,285,000 sq km	Currency	Inti (In)
Capital	Lima		

People

Population	21.3m	Life expectancy: men	60 yrs
Pop. per sq km	17	women	63 yrs
Av. ann. growth		Adult literacy*	82%
in pop. 1983-88	2.6%	Fertility rate (per woman)	4.5
Pop. under 15	39.2%		
Pop. over 65	3.7%		*per 1,000 pop.*
No. men per 100 women	102	Crude birth rate	43.3
Human Development Index	75	Crude death rate	9.2

The economy

GDP	In5,140bn[b]	GDP per head	$1,432
GDP	$30bn	GDP per head in purchasing	
Av. ann. growth in real		power parity (USA=100)	18
GDP 1980-88	0.7%		

Origins of GDP

	% of total
Agriculture	13.1
Industry, of which:	39.7
manufacturing	23.9
Services	47.2

Components of GDP

	% of total
Private consumption	64.8
Public consumption	9.9
Investment	23.1
Exports	19.0
Imports	-16.8

Structure of manufacturing

	% of total
Agric. & food processing	24
Textiles & clothing	11
Machinery & transport	10

	% of total
Other	55
Av. ann. increase in industrial output 1980-88	-

Energy

	'000 TCE		
Total output	14,938	% output exported	26.2
Total consumption	11,692	% consumption imported	11.8
Consumption per head, kg coal equivalent	564		

Inflation and finance

Consumer price			*av. ann. increase 1983-88*
inflation 1989	3,398.6%	Narrow money (M1)	192.3%
Av. ann. inflation 1984-89	371.7%	Broad money	165.0%

Exchange rates

	end 1989		av. 1989
In per $	5,547	Effective rates	1985 = 100
In per SDR	7,264	– nominal	...
In per Ecu	6,640	– real	...

Principal exports

	$m fob		$m fob
Non-traditional products	734	Zinc	263
Copper	607	Petroleum & products	169
Fish & fish products	379	Total incl. others	**2,695**

Main export destinations

	% of total		% of total
USA	21.7	West Germany	6.6
Japan	12.0	UK	5.9

Principal imports

	$m fob		$m fob
Industrial supplies	1,583	Consumer goods	277
Capital goods	688	Total incl. others	**2,750**

Main origins of imports

	% of total		% of total
USA	29.9	Argentina	7.2
West Germany	8.3	Brazil	6.9

Balance of payments, reserves and debt $bn

Visible exports fob	2.7	Overall balance	-2.2
Visible imports fob	-2.8	Change in reserves	-0.1
Trade balance	-0.1	Level of reserves	
Invisibles inflows	1.0	end Dec.	1.1
Invisibles outflows	-2.3	No. months import cover	2.6
Net transfers	0.2	Foreign debt	18.6
Current account balance	-1.1	– as % of GDP	61.2
– as % of GDP	-3.7	Debt service	0.4
Capital balance	-1.3	Debt service ratio	9.6%

Family life

No. households	4.9m	Divorces per 1,000 pop.	...
Av. no. per household	4.6	Cost of living end 1989	
Marriages per 1,000 pop.	6.0	New York = 100	87

a Excluding Indian jungle population.
b Calculated using an amalgam of the various exchange rates in operation in 1988.

PHILIPPINES

Area	300,000 sq km	Currency	Philippine peso (P)
Capital	Manila		

People

Population	58.7m	Life expectancy: men	62 yrs
Pop. per sq km	196	women	65 yrs
Av. ann. growth		Adult literacy	83%
in pop. 1983-88	2.4%	Fertility rate (per woman)	4.3
Pop. under 15	40.1%		
Pop. over 65	3.4%		*per 1,000 pop.*
No. men per 100 women	101	Crude birth rate	33.2
Human Development Index	71	Crude death rate	7.1

The economy

GDP	P827bn	GDP per head	$662
GDP	$39bn	GDP per head in purchasing	
Av. ann. growth in real		power parity (USA=100)	11
GDP 1980-88	1.3%		

Origins of GDP

	% of total
Agriculture	28.9
Industry, of which:	30.3
manufacturing	24.6
Services	40.8

Components of GDP

	% of total
Private consumption	72.9
Public consumption	9.2
Investment	17.1
Exports	26.2
Imports	-23.9

Structure of manufacturing

	% of total		% of total
Agric. & food processing	40	Other	46
Textiles & clothing	7	Av. ann. increase in industrial	
Machinery & transport	7	output 1980-88	0.1%

Energy

	'000 TCE		
Total output	2,401	% output exported	5.3
Total consumption	15,200	% consumption imported	95.0
Consumption per head,			
kg coal equivalent	265		

Inflation and finance

			av. ann. increase 1983-88
Consumer price			
inflation 1989	10.6%	Narrow money (M1)	12.9%
Av. ann. inflation 1984-89	9.4%	Broad money	15.0%

Exchange rates

	end 1989		av. 1989
P per $	22.44	Effective rates	1985 = 100
P per SDR	29.49	– nominal	64
P per Ecu	26.86	– real	76

Principal exports

	$bn fob		$bn fob
Electrical & electronic		Mineral products	0.38
equipment	1.42	Fish & products	0.31
Textiles & clothing	1.32		
Coconuts & products	0.58	Total incl. others	**7.03**

Main export destinations

	% of total		% of total
USA	35.6	Hong Kong	4.9
Japan	20.1	UK	4.6

Principal imports

	$bn cif		$bn cif
Mineral fuels	1.09	Electrical machinery	0.58
Chemicals	1.09	Agric. products & foodstuffs	0.54
Non-electrical machinery	0.71	Total incl. others	**8.72**

Main origins of imports

	% of total		% of total
USA	21.0	Kuwait[a]	4.8
Japan	17.4	Hong Kong	4.6
Taiwan	6.3		

Balance of payments, reserves and debt $bn

Visible exports fob	7.1	Overall balance	0.7
Visible imports fob	-8.2	Change in reserves	1.0
Trade balance	-1.1	Level of reserves	
Invisibles inflows	3.6	end Dec.	2.1
Invisibles outflows	-3.7	No. months import cover	2.1
Net transfers	0.8	Foreign debt	29.4
Current account balance	-0.4	– as % of GDP	75.1
– as % of GDP	-1.0	Debt service	3.4
Capital balance	0.9	Debt service ratio	31.9%

Family life

No. households	9.0m	Divorces per 1,000 pop.	...
Av. no. per household	5.6	Cost of living end 1989	
Marriages per 1,000 pop.	7.0	New York = 100	71

a. 1987.

POLAND

Area	313,000 sq km	Currency	Zloty (Zl)
Capital	Warsaw		

People

Population	37.9m	Life expectancy: men		68 yrs
Pop. per sq km	121		women	73 yrs
Av. ann. growth		Adult literacy		98%
in pop. 1983-88	0.7%	Fertility rate (per woman)		2.2
Pop. under 15	25.2%			
Pop. over 65	10.0%		*per 1,000 pop.*	
No. men per 100 women	95	Crude birth rate		16.4
Human Development Index	91	Crude death rate		9.9

The economy

NMP	Zl24,995bn	GDP per head	$1,719
GDP	$65bn	GDP per head in purchasing	
Av. ann. growth in real		power parity (USA=100)	25
GDP 1980-88	1.0%		

Origins of GDP		Components of GDP	
	% of total		*% of total*
Agriculture	13.0	Private consumption	60.0
Industry, of which:	60.7	Public consumption	8.9
manufacturing	...	Investment	28.8
Services	26.3	Exports	22.6
		Imports	-20.3

Structure of manufacturing

	% of total		*% of total*
Agric. & food processing	15	Other	39
Textiles & clothing	16	Av. ann. increase in industrial	
Machinery & transport	30	output 1980-88	1.3%

Energy

	'000 TCE		
Total output	180,140	% output exported	15.4
Total consumption	181,145	% consumption imported	19.2
Consumption per head,			
kg coal equivalent	4,810		

Inflation and finance

Consumer price			*av. ann. increase 1983-88*
inflation 1989	244.0%	Narrow money (M1)	26.9%
Av. ann. inflation 1984-89	75.6%	Broad money	31.9%

Exchange rates

	end 1989		*av. 1989*
Zlª per $	6,500	Effective rates	*1985 = 100*
Zlª per SDR	8,540	– nominal	...
Zlª per Ecu	7,781	– real	...

Principal exports

	$bn fob		$bn fob
Engineering products	1.74	Metallurgical products	1.16
Agric. products &		Chemicals	0.91
foodstuffs	1.51		
Energy & fuels	0.93	Total incl. others	**13.96**

Main export destinations

	% of total		% of total
USSR	24.5	East Germany	4.4
West Germany	12.4	China	2.4
Czechoslovakia	6.0	EC	28.3
UK	5.0		

Principal imports

	$bn fob		$bn fob
Engineering products	2.01	Metallurgical products	0.59
Agric. products &		Energy & fuels	0.37
foodstuffs	1.56		
Chemicals	1.55	Total incl. others	**12.71**

Main origins of imports

	% of total		% of total
USSR	23.3	Switzerland	4.6
West Germany	13.0	Austria	4.4
Czechoslovakia	6.4	EC	28.3
East Germany	5.0		

Balance of payments, reserves and debt $bn

Visible exports fob	7.7	Overall balance	-3.3
Visible imports fob	-6.9	Change in reserves	0.6
Trade balance	0.8	Level of reserves	
Invisibles inflows	2.0	end Dec.	2.2
Invisibles outflows	-4.8	No. months import cover	2.3
Net transfers	1.7	Foreign debt	39.2
Current account balance	-0.3	– as % of GDP	60.2
– as % of GDP	-0.4	Debt service	5.3
Capital balance	-2.9	Debt service ratio	53.9%

Family life

No. households	11.1m	Divorces per 1,000 pop.	1.3
Av. no. per household	2.9	Cost of living end 1989	
Marriages per 1,000 pop.	6.5	New York = 100	...

a Convertible currency transactions only.

PORTUGAL

Area	92,000 sq km	Currency	Escudo (Esc)
Capital	Lisbon		

People

Population	10.4m	Life expectancy: men	70 yrs
Pop. per sq km	113	women	77 yrs
Av. ann. growth		Adult literacy	84%
in pop. 1983-88	0.8%	Fertility rate (per woman)	1.8
Pop. under 15	21.2%		
Pop. over 65	12.9%		*per 1,000 pop.*
No. men per 100 women	93	Crude birth rate	13.5
Human Development Index	90	Crude death rate	10.1

The economy

GDP	Esc6,008bn	GDP per head	$4,107
GDP	$42bn	GDP per head in purchasing	
Av. ann. growth in real		power parity (USA=100)	34
GDP 1980-88	2.2%		

Origins of GDP		Components of GDP	
	% of total		*% of total*
Agriculture	9.1	Private consumption	64.8
Industry, of which:	39.6	Public consumption	15.2
manufacturing	29.7	Investment	26.5
Services	51.3	Exports	34.4
		Imports	-40.9

Structure of manufacturing

	% of total		*% of total*
Agric. & food processing	17	Other	45
Textiles & clothing	22	Av. ann. increase in industrial	
Machinery & transport	16	output 1980-88	...

Energy

	'000 TCE		
Total output	1,378	% output exported[a]	36.1
Total consumption	13,622	% consumption imported[a]	136.2
Consumption per head,			
kg coal equivalent	1,329		

Inflation and finance

Consumer price			*av. ann. increase 1983-88*
inflation 1989	12.6%	Narrow money (M1)	21.1%
Av. ann. inflation 1984-89	12.5%	Broad money	18.8%

Exchange rates

	end 1989		*av. 1989*
Esc per $	149.8	Effective rates	*1985 = 100*
Esc per SDR	196.9	– nominal	77
Esc per Ecu	179.4	– real	104

Principal exports

	$bn fob		$bn fob
Textiles & clothing	4.08	Food products	0.88
Machinery & transport		Chemicals & plastics	0.75
equipment	1.74		
Forestry products	1.61	Total incl. others	**10.63**

Main export destinations

	% of total		% of total
France	15.4	Netherlands	6.0
West Germany	14.7	USA	6.0
UK	14.2	EC	71.8
Spain	11.4	Efta	10.6

Principal imports

	$bn cif		$bn cif
Machinery & transport		Textiles & clothing	1.62
equipment	6.25	Energy & fuels	1.43
Food products	2.52		
Chemicals & plastics	2.06	Total incl. others	**16.77**

Main origins of imports

	% of total		% of total
West Germany	13.7	UK	8.2
Spain	13.5	Netherlands	4.8
France	11.5	EC	66.4
Italy	9.3	Opec	5.2

Balance of payments, reserves and debt $bn

Visible exports fob	10.7	Overall balance	0.9
Visible imports fob	-15.8	Change in reserves	0.6
Trade balance	-5.1	Level of reserves	
Invisibles inflows	4.0	end Dec.	10.3
Invisibles outflows	-3.9	No. months import cover	6.3
Net transfers	4.3	Foreign debt	17.3
Current account balance	-0.6	– as % of GDP	41.4
– as % of GDP	-1.5	Debt service	4.7
Capital balance	0.1	Debt service ratio	31.8%

Family life

No. households	3.5m	Divorces per 1,000 pop.	0.9
Av. no. per household	2.9	Cost of living end 1989	
Marriages per 1,000 pop.	7.0	New York = 100	76

a Energy trade data are distorted by transitory and oil refining activities.

SAUDI ARABIA

Area	2,150,000 sq km	Currency	Saudi riyal (SR)
Capital	Riyadh		

People

Population	14.0m	Life expectancy:	men	62 yrs
Pop. per sq km	7		women	65 yrs
Av. ann. growth		Adult literacy		51%
in pop. 1983-88	5.6%	Fertility rate (per woman)		7.2
Pop. under 15	45.4%			
Pop. over 65	2.6%			*per 1,000 pop.*
No. men per 100 women	119	Crude birth rate		42.0
Human Development Index	70	Crude death rate		7.6

The economy

GDP	SR281bn	GDP per head	$5,311
GDP	$74bn	GDP per head in purchasing	
Av. ann. growth in real		power parity (USA=100)	47
GDP 1980-88	-5.1%		

Origins of GDP		Components of GDP	
	% of total		*% of total*
Agriculture	6.6	Private consumption	49.3
Industry, of which:	44.8	Public consumption	39.2
manufacturing	8.3	Investment	19.4
Services	48.6	Exports	36.0
		Imports	-43.9

Structure of manufacturing

	% of total		*% of total*
Agric. & food processing	...	Other	...
Textiles & clothing	...	Av. ann. increase in industrial	
Machinery & transport	...	output 1980-88	-8.2%

Energy

	'000 TCE		
Total output	330,869	% output exported	65.8
Total consumption	86,042	% consumption imported	-
Consumption per head,			
kg coal equivalent	6,322		

Inflation and finance

Consumer price			*av. ann. increase 1983-88*
inflation 1989	1.2%	Narrow money (M1)	...
Av. ann. inflation 1984-89	-1.2%	Broad money	...

Exchange rates

	end 1989		*av. 1989*
SR per $	3.75	Effective rates	1985 = 100
SR per SDR	4.92	– nominal	70
SR per Ecu	4.45	– real	60

Principal exports

	$bn fob		$bn fob
Crude oil & refined		Petrochemicals	2.70
petroleum	20.18	Total incl. others	**24.23**

Main export destinations[a]

	% of total		% of total
Japan	22.7	Bahrain	5.1
USA	19.8	Singapore	5.1
Netherlands	6.2	Italy	4.1

Principal imports

	$bn cif		$bn cif
Consumer goods	5.07	Building materials	3.18
Transport equipment	3.70	Agric. products & foodstuffs	3.11
Machinery & equipment	3.29	Total incl. others	**21.18**

Main origins of imports

	% of total		% of total
USA	16.2	West Germany	7.2
Japan	16.0	Italy	6.5
UK	7.3	France	5.2

Balance of payments, reserves and debt $bn

Visible exports fob	23.1	Overall balance	2.6
Visible imports fob	-18.3	Change in reserves	4.4
Trade balance	4.9	Level of reserves	
Invisibles inflows	13.3	end Dec.	20.8
Invisibles outflows	-19.5	No. months import cover	7.3
Net transfers	-8.2	Foreign debt	18.5
Current account balance	-9.6	– as % of GDP	24.9
– as % of GDP	-12.9	Debt service	1.9
Capital balance	12.2	Debt service ratio	5.0%

Family life

No. households	1.7m	Divorces per 1,000 pop.	...
Av. no. per household	6.9	Cost of living end 1989	
Marriages per 1,000 pop.	...	New York = 100	84

a 1987; excluding re-exports.

SINGAPORE

Area	618 sq km	Currency	Singapore dollar (S$)
Capital	Singapore		

People

Population	2.7m	Life expectancy: men	70 yrs
Pop. per sq km	4,288	women	76 yrs
Av. ann. growth		Adult literacy	83%
in pop. 1983-88	1.2%	Fertility rate (per woman)	1.7
Pop. under 15	26.5%		
Pop. over 65	4.7%		*per 1,000 pop.*
No. men per 100 women	103	Crude birth rate	16.5
Human Development Index	90	Crude death rate	5.6

The economy

GDP	S$48bn	GDP per head	$9,019
GDP	$24bn	GDP per head in purchasing	
Av. ann. growth in real		power parity (USA=100)	73
GDP 1980-88	6.6%		

Origins of GDP

	% of total		% of total
		Components of GDP	
Agriculture	0.6	Private consumption	48.2
Industry, of which:	36.6	Public consumption	11.5
manufacturing	28.8	Investment	36.6
Services	62.8	Exports	197.3
		Imports	-193.5

Structure of manufacturing

	% of total		% of total
Agric. & food processing	6	Other	43
Textiles & clothing	5	Av. ann. increase in industrial	
Machinery & transport	46	output 1980-88	2.9%

Energy

	'000 TCE		
Total output	...	% output exported	...
Total consumption	12,465	% consumption imported[a]	545.7
Consumption per head,			
kg coal equivalent	4,776		

Inflation and finance

			av. ann. increase 1983-88
Consumer price			
inflation 1989	2.4%	Narrow money (M1)	6.8%
Av. ann. inflation 1984-89	0.7%	Broad money	10.5%

Exchange rates

	end 1989		av. 1989
S$ per $	1.89	Effective rates	1985 = 100
S$ per SDR	2.49	– nominal	115
S$ per Ecu	2.27	– real	92

Principal exports

	$bn fob		$bn fob
Machinery & equipment	18.88	Crude materials	2.01
Minerals & fuels	5.05	Agric. products & foodstuffs	1.63
Manufactured products	3.25	Textiles & clothing	1.24
Chemicals	2.59	Total incl. others	**42.73**

Main export destinations[b]

	% of total		% of total
USA	23.8	Thailand	5.5
Malaysia	13.6	UK	2.9
Japan	8.6	Australia	2.7
Hong Kong	6.3		

Principal imports

	$bn cif		$bn cif
Machinery & equipment	19.05	Agric. products & foodstuffs	2.68
Manufactured products	6.47	Crude minerals	1.49
Mineral fuels	6.18		
Chemicals	2.89	Total incl. others	**47.95**

Main origins of imports[b]

	% of total		% of total
Japan	21.9	Saudi Arabia	4.4
USA	15.5	China	3.8
Malaysia	14.6	West Germany	3.7
Taiwan	4.5		

Balance of payments, reserves and debt $bn

Visible exports fob	38.0	Overall balance	1.7
Visible imports fob	-40.3	Change in reserves	1.8
Trade balance	-2.3	Level of reserves	
Invisibles inflows	12.3	end Dec.	17.1
Invisibles outflows	-8.0	No. months import cover	4.2
Net transfers	-0.2	Foreign debt	4.7
Current account balance	1.7	– as % of GDP	19.8
– as % of GDP	6.9	Debt service	0.9
Capital balance	0.5	Debt service ratio	1.8%

Family life

No. households	0.5m	Divorces per 1,000 pop.	1.0
Av. no. per household	5.7	Cost of living end 1989	
Marriages per 1,000 pop.	9.0	New York = 100	92

a Energy trade data are distorted by transitory and oil refining activities.
b 1987.

SOUTH AFRICA

Area	1,233,000 sq km	Currency	Rand (R)
Capital	Pretoria		

People

Population	29.6m	Life expectancy: men	58 yrs
Pop. per sq km	24	women	64 yrs
Av. ann. growth		Adult literacy	70%
in pop. 1983-88	2.6%	Fertility rate (per woman)	4.5
Pop. under 15	37.0%		
Pop. over 65	4.2%		*per 1,000 pop.*
No. men per 100 women	100	Crude birth rate	31.7
Human Development Index	73	Crude death rate	9.8

The economy

GDP	R201bn	GDP per head	$2,958
GDP	$88bn	GDP per head in purchasing	
Av. ann. growth in real		power parity (USA=100)	28
GDP 1980-88	1.5%		

Origins of GDP		Components of GDP	
	% of total		*% of total*
Agriculture	5.9	Private consumption	56.3
Industry, of which:	40.5	Public consumption	18.4
manufacturing	24.5	Investment	20.3
Services	53.6	Exports	28.7
		Imports	-23.5

Structure of manufacturing

	% of total		*% of total*
Agric. & food processing	14	Other	61
Textiles & clothing	8	Av. ann. increase in industrial	
Machinery & transport	17	output 1980-88	0.6%

Energy

	'000 TCE		
Total output	134,983	% output exported	31.7
Total consumption	81,382	% consumption imported	28.1
Consumption per head,			
kg coal equivalent	2,816		

Inflation and finance

Consumer price			*av. ann. increase 1983-88*
inflation 1989	14.7%	Narrow money (M1)	19.2%
Av. ann. inflation 1984-89	15.7%	Broad money	19.9%

Exchange rates

	end 1989		av. 1989
R per $	2.54	Effective rates	1985 = 100
R per SDR	3.33	– nominal	62
R per Ecu	3.03	– real	103

Principal exports

	$bn fob		$bn fob
Gold	8.63	Platinum[a]	1.10
Base metals	2.95	Agric. products & foodstuffs	1.06
Mineral products	2.20	Total incl. others	21.5

Main export destinations[b]

	% of total		% of total
Italy	11.2	West Germany	6.8
Japan	8.3	UK	5.8
USA	6.9		

Principal imports

	$bn cif		$bn cif
Machinery & equipment	5.45	Oil[a]	1.50
Transport equipment	2.47	Base metals	0.85
Chemicals		Total incl. others	17.4

Main origins of imports[b]

	% of total		% of total
West Germany	19.4	USA	10.0
Japan	10.4	Italy	4.0
UK	10.1		

Balance of payments, reserves and debt $bn

Visible exports fob	22.4	Overall balance	-1.4
Visible imports fob	-17.2	Change in reserves	-0.8
Trade balance	5.2	Level of reserves	
Invisibles inflows	3.3	end Dec.	2.1
Invisibles outflows	-7.4	No. months import cover	1.0
Net transfers	0.2	Foreign debt	21.2
Current account balance	1.3	– as % of GDP	24.1
– as % of GDP	1.5	Debt service	2.5
Capital balance	-1.6	Debt service ratio	9.6%

Family life

No. households	8.1m	Divorces per 1,000 pop.	...
Av. no. per household	4.0	Cost of living end 1989	
Marriages per 1,000 pop.	...	New York = 100	58

a Estimate; no official figures published.
b Based on partial data only.

SOUTH KOREA

Area	99,000 sq km	Currency	Won (W)
Capital	Seoul		

People

Population	42.0m	Life expectancy: men	66 yrs
Pop. per sq km	423	women	73 yrs
Av. ann. growth		Adult literacy	...
in pop. 1983-88	1.0%	Fertility rate (per woman)	2.0
Pop. under 15	26.5%		
Pop. over 65	4.7%		*per 1,000 pop.*
No. men per 100 women	100	Crude birth rate	18.8
Human Development Index	90	Crude death rate	6.2

The economy

GDP	W128,000bn	GDP per head	$4,081
GDP	$171bn	GDP per head in purchasing	
Av. ann. growth in real		power parity (USA=100)	24
GDP 1980-88	9.0%		

Origins of GDP		Components of GDP	
	% of total		*% of total*
Agriculture	10.8	Private consumption	51.6
Industry, of which:	43.2	Public consumption	10.2
manufacturing	31.6	Investment	29.8
Services	46.0	Exports	40.8
		Imports	-32.3

Structure of manufacturing

	% of total		*% of total*
Agric. & food processing	15	Other	44
Textiles & clothing	17	Av. ann. increase in industrial	
Machinery & transport	24	output 1980-88	10.8%

Energy

	'000 TCE		
Total output	21,437	% output exported	24.2
Total consumption	73,163	% consumption imported	95.8
Consumption per head,			
kg coal equivalent	1,760		

Inflation and finance

			av. ann. increase 1983-88
Consumer price			
inflation 1989	5.6%	Narrow money (M1)	12.4%
Av. ann. inflation 1984-89	4.2%	Broad money	16.4%

Exchange rates

	end 1989		*av. 1989*
W per $	697.6	Effective rates	1985 = 100
W per SDR	893.1	– nominal	...
W per Ecu	808.7	– real	...

Principal exports

	$bn fob		$bn fob
Machinery & transport equipment	23.46	Footwear	3.80
		Textiles	2.77
Clothing	8.70	Total incl. others	60.70

Main export destinations

	% of total		% of total
USA	35.3	West Germany	3.9
Japan	19.8	UK	3.2
Hong Kong	5.9		

Principal imports

	$bn cif		$bn cif
Machinery & transport equipment	18.24	Mineral fuels & lubricants	5.99
		Food & live animals	2.30
Raw materials	7.74		
Chemicals	6.28	Total incl. others	51.81

Main origins of imports

	% of total		% of total
Japan	30.7	Australia	3.5
USA	24.6	Malaysia	2.6
West Germany	4.0		

Balance of payments, reserves and debt $bn

Visible exports fob	59.6	Overall balance	9.3
Visible imports fob	-48.2	Change in reserves	3.7
Trade balance	11.4	Level of reserves	
Invisibles inflows	11.3	end Dec.	12.4
Invisibles outflows	-10.0	No. months import cover	2.6
Net transfers	1.4	Foreign debt	43.2
Current account balance	14.2	– as % of GDP	25.2
– as % of GDP	8.3	Debt service	9.0
Capital balance	-4.3	Debt service ratio	12.7%

Family life

No. households	...	Divorces per 1,000 pop.	0.6
Av. no. per household	...	Cost of living end 1989	
Marriages per 1,000 pop.	8.9	New York = 100	110

SPAIN

Area	505,000 sq km	Currency	Peseta (Pta)
Capital	Madrid		

People

Population	39.1m	Life expectancy: men	74 yrs
Pop. per sq km	77	women	80 yrs
Av. ann. growth		Adult literacy	93%
in pop. 1983-88	0.5%	Fertility rate (per woman)	1.7
Pop. under 15	20.4%		
Pop. over 65	13.0%		*per 1,000 pop.*
No. men per 100 women	91	Crude birth rate	12.8
Human Development Index	97	Crude death rate	9.1

The economy

GDP	Pta39,440bn	GDP per head	$8,668
GDP	$339bn	GDP per head in purchasing	
Av. ann. growth in real		power parity (USA=100)	46
GDP 1980-88	2.6%		

Origins of GDP

	% of total		*% of total*
		Components of GDP	
Agriculture	5.1	Private consumption	63.0
Industry, of which:	37.4	Public consumption	14.3
manufacturing	27.0	Investment	23.9
Services	57.5	Exports	19.5
		Imports	-20.7

Structure of manufacturing

	% of total		*% of total*
Agric. & food processing	17	Other	52
Textiles & clothing	9	Av. ann. increase in industrial	
Machinery & transport	22	output 1980-88	2.3%

Energy

	'000 TCE		
Total output	26,225	% output exported[a]	52.6
Total consumption	81,776	% consumption imported[a]	101.2
Consumption per head,			
kg coal equivalent	2,106		

Inflation and finance

			av. ann. increase 1983-88
Consumer price			
inflation 1989	6.8%	Narrow money (M1)	14.9%
Av. ann. inflation 1984-89	6.9%	Broad money	11.5%

Exchange rates

	end 1989		*av. 1989*
Pta per $	109.7	Effective rates	1985 = 100
Pta per SDR	144.2	– nominal	105
Pta per Ecu	131.3	– real	124

Principal exports

	$bn fob		$bn fob
Non-food consumer goods	12.55	Capital goods	6.65
Raw materials & intermediate products	12.25	Energy products	1.88
Agric. products & foodstuffs	6.90	Total incl. others	**40.34**

Main export destinations

	% of total		% of total
France	18.5	USA	7.9
West Germany	12.0	EC	65.9
UK	9.8	Opec	4.6
Italy	9.7	Latin America	2.6

Principal imports

	$bn cif		$bn cif
Raw materials & intermediate products (excl. fuels)	18.43	Energy products	6.89
Capital goods	15.84	Agric. products & foodstuffs	6.25
Non-foods consumer goods	13.02	Total incl. others	60.53

Main origins of imports

	% of total		% of total
West Germany	16.2	UK	7.1
France	13.5	EC	56.8
Italy	9.6	Opec	6.7
USA	8.9	Latin America	5.0

Balance of payments, reserves and aid $bn

Visible exports fob	39.7	Capital balance	14.6
Visible imports fob	-57.7	Overall balance	8.4
Trade balance	-18.0	Change in reserves	7.1
Invisibles inflows	27.4	Level of reserves	
Invisibles outflows	-17.7	end Dec.	41.9
Net transfers	4.5	No. months import cover	6.7
Current account balance	-3.8	Aid given	0.24
– as % of GDP	-1.1	– as % of GDP	0.07

Family life

No. households	16.0m	Divorces per 1,000 pop.	0.5
Av. no. per household	2.6	Cost of living end 1989	
Marriages per 1,000 pop.	5.3	New York = 100	104

a Energy trade data are distorted by transitory and oil refining activities.

SWEDEN

Area	450,000 sq km	Currency	Swedish krona (Skr)
Capital	Stockholm		

People

Population	8.44m	Life expectancy: men	74 yrs
Pop. per sq km	19	women	80 yrs
Av. ann. growth		Adult literacy	99%
in pop. 1983-88	0.3%	Fertility rate (per woman)	1.65
Pop. under 15	16.5%		
Pop. over 65	18.3%		*per 1,000 pop.*
No. men per 100 women	97	Crude birth rate	11.2
Human Development Index	99	Crude death rate	12.2

The economy

GDP	Skr1,097bn	GDP per head	$21,155
GDP	$179bn	GDP per head in purchasing	
Av. ann. growth in real		power parity (USA=100)	77
GDP 1980-88	1.8%		

Origins of GDP		Components of GDP	
	% of total		*% of total*
Agriculture	4.5	Private consumption	51.0
Industry, of which:	42.1	Public consumption	28.6
manufacturing	31.8	Investment	20.2
Services	53.4	Exports	35.9
		Imports	-35.7

Structure of manufacturing

	% of total		*% of total*
Agric. & food processing	10	Other	53
Textiles & clothing	2	Av. ann. increase in industrial	
Machinery & transport	35	output 1980-88	2.1%

Energy

	'000 TCE		
Total output	17,202	% output exported	64.1
Total consumption	42,034	% consumption imported	85.7
Consumption per head,			
kg coal equivalent	5,004		

Inflation and finance

Consumer price		*av. ann. increase 1983-88*	
inflation 1989	6.5%	Narrow money (M1)	6.1%
Av. ann. inflation 1984-89	5.6%	Broad money	8.4%

Exchange rates

	end 1989		*av. 1989*
Skr per $	6.23	Effective rates	*1985 = 100*
Skr per SDR	8.18	– nominal	95
Skr per Ecu	7.45	– real	112

Principal exports

	$bn fob		$bn fob
Machinery incl. electricals	13.43	Transport equipment	7.87
		Iron & steel	3.15
Wood products, pulp & paper	9.12	Agric. products & foodstuffs	0.85
		Total incl. others	**49.76**

Main export destinations

	% of total		% of total
West Germany	12.1	Denmark	6.9
UK	11.2	EC	52.2
USA	9.9	Efta	19.9
Norway	9.4		

Principal imports

	$bn cif		$bn cif
Machinery incl. electricals	12.23	Mineral fuels	3.12
		Textiles & clothing	3.67
Transport equipment	5.83	Agric. products & foodstuffs	2.88
Chemicals	4.58	Total incl. others	**45.78**

Main origins of imports

	% of total		% of total
West Germany	21.2	Denmark	6.7
UK	8.6	EC	56.0
USA	7.5	Efta	16.5
Finland	7.0		

Balance of payments, reserves and aid $bn

Visible exports fob	49.3	Capital balance	2.9
Visible imports fob	-44.6	Overall balance	-1.7
Trade balance	4.7	Change in reserves	0.3
Invisibles inflows	12.9	Level of reserves	
Invisibles outflows	-18.6	end Dec.	8.8
Net transfers	-1.6	No. months import cover	1.7
Current account balance	-2.5	Aid given	1.53
– as % of GDP	-1.4	– as % of GDP	0.87

Family life

No. households	4.0m	Divorces per 1,000 pop.	2.3
Av. no. per household	2.2	Cost of living end 1989	
Marriages per 1,000 pop.	5.2	New York = 100	109

SWITZERLAND

Area	41,000 sq km	Currency	Swiss franc (Swfr)
Capital	Berne		

People

Population	6.62m	Life expectancy: men		74 yrs
Pop. per sq km	160		women	80 yrs
Av. ann. growth		Adult literacy		99%
in pop. 1983-88	0.4%	Fertility rate (per woman)		1.6
Pop. under 15	16.4%			
Pop. over 65	15.3%			*per 1,000 pop.*
No. men per 100 women	95	Crude birth rate		11.7
Human Development Index	99	Crude death rate		10.2

The economy

GDP	Swfr270bn	GDP per head	$27,748
GDP	$184bn	GDP per head in purchasing	
Av. ann. growth in real		power parity (USA=100)	87
GDP 1980-88	1.9%		

Origins of GDP[a]		Components of GDP	
	% of total		*% of total*
Agriculture	3.5	Private consumption	57.9
Industry, of which:	34.5	Public consumption	12.9
manufacturing	25.0	Investment	29.1
Services	62.0	Exports	35.9
		Imports	-35.8

Structure of manufacturing

	% of total		*% of total*
Agric. & food processing	...	Other	...
Textiles & clothing	...	Av. ann. increase in industrial	
Machinery & transport	...	output 1980-88[b]	1.8%

Energy

	'000 TCE		
Total output	6,892	% output exported	40.4
Total consumption	25,040	% consumption imported	84.6
Consumption per head,			
kg coal equivalent	3,794		

Inflation and finance

Consumer price			*av. ann. increase 1983-88*
inflation 1989	3.2%	Narrow money (M1)	3.0%
Av. ann. inflation 1984-89	2.1%	Broad money	6.3%

Exchange rates

	end 1989		*av. 1989*
Swfr per $	1.55	Effective rates	*1985 = 100*
Swfr per SDR	2.03	– nominal	107
Swfr per Ecu	1.85	– real	105

Principal exports

	$bn fob		$bn fob
Machinery	15.15	Metals & metal manufactures	4.41
Chemicals	10.87	Textiles & clothing	3.02
Precision instruments, watches & jewellery	10.33	Total incl. others	**50.73**

Main export destinations

	% of total		% of total
West Germany	21.0	UK	7.9
France	9.4	OECD	78.6
USA	8.5	EC	56.0
Italy	8.3	Efta	7.0

Principal imports

	$bn cif		$bn cif
Machinery	11.61	Textiles & clothing	5.29
Chemicals	6.42	Agric. products	5.10
Motor vehicles	6.34	Energy & fuels	2.2
Precision instruments, watches & jewellery	6.13	Total incl. others	**56.44**

Main origins of imports

	% of total		% of total
West Germany	34.0	USA	5.5
France	10.6	Japan	5.0
Italy	10.1	EC	71.3
UK	5.7	Efta	7.2

Balance of payments, reserves and aid $bn

Visible exports fob	59.6	Capital balance	-13.5
Visible imports fob	-48.7	Overall balance	-2.4
Trade balance	10.9	Change in reserves	-3.3
Invisibles inflows	32.1	Level of reserves	
Invisibles outflows	-33.0	end Dec.	32.1
Net transfers	-1.7	No. months import cover	4.7
Current account balance	8.3	Aid given	0.6
– as % of GDP	4.5	– as % of GDP	0.32

Family life

No. households	3.1m	Divorces per 1,000 pop.	1.8
Av. no. per household	2.3	Cost of living end 1989	
Marriages per 1,000 pop.	6.8	New York = 100	116

a 1985.
b Based on index of manufacturing output.

TAIWAN

Area	36,000 sq km	Currency	New Taiwan dollar (NT$)
Capital	Taipei		

People

Population	19.9m	Life expectancy: men	...
Pop. per sq km	553	women	...
Av. ann. growth		Adult literacy	92%
in pop. 1983-88	1.1%	Fertility rate (per woman)	2.6
Pop. under 15	...		
Pop. over 65	...		*per 1,000 pop.*
No. men per 100 women	...	Crude birth rate	22.3
Human Development Index	...	Crude death rate	7.0

The economy

GDP	NT$3,500bn	GDP per head	$5,975
GDP	$119bn	GDP per head in purchasing	
Av. ann. growth in real		power parity (USA=100)	...
GDP 1980-88	7.5%		

Origins of GDP		Components of GDP	
	% of total		*% of total*
Agriculture	6.1	Private consumption	50.2
Industry, of which:	46.1	Public consumption	15.1
manufacturing	38.1	Investment	24.0
Services	47.8	Exports	57.1
		Imports	-46.4

Structure of manufacturing

	% of total		*% of total*
Agric. & food processing	...	Other	...
Textiles & clothing	...	Av. ann. increase in industrial	
Machinery & transport	...	output 1980-88	8.0%

Energy

	'000 TCE		
Total output	...	% output exported	3.3
Total consumption	...	% consumption imported	76.7
Consumption per head,			
kg coal equivalent	...		

Inflation and finance

Consumer price		*av. ann. increase 1983-88*	
inflation 1989	4.4%	Narrow money (M1)	26.1
Av. ann. inflation 1984-89	1.3%	Broad money	22.6

Exchange rates

	end 1989		*av. 1989*
NT$ per $	25.75	Effective rates	*1985 = 100*
NT$ per SDR	33.84	– nominal	...
NT$ per Ecu	30.82	– real	...

Principal exports[a]

	$bn fob		$bn fob
Electronic products	10.60	Toys & sporting goods	3.26
Clothing	4.43	Metal products	3.23
Textiles	3.40		
Footware	3.77	Total incl. others	**60.59**

Main export destinations

	% of total		% of total
USA	38.7	UK	3.1
Japan	14.5	Singapore	2.8
Hong Kong	9.2	Canada	2.6
West Germany	3.9		

Principal imports[a]

	$bn cif		$bn cif
Crude petroleum	2.52	Iron & steel	2.33
Electronic products	4.26	Agric. products & foodstuffs	1.48
Chemicals	3.61		
Machinery	3.77	Total incl. others	**49.66**

Main origins of imports[a]

	% of total		% of total
Japan	29.9	Australia	2.7
USA	26.2	Saudi Arabia	2.5
West Germany	4.3	South Korea	1.8
Hong Kong	3.9		

Balance of payments, reserves and debt $bn

Visible exports fob	60.3	Overall balance	-1.4
Visible imports fob	-46.5	Change in reserves	-0.2
Trade balance	13.8	Level of reserves	
Invisibles inflows	11.2	end Dec.[a]	73.9
Invisibles outflows	-13.0	No. months import cover	14.9
Net transfers	-1.9	Foreign debt	13.9
Current account balance	10.2	– as % of GDP	11.6
– as % of GDP	8.6	Debt service	1.3
Capital balance	-12.9	Debt service ratio	1.9%

Family life

No. households	4.5m	Divorces per 1,000 pop.	...
Av. no. per household	4.3	Cost of living end 1989	
Marriages per 1,000 pop.	7.5	New York = 100	145

a Excluding gold.

THAILAND

Area	514,000 sq km	Currency	Baht (Bt)
Capital	Bangkok		

People

Population	54.5m	Life expectancy: men	63 yrs
Pop. per sq km	106	women	67 yrs
Av. ann. growth		Adult literacy	88%
in pop. 1983-88	1.9%	Fertility rate (per woman)	2.6
Pop. under 15	32.7%		
Pop. over 65	3.9%		*per 1,000 pop.*
No. men per 100 women	101	Crude birth rate	22.3
Human Development Index	78	Crude death rate	7.0

The economy

GDP	Bt1,466bn	GDP per head	$1,063
GDP	$58bn	GDP per head in purchasing	
Av. ann. growth in real		power parity (USA=100)	17
GDP 1980-88	5.5%		

Origins of GDP

	% of total		*% of total*
Agriculture	19.9	Private consumption	62.6
Industry, of which:	32.1	Public consumption	11.0
manufacturing	24.4	Investment	28.1
Services	48.0	Exports	35.2
		Imports	-36.9

Components of GDP

Structure of manufacturing

	% of total		*% of total*
Agric. & food processing	30	Other	39
Textiles & clothing	17	Av. ann. increase in industrial	
Machinery & transport	14	output 1980-88	5.6%

Energy

	'000 TCE		
Total output	11,688	% output exported	5.8
Total consumption	26,425	% consumption imported	61.6
Consumption per head,			
kg coal equivalent	493		

Inflation and finance

Consumer price		*av. ann. increase 1983-88*	
inflation 1989	5.5%	Narrow money (M1)	12.7%
Av. ann. inflation 1984-89	3.2%	Broad money	16.4%

Exchange rates

	end 1989		*av. 1989*
Bt per $	25.69	Effective rates	1985 = 100
Bt per SDR	33.76	– nominal	...
Bt per Ecu	30.75	– real	...

Principal exports

	$bn fob		$bn fob
Textiles & clothing	2.30	Tapioca	0.86
Rice	1.37	Precious stones	0.53
Rubber	1.03	Total incl. others	**15.90**

Main export destinations

	% of total		% of total
USA	20	Netherlands	5
Japan	16	West Germany	5
Singapore	8		

Principal imports

	$bn cif		$bn cif
Non-electrical machinery	3.47	Iron & steel	1.59
Electrical machinery	1.98	Energy & fuel	1.43
Chemicals	1.79	Total incl. others	**19.80**

Main origins of imports

	% of total		% of total
Japan	29	West Germany	5
USA	14	Malaysia	4
Singapore	7		

Balance of payments, reserves and debt $bn

Visible exports fob	15.8	Overall balance	2.6
Visible imports fob	-17.9	Change in reserves	2.5
Trade balance	-2.0	Level of reserves	
Invisibles inflows	5.9	end Dec.	7.1
Invisibles outflows	-5.7	No. months import cover	3.6
Net transfers	0.2	Foreign debt	21.8
Current account balance	-1.7	– as % of GDP	39.2
– as % of GDP	-2.9	Debt service	2.7
Capital balance	3.8	Debt service ratio	12.6%

Family life

No. households	9.2m	Divorces per 1,000 pop.	0.6
Av. no. per household	5.1	Cost of living end 1989	
Marriages per 1,000 pop.	6.3	New York = 100	65

UK

Area	244,000 sq km	Currency	Pound (£)
Capital	London		

People

Population	57.1m	Life expectancy: men	72 yrs
Pop. per sq km	234	women	78 yrs
Av. ann. growth		Adult literacy	99%
in pop. 1983-88	0.3%	Fertility rate (per woman)	1.8
Pop. under 15	18.9%		
Pop. over 65	15.5%		*per 1,000 pop.*
No. men per 100 women	95	Crude birth rate	13.4
Human Development Index	97	Crude death rate	11.9

The economy

GDP	£464bn	GDP per head	$14,477
GDP	$826bn	GDP per head in purchasing	
Av. ann. growth in real		power parity (USA=100)	66
GDP 1980-88	2.8%		

Origins of GDP		Components of GDP	
	% of total		*% of total*
Agriculture	1.4	Private consumption	64.6
Industry, of which:	35.7	Public consumption	19.2
manufacturing	23,7	Investment	19.9
Services	62.9	Exports	28.4
		Imports	-32.0

Structure of manufacturing

	% of total		*% of total*
Agric. & food processing	14	Other	48
Textiles & clothing	6	Av. ann. increase in industrial	
Machinery & transport	32	output 1980-88	2.4%

Energy

	'000 TCE		
Total output	332,066	% output exported	42.5
Total consumption	290,742	% consumption imported	32.9
Consumption per head,			
kg coal equivalent	5,107		

Inflation and finance

Consumer price		*av. ann. increase 1983-88*	
inflation 1989	7.8%	Narrow money (M1)	18.4%
Av. ann. inflation 1984-89	5.3%	Broad money	17.2%

Exchange rates

	end 1989		*av. 1989*
£ per $	0.62	Effective rates	*1985 = 100*
£ per SDR	1.22	– nominal	87
£ per Ecu	0.74	– real	105

Principal exports

	$bn fob		$bn fob
Finished manufactured products	73.0	Fuels	10.1
Semi-manufactured products	40.2	Basic materials	3.8
Agric. products & foodstuffs	10.7	Total incl. others	**153.4**

Main export destinations

	% of total		% of total
USA	12.9	Bel/Lux	5.2
West Germany	11.7	Italy	5.0
France	10.2	EC	50.2
Netherlands	6.9		

Principal imports

	$bn cif		$bn cif
Finished manufactured products	99.1	Basic materials	10.6
Semi-manufactured products	49.1	Fuels	10.2
Agric. products & foodstuffs	18.7	Total incl. others	**197.9**

Main origins of imports

	% of total		% of total
West Germany	16.6	Japan	6.1
USA	10.1	Italy	5.5
France	8.8	EC	52.4
Netherlands	7.8		

Balance of payments, reserves and aid $bn

Visible exports fob	143.5	Capital balance	2.4
Visible imports fob	-180.5	Overall balance	-1.7
Trade balance	-37.0	Change in reserves	2.4
Invisibles inflows	148.4	Level of reserves	
Invisibles outflows	-130.9	end Dec.	44.1
Net transfers	-6.4	No. months import cover	1.7
Current account balance	-26.0	Aid given	2.6
– as % of GDP	-3.1	– as % of GDP	0.32

Family life

No. households	23.1m	Divorces per 1,000 pop.	4.8
Av. no. per household	2.6	Cost of living end 1989	
Marriages per 1,000 pop.	9.7	New York = 100	104

USA

Area	9,373,000 sq km	Currency	US dollar ($)
Capital	Washington DC		

People

Population	246.33m	Life expectancy:	men	72 yrs
Pop. per sq km	26		women	79 yrs
Av. ann. growth		Adult literacy		...
in pop. 1983-88	1.0%	Fertility rate (per woman)		1.8
Pop. under 15	21.5%			
Pop. over 65	12.6%			*per 1,000 pop.*
No. men per 100 women	95	Crude birth rate		15.1
Human Development Index	96	Crude death rate		8.8

The economy

GDP	$4,881bn	GDP per head	$19,815
		GDP per head in purchasing	
Av. ann. growth in real		power parity (USA=100)	100
GDP 1980-88	3.0%		

Origins of GDP

	% of total	**Components of GDP**	*% of total*
Agriculture	2.1	Private consumption	66.4
Industry, of which:	25.6	Public consumption	19.8
manufacturing	18.9	Investment	15.6
Services	72.3	Exports	10.7
		Imports	-12.6

Structure of manufacturing

	% of total		*% of total*
Agric. & food processing	12	Other	48
Textiles & clothing	5	Av. ann. increase in industrial	
Machinery & transport	35	output 1980-88	2.8%

Energy

	'000 TCE		
Total output	1,987,250	% output exported	5.0
Total consumption	2,327,580	% consumption imported	20.9
Consumption per head,			
kg coal equivalent	9,452		

Inflation and finance

Consumer price		*av. ann. increase 1983-88*	
inflation 1989	4.8%	Narrow money (M1)	8.4%
Av. ann. inflation 1984-89	3.6%	Broad money	7.4%

Exchange rates

	end 1989		*av. 1989*
$ per SDR	1.31	Effective rates	*1985 = 100*
$ per Ecu	1.20	– nominal	68
		– real	68

Principal exports

	$bn fob		$bn fob
Machinery	88.4	Chemicals	32.3
Transport equipment	46.7	Agric. products & foodstuffs	31.0
Crude materials	34.8	Total incl. others	**322.43**

Main export destinations

	% of total		% of total
Canada	22.0	West Germany	4.5
Japan	11.7	Taiwan	3.8
Mexico	6.4	South Korea	3.5
UK	5.7	EC	23.6

Principal imports

	$bn fob		$bn fob
Machinery	117.3	Agric. products & foodstuffs	19.9
Transport equipment	79.8	Chemicals	19.9
Crude materials	55.3	Total incl. others	**459.54**

Main origins of imports

	% of total		% of total
Japan	20.3	Mexico	5.3
Canada	18.5	South Korea	4.6
West Germany	6.0	UK	4.1
Taiwan	5.6	EC	19.2

Balance of payments, reserves and aid $bn

Visible exports fob	319.7	Capital balance	100.6
Visible imports fob	-446.5	Overall balance	-36.3
Trade balance	-126.8	Change in reserves	1.8
Invisibles inflows	210.5	Level of reserves	
Invisibles outflows	-195.2	end Dec.	47.8
Net transfers	-14.7	No. months import cover	0.9
Current account balance	-126.2	Aid given	10.14
– as % of GDP	-2.6	– as % of GDP	0.21

Family life

No. households	88.1m	Divorces per 1,000 pop.	4.8
Av. no. per household	2.7	Cost of living end 1989	
Marriages per 1,000 pop.	9.7	New York = 100	100

USSR

Area	22,403,000 sq km	Currency	Rouble (Rb)
Capital	Moscow		

People

Population	283.7m	Life expectancy: men		65 yrs
Pop. per sq km	13	women		74 yrs
Av. ann. growth		Adult literacy		...
in pop. 1983-88	0.8%	Fertility rate (per woman)		2.4
Pop. under 15	25.5%			
Pop. over 65	9.6%			*per 1,000 pop.*
No. men per 100 women	90	Crude birth rate		18.4
Human Development Index	92	Crude death rate		10.6

The economy

NMP[a]	Rb619bn	GDP per head[b]	2,055$
GDP[b]	$583bn	GDP per head in purchasing	
Av. ann. growth in real		power parity (USA=100)	...
GDP 1980-88	3.4%		

Origins of NMP[c]		Components of NMP[c]	
	% of total		*% of total*
Agriculture	21.0	Private consumption[d]	74.0
Industry, of which:	56.0	Public consumption	...
manufacturing	...	Investment	26.0
Services	23.0	Exports	2.0
		Imports	-2.0

Structure of manufacturing

	% of total		*% of total*
Agric. & food processing	...	Other	...
Textiles & clothing	...	Av. ann. increase in industrial	
Machinery & transport	...	output 1980-88	3.9%

Energy

	'000 TCE		
Total output	2,335,805	% output exported	17.5
Total consumption	1,878,085	% consumption imported	1.9
Consumption per head,			
kg coal equivalent	6,634		

Inflation and finance

			av. ann. increase 1984-88
Consumer price			
inflation 1989	...	Narrow money (M1)	...
Av. ann. inflation 1984-89	...	Broad money	...

Exchange rates

	end 1989		*av. 1989*
Rb[e] per $	0.62	Effective rates	1985 = 100
Rb[e] per SDR	0.82	– nominal	...
Rb[e] per Ecu	0.75	– real	...

Principal exports

	$bn fob		$bn fob
Petroleum products	32.3	Electric power equipment	2.3
Natural gas	9.7		
Steel products	5.0	Total incl. others[f]	**109.8**

Main export destinations

	% of total		% of total
East Germany	10.7	Socialist area	63.9
Czechoslovakia	9.5	Non-socialist area:	
Poland	9.4	developed	21.8
Bulgaria	9.1	LDC	14.3
West Germany	3.6		

Principal imports

	$bn fob		$bn fob
Machinery & equipment	43.5	Chemicals	5.3
Agric. products &		Wood & paper products	1.3
foodstuffs	16.8		
Ores & metals	8.5	Total incl. others	**106.5**

Main origins of imports

	% of total		% of total
Poland	10.9	Socialist area	66.7
East Germany	10.8	Non-socialist area:	
Bulgaria	10.6	developed	25.1
Czechoslovakia	10.5	LDC	8.2
West Germany	5.0		

Balance of payments, reserves and debt $bn

Visible exports fob	109.8	Overall balance	...
Visible imports fob	-106.4	Change in reserves	...
Trade balance	3.4	Level of reserves	
Invisibles inflows	...	end Dec.	
Invisibles outflows	...	No. months import cover	...
Net transfers	...	Foreign debt [g]	40.9
Current account balance	-1.5	– as % of GDP[h]	10.5
– as % of GDP	-0.3	Debt service	...
Capital balance	...	Debt service ratio[i]	27.0%

Family life

No. households	84.6m	Divorces per 1,000 pop.	3.4
Av. no. per household	4.0	Cost of living end 1989	
Marriages per 1,000 pop.	9.8	New York = 100	115

---

a Net Material Product.
b The Economist Books estimate of GDP based on a compromise exchange rate of $1 = Rb1.22 (see page 22).
c 1986.
d Private and public consumption.

e Official rate.
f Excluding gold and coins.
g Convertible currency debt only.
h At official exchange rate.
i 1989. Calculated as a % convertible currency exports excluding gold sales.

VENEZUELA

Area	912,000 sq km	Currency	Bolivar (Bs)
Capital	Caracas		

People

Population	18.8m	Life expectancy: men	67 yrs
Pop. per sq km	21	women	73 yrs
Av. ann. growth		Adult literacy	85%
in pop. 1983-88	2.7%	Fertility rate (per woman)	3.8
Pop. under 15	38.3%		
Pop. over 65	3.7%		*per 1,000 pop.*
No. men per 100 women	102	Crude birth rate	30.7
Human Development Index	86	Crude death rate	5.4

The economy

GDP	Bs924bn	GDP per head	$3,400
GDP	$64bn	GDP per head in purchasing	
Av. ann. growth in real		power parity (USA=100)	24
GDP 1980-88	0.9%		

Origins of GDP

	% of total		% of total
		Components of GDP	
Agriculture	5.9	Private consumption	65.7
Industry, of which:	35.6	Public consumption	9.5
manufacturing	16.5	Investment	30.4
Services	58.5	Exports	21.8
		Imports	-27.4

Structure of manufacturing

	% of total		% of total
Agric. & food processing	23	Other	60
Textiles & clothing	8	Av. ann. increase in industrial	
Machinery & transport	9	output 1980-88	0.9%

Energy

	'000 TCE		
Total output	175,296	% output exported	60.7
Total consumption	55,139	% consumption imported	0.1
Consumption per head,			
kg coal equivalent	3,018		

Inflation and finance

Consumer price		*av. ann. increase 1983-88*	
inflation 1989	84.5%	Narrow money (M1)	18.8%
Av. ann. inflation (1984-89)	30.6%	Broad money	20.5%

Exchange rates

	end 1989		av. 1989
Bs per $	43.08	Effective rates	1985 = 100
Bs per SDR	56.61	– nominal	19
Bs per Ecu	51.57	– real	50

Principal exports

	$bn fob		$bn fob
Petroleum & products	8.16	Steel	0.22
Aluminium	0.68		
Gold	0.30	Total incl. others	**10.23**

Main export destinations

	% of total		% of total
USA	48.9	Canada	3.6
West Germany	5.5	Chile	1.4
Japan	4.1		

Principal imports

	$bn cif		$bn cif
Raw materials	4.80	Construction materials	0.35
Machinery & equipment	3.12		
Transport materials	1.69	Total incl. others	**11.58**

Main origins of imports

	% of total		% of total
USA	44.0	Japan	5.3
West Germany	7.3	Brazil	4.8
Italy	5.7		

Balance of payments, reserves and debt $bn

Visible exports fob	10.2	Overall balance	-4.9
Visible imports fob	-11.6	Change in reserves	-4.2
Trade balance	-1.3	Level of reserves	
Invisibles inflows	2.6	end Dec.	6.5
Invisibles outflows	-5.8	No. months import cover	4.5
Net transfers	-0.2	Foreign debt	34.7
Current account balance	-4.7	– as % of GDP	54.4
– as % of GDP	-7.4	Debt service	5.4
Capital balance	-0.6	Debt service ratio	42.5%

Family life

No. households	3.7m	Divorces per 1,000 pop.	0.4
Av. no. per household	4.9	Cost of living end 1989	
Marriages per 1,000 pop.	5.4	New York = 100	49

YUGOSLAVIA

Area	226,000 sq km	Currency	Yugoslav dinar (YuD)
Capital	Belgrade		

People

Population	23.6m	Life expectancy: men	67 yrs
Pop. per sq km	104	women	75 yrs
Av. ann. growth		Adult literacy	90%
in pop. 1983-88	0.7%	Fertility rate (per woman)	2.0
Pop. under 15	22.9%		
Pop. over 65	9.1%		*per 1,000 pop.*
No. men per 100 women	98	Crude birth rate	15.0
Human Development Index	91	Crude death rate	8.8

The economy

GDP[a]	YuD148,561bn	GDP per head	$2,279
GDP	$54bn	GDP per head in purchasing	
Av. ann. growth in real		power parity (USA=100)	29
GDP 1980-88	0.5%		

Origins of GDP[b]

	% of total		% of total
		Components of GDP[c]	
Agriculture	11.5	Private consumption	50.4
Industry, of which:	54.6	Public consumption	14.3
manufacturing	...	Investment	36.0
Services	33.9	Exports	16.1
		Imports	-16.8

Structure of manufacturing

	% of total		% of total
Agric. & food processing	13	Other	45
Textiles & clothing	17	Av. ann. increase in industrial	
Machinery & transport	25	output 1980-88	...

Energy

	'000 TCE		
Total output	35,692	% output exported	4.3
Total consumption	56,747	% consumption imported	46.0
Consumption per head,			
kg coal equivalent	2,423		

Inflation and finance

Consumer price			*av. ann. increase 1983-88*
inflation 1989	1,250%	Narrow money (M1)	94.1%
Av. ann. inflation 1984-89	345.2%	Broad money	102.3%

Exchange rates

	end 1989		av. 1989
YuD per $	118,160	Effective rates	1985 = 100
YuD per SDR	155,281	– nominal	...
YuD per Ecu	141,428	– real	...

Principal exports

	$bn fob		$bn fob
Manufactures excl.		Food, drink & tobacco	1.05
machinery	3.22	Raw materials	0.68
Machinery	2.60	Ships	0.47
Chemicals	1.16	Total incl. others	**12.60**

Main export destinations

	% of total		% of total
USSR	18.4	OECD	52.8
Italy	15.4	Developing countries	14.0
West Germany	11.7	EC	38.0
USA	6.1		

Principal imports

	$bn cif		$bn cif
Machinery	2.74	Transport equipment	0.88
Energy & fuels	2.39	Food, drink & tobacco	0.79
Chemicals	2.29		
Raw materials excl. fuels	1.44	Total incl. others	**13.15**

Main origins of imports

	% of total		% of total
West Germany	17.1	OECD	56.0
USSR	13.8	Developing countries	16.0
Italy	10.5	EC	38.9
USA	5.5		

Balance of payments, reserves and debt $bn

Visible exports fob	12.8	Overall balance	2.0
Visible imports fob	-12.0	Change in reserves	2.1
Trade balance	0.8	Level of reserves	
Invisibles inflows	4.9	end Dec.	2.4
Invisibles outflows	-8.1	No. months import cover	1.4
Net transfers	4.9	Foreign debt	21.7
Current account balance	2.5	– as % of GDP	40.4
– as % of GDP	4.6	Debt service	3.3
Capital balance	-0.7	Debt service ratio	18.9%

Family life

No. households	7.0m	Divorces per 1,000 pop.	0.9
Av. no. per household	3.0	Cost of living end 1989	
Marriages per 1,000 pop.	6.8	New York = 100	50

a   Gross Material Product.
b   As % of NMP.
c   1986.

ZAIRE

Area	2,344,000 sq km	Currency	Zaire (Z)
Capital	Kinshasa		

People

Population	33.5m	Life expectancy: men	51 yrs
Pop. per sq km	14	women	54 yrs
Av. ann. growth		Adult literacy	62%
in pop. 1983-88	2.9%	Fertility rate (per woman)	6.1
Pop. under 15	46.2%		
Pop. over 65	2.6%		*per 1,000 pop.*
No. men per 100 women	98	Crude birth rate	45.6
Human Development Index	29	Crude death rate	13.9

The economy

GDP	Z326.9bn	GDP per head	$193
GDP	$6.5bn	GDP per head in purchasing	
Av. ann. growth in real		power parity (USA=100)	1
GDP 1980-88	1.5%		

Origins of GDP[a]		Components of GDP	
	% of total		*% of total*
Agriculture	27.5	Private consumption	72.7
Industry, of which:	32.3	Public consumption	17.4
manufacturing	1.6	Investment	12.7
Services	40.2	Exports	...
		Imports	...

Structure of manufacturing

	% of total		*% of total*
Agric. & food processing	40	Other	36
Textiles & clothing	16	Av. ann. increase in industrial	
Machinery & transport	8	output 1980-88	3.2%

Energy

	'000 TCE		
Total output	2,578	% output exported	61.4
Total consumption	2,077	% consumption imported	65.9
Consumption per head,			
kg coal equivalent	64		

Inflation and finance

Consumer price		*av. ann. increase 1983-88*	
inflation 1989	104.1%	Narrow money (M1)	64.1%
Av. ann. inflation 1984-89	69.6%	Broad money	66.8%

Exchange rates

	end 1989		*av. 1989*
Z per $	454.6	Effective rates	*1985 = 100*
Z per SDR	597.4	– nominal	13
Z per Ecu	544.2	– real	73

Principal exports

	$m fob		$m fob
Copper & cobalt	1,075	Coffee	142
Crude petroleum	211	Gold	44
Diamonds	204	Total incl. others	**1,744**

Main export destinations[b]

	% of total		% of total
Bel/Lux	43	West Germany	11
USA	19	Italy	8

Principal imports[c]

	$m fob		$m fob
Imports for Gécamines[d]	362	Transport equipment	95
Petroleum products	169		
Agric. products &			
foodstuffs	147	Total incl. others	**1,395**

Main origins of imports[b]

	% of total		% of total
China	43	France	7
Bel/Lux	13	USA	5

Balance of payments, reserves and debt $m

Visible exports fob	2,207	Overall balance	-779
Visible imports fob	-1,644	Change in reserves	187
Trade balance	563	Level of reserves	
Invisibles inflows	185	end Dec.	372
Invisibles outflows	-1,570	No. months import cover	1.4
Net transfers	129	Foreign debt	8,474
Current account balance	-693	– as % of GDP	121.4
– as % of GDP	-10.7	Debt service	216
Capital balance	-46	Debt service ratio	9.0%

Family life

No. households	5.2m	Divorces per 1,000 pop.	...
Av. no. per household	5.9	Cost of living end 1989	
Marriages per 1,000 pop.	...	New York = 100	...

a 1985.
b Estimates.
c 1987.
d Gécamines is the giant government-owned mining company, producing all Zairean cobalt, zinc, coal and copper.

ZIMBABWE

Area	391,000 sq km	Currency	Zimbabwe dollar (Z$)
Capital	Harare		

People

Population	8.9m	Life expectancy: men	57 yrs
Pop. per sq km	23	women	60 yrs
Av. ann. growth		Adult literacy	74%
in pop. 1983-88	2.8%	Fertility rate (per woman)	5.8
Pop. under 15	44.8%		
Pop. over 65	2.7%		*per 1,000 pop.*
No. men per 100 women	98.3	Crude birth rate	41.7
Human Development Index	58	Crude death rate	10.2

The economy

GDP[a]	Z$8.3bn	GDP per head	$518
GDP[a]	$4.6bn	GDP per head in purchasing	
Av. ann. growth in real		power parity (USA=100)	10
GDP 1980-88	3.1%		

Origins of GDP

	% of total
Agriculture	15.5
Industry, of which:	34.9
manufacturing	26.5
Services	49.6

Components of GDP

	% of total
Private consumption	54.2
Public consumption	19.3
Investment	22.5
Exports	28.8
Imports	-24.8

Structure of manufacturing

	% of total		*% of total*
Agric. & food processing	28	Other	46
Textiles & clothing	16	Av. ann. increase in industrial	
Machinery & transport	10	output 1980-88	3.9%

Energy

	'000 TCE		
Total output	5,149	% output exported	1.6
Total consumption	6,316	% consumption imported	24.3
Consumption per head,			
kg coal equivalent	731		

Inflation and finance

Consumer price			*av. ann. increase 1983-88*
inflation 1989	12.8%	Narrow money (M1)	16.4%
Av. ann. inflation 1984-89	11.3%	Broad money	15.4%

Exchange rates

	end 1989		*av. 1989*
Z$ per $	2.27	Effective rates	1985 = 100
Z$ per SDR	2.98	– nominal	...
Z$ per Ecu	2.72	– real	...

Principal exports[b]

	$m fob		$m fob
Gold	265	Cotton	73
Tobacco	256	Nickel	56
Ferro-alloys	150	Total incl. others	1,404

Main export destinations[bc]

	% of total		% of total
UK	12.9	South Africa	9.8
West Germany	10.2	USA	6.8

Principal imports[b]

	$m fob		$m fob
Machinery & transport		Petroleum products &	
equipment	383	electricity	144
Manufactured products	242		
Chemicals	187	Total incl. others	1,048

Main origins of imports[b]

	% of total		% of total
South Africa	20.8	USA	9.4
UK	11.5	West Germany	8.7

Balance of payments, reserves and debt $m

Visible exports fob	1,585	Overall balance	102
Visible imports fob	-1,193	Change in reserves	94.0
Trade balance	392	Level of reserves	
Invisibles inflows	217	end Dec.	257
Invisibles outflows	-658	No. months import cover	1.7
Net transfers	58	Foreign debt	2,659
Current account balance	9.0	– as % of GDP[d]	42.8
– as % of GDP	0.2	Debt service	501
Capital balance	44.0	Debt service ratio	27.8%

Family life

No. households	2.0m	Divorces per 1,000 pop.	...
Av. no. per household	4.2	Cost of living end 1989	
Marriages per 1,000 pop.	...	New York = 100	50

a At factor cost.
b 1987. Excluding re-exports.
c Excluding gold.
d Estimated on % of GDP at market prices.

Glossary

Asean Association of Southeast Asian Nations. Founded in 1967 and based in Jakarta, Asean incorporates Brunei, Indonesia, Malaysia, Philippines, Singapore and Thailand.

Balance of payments The record of a country's transactions with the rest of the world. The **current account** of the balance of payments consists of: exports of visible trade (goods) less imports of visible trade; "invisible" trade: receipts and payments for services such as banking, tourism and shipping plus dividend and interest payments and profit remittances; private transfer payments, such as remittances from those working abroad; official transfers, including payments to international organizations and some current expenditure aid flows (such as famine relief). Visible imports and exports are normally compiled on rather different definitions to those used in the trade statistics (shown in principal imports and exports) and therefore the statistics do not match. The **capital account** consists of long- and short-term transactions relating to a country's assets and liabilities (for example loans and borrowings). Adding the current to the capital account gives the overall balance. This is compensated by net monetary movements and changes in reserves. In practice methods of statistical recording are neither complete nor accurate and an errors and omissions item, sometimes quite large, will appear. In the country pages of this book this item is included in the overall balance. Changes in reserves are shown without the practice of reversing the sign often followed in balance of payments presentations. They exclude monetary movements and therefore do not equal the overall balance.

CFA Communauté Financière Africaine. Its members, most of the francophone African nations, share a common currency, the CFA franc, which is maintained at a fixed rate of 1Ffr = 50 CFAfr by the French treasury.

Cif/fob When goods pass through customs and are recorded in trade statistics they are normally registered at their value at the point of passage through customs. Imports, which are valued at the point of entry to a country, will include the cost of "carriage, insurance and freight" (cif) from the exporting country to the importing one. The value of exports does not include these elements and is recorded "free on board" (fob). The value of imports will therefore automatically be greater than the equivalent amount of exports – in many cases by a factor of 10-12 per cent. In most (but not all) countries the crude trade statistics record imports cif and exports fob; balance of payments statistics are generally adjusted so that imports are shown fob.

CMEA The Council for Mutual Economic Assistance (also known as Comecon). A 10-member trading bloc of communist (or former communist) states. Members are: Bulgaria, Cuba, Czechoslovakia, East Germany (prior to German unification), Hungary, Mongolia, Poland, Romania, the USSR and Vietnam.

Cost of living The index shown is compiled by Business International for use by companies in determining expatriate compensation. It is a comparison of the cost of maintaining a typical western life style, rather than a comparison of the purchasing power of a citizen of the country, based on typical prices an international executive and family will face when living abroad in the country's largest city. It is scaled so that the cost of living in New York = 100. The index will reflect relative exchange rates. Thus in countries where the exchange rate is overvalued (eg Iran or African countries using the CFA franc), the cost of living is automatically high.

Crude birth rate The number of live births in a year per 1,000 population. The crude rate will automatically be relatively high if a large proportion of the population is of childbearing age and low if this is not the case.

Crude death rate The number of deaths in one year per 1,000 population. Like the crude birth rate this is affected by the population's age structure. It will be relatively high if there is a high proportion of old people in the population.

Debt, foreign Financial obligations owed by a country to the rest of the world and repayable in foreign currency. **Debt service** consists of interest payments on outstanding debt plus any principal repayments due. **The debt service ratio** is debt service expressed as a percentage of the country's earnings from exports of goods and services.

EC European Community. Members are: Belgium, Denmark, France, Germany, Greece, Ireland, Italy, Luxembourg, Netherlands, Portugal, Spain and the UK. Since all statistics in this book refer to the period before German unification on October 3 1990, statistics for the EC will include West Germany only.

Ecu The European currency unit. Technically an accounting measure used within the EC and composed of a weighted basket of the currencies of all EC member countries. The weights are approximately proportional to each country's GDP and foreign trade.

Effective exchange rate This measures a currency's depreciation (figures below 100) or appreciation (figures over 100) against a trade weighted basket of the currencies of the country's main trading partners. Real effective exchange rates

adjust the nominal rates for differences in price movements.

Efta European Free Trade Association. An organization of West European states that are not members of the European Community. It was set up to promote free trade in West Europe but without the aim of developing the closer links envisaged by the EC. Members are: Austria, Finland, Iceland, Norway, Sweden and Switzerland.

Fertility rate The average number of children born to a woman who completes her childbearing years.

GDP Gross Domestic Product. It is the sum of all output produced by economic activity within that country. Economic activity normally refers to goods and services that are exchanged for money or traded in a market system (activities such as housework, childcare by parents and household repairs or improvements carried out by occupiers are excluded). Subsistence farming and other activities that could potentially be exchanged for money are theoretically also included but national statistics vary in the extent to which they cover them.

GDP can be measured in three ways: by summing the output of all production (origins of GDP); by measuring all expenditure on a country's production and adding stockbuilding (components of GDP); or by measuring the income of businesses and individuals generated by the production of goods and services. The exports and imports figures shown in national accounts statistics are defined differently from visible and invisible exports and imports used in the balance of payments, notably by excluding interest, profits and dividends payments.

GDP can be measured either at "market prices", the prices at which goods and services are bought by consumers, or at "factor cost", the cost of producing an item excluding taxes and subsidies. In general the expenditure breakdown is shown at market prices and the production breakdown at factor cost. Data on total GDP generally refer to market prices.National income is obtained by deducting an estimate of depreciation of capital goods (capital consumption) from GDP.

The average annual increase in real GDP shows the growth in GDP excluding any increase due solely to the rise in prices.

Human Development Index This new index is an attempt by the United Nations Development Programme to assess relative levels of human development in various countries. It combines three measures: life expectancy, literacy and whether the average income, based on purchasing power parity (PPP) estimates (see below), is sufficient to meet basic needs. For each component a country's score is scaled according to where it falls between the minimum and maximum country scores; for income adequacy the maximum is taken as the official "poverty line" incomes in nine industrial countries. The scaled scores on the three measures are averaged to give the Human Development Index, shown here scaled from 0 to 100. Countries scoring less than 50 are classified as low human development, those from 50 to 80 as medium and those above 80 as high.

As with any statistical exercise of this sort the results are subject to caveats and the small number of indicators used places some limitations on its usefulness. The index should not be taken as a quality of life indicator since in particular it excludes any direct notion of freedom.

Inflation The rate at which prices are increasing. The most common measure

and the one shown here (but not the only one) is to take the increase in the consumer price index.

Life expectancy rates refer to the average length of time a baby born today can expect to live.

Literacy is defined by UNESCO as the ability to read and write a simple sentence, but definitions can vary from country to country.

Money supply A measure of the "money" available to buy goods and services. Technically it should not include savings. However, it is impossible to know whether money invested in interest-bearing accounts is regarded by the investor as a means of saving or simply of efficiently storing money until required - or both. Thus various definitions of money supply exist.

The measures shown here are based on definitions used by the IMF and may differ from measures used nationally. Narrow money (M1)consists of cash in circulation and demand deposits (bank deposits that can be withdrawn on demand). "Quasi-money" (time, savings and foreign currency deposits which may be regarded by investors either as a means of saving or as a means of holding money) is added to this to create broad money.

NMP Net Material Product. The equivalent measure to GDP used in Marxist national accounting; a system used in East Europe and certain other planned economies. It differs from GDP in excluding certain services and in deducting capital consumption. **Gross Material Product** is equal to NMP plus consumption. In general, NMP is between 80-90% of GDP.

OECD Organization for Economic Cooperation and Development. The "rich countries" club was established in 1961 to promote economic growth and the expansion of world trade. It is based in Paris and has 24 members.

Opec Organization of Petroleum Exporting Countries. Set up in 1960 and based in Vienna, Opec is mainly concerned with oil pricing and production issues. Members are; Algeria, Ecuador, Gabon, Indonesia, Kuwait, Libya, Nigeria, Qatar, Saudi Arabia, UAE and Venezuela.

PPP Purchasing Power Parity. Comparing GDP per head is an unsatisfactory way of comparing relative living standards since it does not take account of differences in prices of goods and services (the cost of living). PPP statistics adjust for cost of living differences by replacing normal exchange rates with rates designed to equalize the prices of a standard "basket" of goods and services. These are used to obtain PPP estimates of GDP per head. PPP estimates are normally shown on a scale of 1 to 100, taking the USA, where the average standard of living is highest, as 100.

Real terms Figures adjusted to allow for inflation.

SDR Special Drawing Right. The reserve currency, introduced by the IMF in 1970, was intended to replace gold and national currencies in settling international transactions. The IMF uses SDRs for book-keeping purposes and issues them to member countries. Their value is based on a basket of the five most widely traded currencies: the US dollar, Deutschemark, pound sterling, Japanese yen and French franc.

Sources

The Brewers' Society, *Statistical Handbook*.

Bureau Internationale de l'Union Postale Universelle, *Statistiques des Services Postaux*.

Business International, *Cost of Living Survey*.

Commonwealth Secretariat, *Wool Quarterly*.

ERC Statistics International, *The World Cigarette Market*.

The Economist Intelligence Unit, *Country Reports*.
The Economist Intelligence Unit, *Country Risk Service*.
The Economist Intelligence Unit, *World Commodity Outlook*.

Euromonitor, *International Marketing Data and Statistics*.
Euromonitor, *European Marketing Data and Statistics*.

FAO, *Production Yearbook*.

Financial Times Business Information, *The Banker*.

ILO, *Year Book of Labour Statistics*.

IMF, *International Financial Statistics*.
IMF, *Direction of Trade Statistics*.

International Cocoa Organization, *Quarterly Bulletin of Cocoa Statistics*.

International Civil Aviation Organization, *ICAO Bulletin*.

International Cotton Advisory Committee, *Bulletin*.

International Criminal Police Organisation (Interpol), *International Crime Statistics*.

International Finance Corporation, *Emerging Stock Markets Factbook*.

International Rubber Study Group, *Rubber Statistics Bulletin*.

International Sugar Organization, *Sugar Yearbook*.

International Tea Committee, *Annual Bulletin of Statistics*.

International Wheat Council, *Report for Crop Year 1987/88*.

OECD, *Main Economic Indicators*.
OECD, *Development Co-operation in the 1990s*.OECD, *Environmental Data*.

Society of Motor Manufacturers and Traders, *World Automotive Statistics*.

Time Inc. Magazines, *Fortune International*.

US Department of Agriculture, *Situation Reports on individual commodities*.
US Department of Energy, *International Energy Annual*.

UN, *Monthly Bulletin of Statistics*.
UN, *World Population Prospects*.
UN, *National Accounts*.
UN, *Energy Statistics Yearbook*.
UN, *International Trade Statistics Yearbook*.
UN, *Review of Maritime Transport*.
UN, *Demographics Yearbook*.
UN, *Statistical Yearbook*.
UNCTAD, *Iron Ore Statistics*.
UN Development Programme, *Human Development Report*.
UNESCO, *Statistical Yearbook*.

Union International des Chemins de Fer, *Statistiques Internationales des Chemins de Fer*.

WHO, *World Health Statistics*.

World Bank, *World Debt Tables*.
World Bank, *World Development Report*.

World Bureau of Metal Statistics, UK, *World Metal Statistics*.

World Road Federation, *World Road Statistics*.

World Tourist Organization, *Yearbook of Tourism Statistics*.